Practical Apache Struts2 Web 2.0 Projects

■ ■ ■

Ian Roughley

Apress®

Practical Apache Struts2 Web 2.0 Projects

Copyright © 2007 by Ian Roughley

ISBN-13 (pbk): 978-1-59059-903-7

ISBN-10 (pbk): 1-59059-903-9

Printed and bound in the United States of America 9 8 7 6 5 4 3 2 1

Lead Editor: Steve Anglin
Technical Reviewer: Frank Zammetti
Editorial Board: Steve Anglin, Ewan Buckingham, Tony Campbell, Gary Cornell, Jonathan Gennick, Jason Gilmore, Kevin Goff, Jonathan Hassell, Matthew Moodie, Joseph Ottinger, Jeffrey Pepper, Ben Renow-Clarke, Dominic Shakeshaft, Matt Wade, Tom Welsh
Project Manager: Candace English
Copy Editor: Julie McNamee
Associate Production Director: Kari Brooks-Copony
Production Editor: Candace English
Compositor: Linda Weidemann, Wolf Creek Press
Proofreader: Lisa Hamilton
Indexer: Broccoli Information Management
Cover Designer: Kurt Krames
Manufacturing Director: Tom Debolski

Distributed to the book trade worldwide by Springer-Verlag New York, Inc., 233 Spring Street, 6th Floor, New York, NY 10013. Phone 1-800-SPRINGER, fax 201-348-4505, e-mail orders-ny@springer-sbm.com, or visit http://www.springeronline.com.

For information on translations, please contact Apress directly at 2855 Telegraph Avenue, Suite 600, Berkeley, CA 94705. Phone 510-549-5930, fax 510-549-5939, e-mail info@apress.com, or visit http://www.apress.com.

The source code for this book is available to readers at http://www.apress.com.

For Skooter.

Contents at a Glance

Contents

Foreword

Apache Struts is one of the most successful open source projects ever created. With the exception of "infrastructure" projects such as Linux, MySQL, and various programming languages, few other open source frameworks have managed to have the success, popularity, market dominance, and ability to change the way developers think as Struts has.

As one of the creators of the original Struts 2.0 codebase, I am overwhelmed with pride and joy to see so many people contribute and use the project. With literally hundreds of thousands of projects developed on top of Struts, and countless more developers experienced with it, the decision to update Struts from version 1.x to 2.x was not a trivial one. And yet through the experience and leadership of the Struts team, the new 2.x version, which this book is about, has been met with wonderful reception among the developer community.

Ian Roughly is a good friend of mine: Over the past 4+ years, he and I both dedicated far too much time on WebWork, the project that merged with Struts and became the foundation for Struts 2.0. Although Ian is not an original Struts developer—in fact, we both got involved with WebWork because, ironically, we didn't feel Struts 1.x was exactly what we needed—he is definitely one of the most qualified people to write a book about Struts.

With a next generation of Struts gaining momentum among classic Struts users as well as new ones, the time is right for a book on this updated, modern technology. Whether you want to learn about AJAX integration, plug-in-oriented development, or just how to build quality web apps, I can think of no one better than Ian to be your guide.

I am certain you will enjoy this book. It's about a great technology, and it's written by an expert who not only created much of this technology but also uses it on a daily basis in his own practice. Ian's words and advice come from real experience—he's not some disconnected architect who doesn't actually write web apps anymore. He's the real deal. He knows what it takes to build quality web applications, all the way from setting up a build system that works well for web development teams, to building complex wizards and workflows, to properly securing your application in a more complicated world dominated by AJAX.

You are in good hands, both in terms of your guide as well as a technology choice. Struts is an evolving framework for building modern web applications, and I encourage you to join the community after you are done with this book so that you may continue to participate in the evolution and be part of one of the most interesting Java web frameworks today.

Enjoy the book!

Patrick Lightbody
Co-creator, Struts 2.0

About the Author

IAN ROUGHLEY is a speaker, author, and consultant based in Boston, MA, where he runs From Down & Around, Inc., a consultancy specializing in architecture, development, and process improvement services. For more than 10 years, he has been helping clients ranging in size from Fortune 10 companies to start-ups.

Focused on a pragmatic and results-based approach, he is a proponent for open source, as well as process and quality improvements through agile development techniques. Ian is a committer on the XWork and WebWork projects; member of the Apache Struts PMC; and speaks at conferences in the United States and abroad. He is also a Sun Certified Java Programmer and J2EE Enterprise Architect and an IBM Certified Solutions Architect.

You can reach Ian at ian@fdar.com, or via the web at http://www.fdar.com.

About the Technical Reviewer

FRANK W. ZAMMETTI is a web architect/developer for a worldwide financial company by day and a jack-of-all-trades by night. Frank has authored a number of books and articles on topics ranging from AJAX to DataVision. Frank is an active participant in a variety of open source projects both small and large; some he leads, and a few he has founded himself. Frank has been involved with computers, in one form another, for more than 25 years, 15 of that being "professional," which just means he was being paid to pretend he knew what he was doing! Frank is an avid indoorsman, shunning the sun like the uncle no one talks about. Frank lives in the United States with his wife, two children who never stop talking, and an assortment of voices in his head that won't stop singing the theme songs from '80s television shows.

Acknowledgments

It has been a remarkable experience being involved with open source development, what I believe to be the real "beta" of Web 2.0 sharing and collaboration. Where else can you combine talented individuals from around the world, without significant management, to produce a product that hundreds of thousands of companies depend upon every day? I'd like to thank everyone involved in the XWork, WebWork, and Apache Struts projects; without their tireless commitment and contributions, I would have nothing to write about. In particular I'd like to thank Don Brown, Patrick Lightbody, Philip Luppens, Rainer Hermanns, and Rene Gielen; they have always been there when I had a particularly tricky question that needed answering.

I would like to thank Steve Anglin, Candace English, and Julie McNamee from Apress, as well as all of the people behind the scenes that I haven't had the opportunity to meet personally. Without your ongoing support and assistance, this book would not have been possible.

I'd also like to thank Frank Zammetti, my technical reviewer and Struts2 community member, for keeping me on my toes, always questioning, and always making sure that the information presented was at its very best.

Finally, I would like to thank my remarkable wife LeAnn. Her continuing support and ongoing review and nongeek analysis of the manuscript has been invaluable.

Introduction

Web application development has been around for a long time. In fact, it has been around long enough that a new term, Web 2.0, is being used to describe the next generation of web applications. Web 2.0 is an intersection of new business models, new ideas, and multifaceted sharing and collaboration—with iterative development techniques getting new features to users at a much faster pace. Along with Web 2.0 came a revival of scripting languages (and even a few new ones), all dynamic and supporting fast-paced and highly productive development environments.

Around the same time, Struts (the first, and most popular Java web application framework ever) was reaching an important milestone—its second major release. This was not only an important milestone for the framework in terms of functionality but also for the improvements made to increase developer productivity. By decreasing coupling within the framework, reducing configuration, providing default and different configuration options (via annotations), and providing a plug-in mechanism to easily extend the base features, Struts2 is providing a platform that can be built upon for the next generation of web applications. With these new enhancements, Struts2 is poised to compete as the development framework of choice for Web 2.0 applications.

To use a new framework, you first have to know the features that are available, and learning a new technology from scratch using reference manuals and disconnected examples can be difficult. In writing this book, my goal was to provide the information to you, on how to develop a Web 2.0 application using Apache Struts2 in a practical and hands-on manner. You will achieve this goal by understanding the architecture of Struts2, by knowing the features that Struts2 provides, by seeing how these features are used, and by using and further exploring each of the features through the code provided. Each chapter builds on the last, providing more and more information until a complete web application emerges.

Time to get started!

■ ■ ■

## CHAPTER 1

Web 2.0 and Struts2

Before charging forward with developing a Web 2.0 application, you need to understand what a Web 2.0 application really is. In this chapter, you will learn what Web 2.0 means from a development as well as end user perspective.

With Struts2 being the technology of choice, you will also learn how Struts2 provides the features to make developing a Web 2.0 application easy.

What Is Web 2.0?

One of the questions that needs to be answered before embarking on developing a Web 2.0 application is "What is Web 2.0?" As it turns out, this is a particularly difficult question to answer.

From a programming perspective, Web 2.0 is synonymous with AJAX (Asynchronous JavaScript and XML). The term AJAX was coined in February 2005 by Jesse James Garrett and is used to describe the interaction between many technologies. At the core is the XMLHttpRequest object, which is supplied by the web browser. This object was first present in Microsoft Internet Explorer 5 (released in March 1999), although similar techniques using IFRAMES and LAYER elements have been available since 1996.

Along with the XMLHttpRequest object, the technologies that make up an AJAX interaction are the following:

- *HTML/XHTML (Hypertext Markup Language)*: Used to present information to the user from within the web browser.

- *DOM (Document Object Model)*: The object structure of the HTML document in the web browser. By manipulating the DOM with JavaScript, the page rendered to the user can be modified dynamically without reloading the current page.

- *CSS (Cascading Style Sheets)*: Used to format and style the HTML presented. By separating formatting from structure, the code can be modified consistently and maintained more easily. Similarly to the DOM, CSS for the current page can be modified via JavaScript to dynamically change the formatting without reloading the current page.

- *JavaScript*: A programming language that can be embedded within HTML documents. JavaScript code or functions can be executed inline (as the page is processed), in response to HTML events (by providing JavaScript in the value of HTML attributes), or triggered by browser events (for example, timers or user events).

- *XML (eXtensible Markup Language)*: The format of the data returned by the server in response to the asynchronous call from the web browser. The XML response returned is processed by JavaScript in the web browser, causing changes in the HTML (by manipulating the DOM or CSS).

Recently, another data format has been gaining popularity: JSON (JavaScript Object Notation). Similar to XML, JSON returns data that can be processed within the web browser using JavaScript. The advantage of JSON is that it can be very easily parsed by JavaScript; in fact, to convert a response of any size from the JSON transport format to JavaScript objects involves a single call of `eval('('+responseJSON+')')` (where `responseJSON` is the JSON data represented as text or a string). Using JavaScript to process XML is much more involved and requires at least one line of code to assign a value from the XML document to a JavaScript object.

EVALUATING VS. PARSING

There is a security concern when calling `eval()` on a JSON string, especially when the JSON is obtained from a source external to the code currently being executed. The problem lies in the fact that the `eval()` function compiles and executes any JavaScript code in the text string being parsed to create the object representation. For this reason, you need to be sure that you trust the source of the JSON text. Even better still, you can use a JSON parser, which avoids the problems associated with the `eval()` function.

One such parser can be found at `http://www.json.org/json.js` (the web site `http://www.json.org` is the gateway to all things JSON). When using this JavaScript script, additional methods are added to the basic JavaScript objects to both generate JSON and parse JSON. When provided with a JSON string to be parsed (say `jsonText`), the following code is used:

```
jsonText.parseJSON(filter);
```

The parameter `filter` is an optional JavaScript function, which can be used to further filter and transform the result. To generate JSON, use the `toJSONString()` method. For example, to convert a boolean `myBoolean`, use the following:

```
myBoolean.toJSONString();
```

By using a JavaScript JSON parser, the JSON text can be converted just as simply but without security concerns.

By using AJAX interactions, developers can make the user experience less awkward. Rather than requiring the entire HTML page to be reloaded from the server (along with processing the request on the server) and rerendered to update values in a drop-down selection box, now a smaller request to the server can be made. More importantly, the page is not rerendered; instead, the only change to the HTML is that the values for the drop-down selection box have now been changed.

Smaller and more targeted information requests to the server means that the time spent waiting for the network and server processing will be less. Not having to rerender the entire browser page on each server request will also be perceived as the web application performing faster. With these pieces working together in an AJAX interaction, the web browser will become more responsive and act more like a traditional desktop application—increasing the usability and overall user experience.

It also means that developers need to think differently. In fact, developers need to reexamine the fundamental way that a web application is constructed; rather than thinking of a page as a unit of work, they need to think of functionality from a page as being the unit of work, with many functions being combined to create the final page. Furthermore, the same functionality can now be easily shared among pages.

THE PAVLOV EFFECT

Changing the user interaction (even for the better) has its own problems. Users have been trained to understand that nothing on HTML pages changes until you click a link or a form submit button. All of a sudden, things are different. Now, at any time, any part of the HTML page has the potential of being updated or removed, and new information can be added.

To help transition users to the new browser interaction model, as well as to provide developers with guidelines of when and how to use AJAX in web applications, a series of patterns has emerged. AJAX patterns cover a wide range of topics, including how to signal the user that a UI element has changed; when to make server calls to obtain data; options for introducing AJAX into non-AJAX web applications; how to manage technical aspects such as server timeouts; and ways to provide a non-AJAX fall-back when JavaScript is not available on the user's browser.

From a marketing or end-user perspective, things are a little different. There is no doubt that more interactive user interfaces can make the overall web application's usability better, however, the shift from Web 1.0 to Web 2.0 is more than user interfaces.

In September 2005, Tim O'Reilly published an article titled "What Is Web 2.0" (`http://www.oreillynet.com/pub/a/oreilly/tim/news/2005/09/30/what-is-web-20.html`). This article explored what Web 2.0 was by comparing a new breed of web sites that were available to those that had been around for some time. The result was that no hard boundaries of principles or technologies signified an application as a Web 2.0 application. Instead, there were guiding principles that, when adopted, resulted in a web application that is more Web 2.0 than when the principles were not used. Following is the list of proposed principles:

- *Web as a platform*: Applications should take advantage of the Web as a platform rather than simply providing a presence on the Web. By working symbiotically with the openness and connectedness of the Web, services can reach out to all users. And in doing so, will get better as more people use the service.

- *Harness collective intelligence*: Hyperlinking has been the foundation of the Web, allowing users to explore related content, but it has always been provided by the web site being visited. The new breed of applications takes this a step further, allowing users to provide information to the web application in the form of content and metadata (information about the content, such as ranking or popularity). Individual publishing, via blogging, has also become popular, allowing anyone to become a publisher of information and opinions.

- *Data is the next "Intel inside"*: Originally, companies owned and provided data to users of their application. Although an initial set of data is still this way, a new and much more valuable set of data is being provided by users of the application. Now the race is on for companies to own a particular category of user-provided data, leading to the question, "who owns the data?"

- *End of the software release cycle*: With software being delivered as a service rather than a product, all users of a web application can take advantage of new features being provided immediately. In a sense, users then become codevelopers and can be monitored to determine which features are used, and how often—shaping the features of the final product. Releasing often also requires operations to become a core competency.

- *Lightweight programming models*: There is a preference to use simple protocols, such as REST (Representation State Transfer) rather than SOAP (Simple Object Access Protocol), and RSS (Really Simple Syndication) to provide syndication and remixability. The innovation is that combining many loosely coupled services together in a unique or novel manner provides value in the assembly.

- *Software above the level of a single device*: In a connected world, the browser is no longer the single device of choice. Web applications will need to interact with devices accessing them from web browsers and cell phones, as well as more specialized devices such as iPods, PDAs, and cable boxes.

- *Rich user experiences*: Services are becoming RIAs (Rich Internet Applications), providing dynamic and responsive interactions with users. AJAX (which was explained earlier) as well as Java applets and proprietary solutions such as Macromedia Flash, are all enabling technologies.

Almost one year later in August 2006, Tim O'Reilly gathered a group of people together to build on his initial paper. Gregor Hohpe was one of those people invited, and he blogged (http://www.eaipatterns.com/ramblings/45_web20.html) about the values, principles, and patterns that were discussed.

As an agile developer, the style the values were presented in hit an accord. Using the same format as the Agile Manifesto, it presented the differences between a Web 1.0 and Web 2.0 application as a range. The closer the application is represented by the descriptions on the left, the more Web 2.0 the web application is. In the end, whether an application is Web 1.0 or

Web 2.0 is still subjective, but grading the level of Web 2.0-ness is easier. The values, with my interpretation, are provided here:

- *Simplicity over Completeness*: Application features do not need to be absolutely complete, having every variation and every option possible. Instead, the most used options are all that is required, making the application much simpler to use and quicker to market.

- *Long Tail over Mass Audience*: Business models are focusing on selling smaller volumes of a large variety of hard-to-find or unique items rather than selling large volumes of a small number of popular items. The same can be said about knowledge (see the Wikipedia entry for more information on the Long Tail `http://en.wikipedia.org/wiki/The_Long_Tail`).

- *Share over Protect*: Web sites are no longer gated enclosures; instead, information and services are shared using techniques such as web services and feeds.

- *Advertise over Subscribe*: The preferred revenue model for Web 2.0 sites is advertisement rather than subscription (although of all the values, this is the one that is most controversial because as applications move from products to Web 2.0 services, a subscription model will be required).

- *Syndication over Stickiness*: An early goal of web applications was to keep users on the site for as long as possible. By providing services, the information that could only reach users on the site can now have a much farther reach by syndication (with links leading them back to the application).

- *Early Availability over Correctness*: Rather than working behind closed doors to perfect a web application feature, it's more important to get the features out to users so they can assist as codevelopers in the perfecting the features.

- *Select by Crowd over Editor*: The opinions and aggregated wisdom of many people is far more valuable than the opinion of a single person.

- *Honest Voice over Corporate Speak*: The opinions of experts participating in or using a service or product are more valuable than marketing information that has no personal insight.

- *Participation over Publishing*: Whenever possible, it's better to allow the users to participate and share their experience, rather than publishing edited information.

- *Community over Product*: Creating a community and then taking advantage of the collective knowledge of the community is more important than providing a product with individual user access.

The interesting thing is that in this second phase of the Web, the focus is once again on collaboration and sharing information and opinions. This was an original goal of the Internet (`http://en.wikipedia.org/wiki/History_of_the_Internet`) when universities were exploring ways to collaborate.

Web Application Development 2.0

After reviewing the values and principles that make up a Web 2.0 application, you might be asking yourself "how is this different from what I am doing now?" We have reviewed AJAX interactions in the previous section, and this is by far the most significant change from a development perspective. Other changes are at a far more fundamental software development level and less visible to the end user:

- *Development process agility*: As a service, software features can be changed at lightning speed. It could be at a client's request or as new business requirements are introduced, but either way, a process must be in place to efficiently introduce new features and validate that the new code has not broken existing features. More than ever, unit testing, continuous integration, and automated deployment processes are required to support the development efforts.

- *Syndication and integration*: Two sides of the same coin, syndication and integration allow your application to share data with other external applications as well as use services from external sources. When architecting your web application, thought needs to be put into determining how the application will technically achieve these objectives, as well as what format the data and services being provided will take.

- *Web framework agility*: Having a web development environment that works with the developer to provide an environment that is flexible, productive, and encompasses the values of Web 2.0 is of utmost importance. With Web 2.0, there has been a resurgence of development in existing dynamic languages, such as PHP, as well as newer languages and frameworks, such as Ruby and Ruby on Rails. Struts2 is one of many Java frameworks that provide the maturity, experience, and features to compete with dynamic language frameworks.

The features listed previously are not technical features of web development frameworks, and this is important. As web development matures into a second phase of growth, the focus is on business models and features provided to the users. Technically, the difference is on how the applications are developed—by integrating services (that may be provided by other applications, known as mashups) and data together to provide value.

Web Framework Agility with Struts2

Because the focus of this book is on web development, we will explore how Struts2 provides agility as a web application framework. However, before getting to Struts2, we need to talk briefly about a new web framework that made its debut around the same time that web applications were releasing Web 2.0 features. This framework is Ruby on Rails.

When Ruby on Rails was released in August 2004, many (if not all) existing web application frameworks went through a period of self-examination; new frameworks were also created (Grails, for example). Several driving factors made Rails so compelling to use as a developer:

- *Full web application stack*: All the basic elements necessary to build a web application were provided in the base distribution.

- *Convention over configuration*: Rather than configuring every element of the application, conventions were used (that could be overridden). A standard directory structure (where each development artifact had a known location) and standard naming conventions are a large part of the conventions.

- *Scaffolding*: The framework can provide fully functional basic user interfaces (with controller logic) for model objects, allowing the application to be used while the real production code is being developed.

- *Interpreted development language*: The underlying development language is Ruby, which is dynamic, object-oriented, and interpreted.

All these features allow developers to be more productive from the initial download and setup of the framework, to the day-to-day development of new web application features.

Struts was first released in July 2001 and was an overwhelming success. It provided an MVC (Model View Controller) pattern implementation for Java web development, allowing web applications written in Java to segment code (rather than writing HTML code in servlets or Java code in JSPs) and to manage reusability and maintenance of existing code.

Over time, developing in Struts required more developer-provided code to implement the necessary web application features, and a proposal for the next generation of Struts was suggested. Architecturally, the changes necessary to implement the proposed features were significant and, rather than starting from scratch, Struts developers approached other open source Java frameworks with a proposal for a merger. Without covering all the details, the result was that WebWork (an OpenSymphony project that itself was an early fork of the Struts code base) merged with Apache to become the basis of Struts2.

■**Note** The history of Struts Ti and the WebWork/Struts merger is documented by Don Brown at
`http://www.oreillynet.com/onjava/blog/2006/10/my_history_of_struts_2.html`.

Interestingly, one of the WebWork lead developers, Pat Lightbody, had been reviewing features of Ruby on Rails with the goal of making WebWork more productive and easier for developers to use. Some of these features are now part of the Struts2 feature set, and some (because of the Java language constraints as well as maturity reasons) did not make the transition.

Following is a list of Struts2 features that drive the framework forward to be more developer friendly and productive:

- *Java*: The Java language has been around for 10 years now and has matured to a point where most of the features (nonbusiness-related) already exist as libraries. Java is typed (a plus for some developers) and can access an organizational infrastructure that has already been developed (although JRuby and Groovy have options for calling existing Java classes via dynamic languages).

- *Plug-ins*: Functionality provided as core or third-party plug-ins can be added as needed, rather than requiring the core framework to include everything. As well, the plug-in development life cycle (and hence the introduction of new features) is no longer tied to the core framework, allowing more frequent upgrades.

- *Convention over configuration*: Wherever possible, configuration has been eliminated. By using zero-configuration, class names can provide action mappings, and returned result values can provide names for JSPs to be rendered.

- *Annotations rather than XML configuration*: There are two benefits to using annotations: first is a reduction in XML configuration, and second is the configuration is closer to the action class (reducing the effort necessary to determine the action configuration).

- *Data conversion*: The conversion of string-based form field values to objects or primitive types is handled by the framework (and vice-versa), removing the necessity of providing this infrastructure code in the action class.

- *Dependency injection*: All the objects that the action needs to interact with to perform the logic of the action are provided via setters. This reduces the coupling between application layers, and makes the application simpler and easier to test.

- *Testability*: Testing Struts2 actions, interceptor, and other classes is very easy.

- *MVC pattern*: Struts2 continues to use the MVC pattern, providing a layer of abstraction between the view (usually rendered as HTML) and the framework by using a URL. This is important because it doesn't tie the framework to a particular device or rendering style (such as, always refresh an entire page; partial HTML updates; and processing events supplied as AJAX requests).

A lot of work is still needed to get to the productivity level that Ruby on Rails is today, and some features will just never make it (due to the restrictions of the Java language). However, in choosing a web application framework, many factors are involved, and the selection of a programming language that can take advantage of the organization infrastructure that is already in place is one of the most important. With numerous options available to choose from for Java web application frameworks, Struts2 is just as strong of a contender today as it was when Struts was first released—providing the developer productivity features and Web 2.0 functionality that is needed to develop today's web applications.

Using this Book

Throughout the course of this book, the Struts2 framework will be used to develop a Web 2.0 application. As we have already discussed, Web 2.0 characteristics mostly focus around business features and the underlying business model of the organization. However, to develop a fully featured application, you need to understand the framework, concepts, configuration, and the (non-Web 2.0 specific) features. With this in mind, this book is divided into four sections:

- Chapter 2 and Chapter 3 provide the fundamentals on Struts2 with information on how to get up and running, how a request is processed, background information on the framework, and configuration information and extension points.

- Chapter 4 provides the background information on the application that is to be developed throughout the course of the book, including the development process to be used, an overview of the application, the use cases that will be developed, and supporting technologies (that are used in combination with Struts2).

- Chapters 5 through 8 describe the core features of any web application: data manipulation, wizards and workflows, security, and rendering information.

- Chapter 9 and Chapter 10 focus on the Web 2.0 features of the application, including syndication, integration, and ways that AJAX can be integrated into the application.

■**Note** The code was developed using Struts version 2.0.9. In most cases, the provided code should be compatible with any 2.0.x release; however, if you do choose to use a more recent version, there may be some incompatibilities.

Because the concepts and features being introduced are built upon the knowledge from previous chapters, reading the book forward from start to finish is recommended. If you are familiar with Java web application frameworks and don't want to read the entire book, start with Chapter 2 and Chapter 3. These provide the necessary Struts2-specific information so that you can pick and choose the other chapters to read. If you are familiar with Struts2 and are looking for specific implementation information, Chapters 1 through 4 can be safely skipped.

Finally, the application developed in this book illustrates the most common technologies used when developing web applications today: JSPs, the Spring Framework, and JPA. By using Struts2, you have many other options for the view, business tier, and data tier. Plug-ins are the most common mechanism for integrating new technologies, and the list of all the current plug-ins can be found at `http://cwiki.apache.org/S2PLUGINS/home.html`. When considering alternatives, this is the first place you should look.

The other reference you should keep handy is the Struts2 official document site: `http://struts.apache.org/2.x/docs/guides.html`. Here you will find the most up-to-date information on Struts2, as well as reference documentation, guides, tutorials, and release notes for released versions.

CHAPTER 2

■■■

Getting Up and Running

Starting to work with a new technology or framework can be intimidating. Where do you start learning? How do you know that you are implementing classes correctly? How do you know that the configuration is correct? The easiest way to start out is to follow an example, and Struts2 provides just that, but not in the traditional sense. By using a build tool called *Maven2*, Struts2 is able to generate an example project's files and configuration.

In this chapter, you will learn everything you need to get started with Struts2. Starting with information on the build process, you will continue on to generate an example application. You will run the example project on an application server, and with a running example, learn how the different parts of a basic Struts2 application interact.

The Build Process

The build process represents an independent, consistent, and repeatable method to package an application in a state that can be deployed or distributed. When presented like this, it is incomprehensible to think that any organization would not be employing such a process. It's easy, right? However, widespread use is limited. Either organizations have no common process, or there is a process, but it is specific to the developers' environment—clicking the Build Project button, using a script that was developed locally, using a common build script that contains hard-coded environmental information, and so on. Each of these scenarios will lead to equally disastrous outcomes when used on a system other than the one where the process was created.

To facilitate good development processes, we will start out using a build process that can be utilized in any environment: on a developer's workstation, on the integration server, on the test server, or on the build server that creates the final distribution packages. The tool we will be using is *Maven2* from the *Apache Foundation*.

■**Note** There is no requirement to use Maven2 to create a Struts2 application; you could use ANT scripts or your IDE to create the WAR file. The important thing is to have the process independent, consistent, and repeatable.

Maven2

Maven2 is a command-line tool that is used to build, test, report on, and package projects. It provides many features that will make developing your project easier. Here are a few of the features that you will be taking advantage of:

- *Standard directory structure*: Each project that uses Maven2 will have the same directory structure; this makes it easier when developers are working across multiple projects.

- *Plug-in architecture*: Each function of Maven2 is performed by a plug-in, whether the function is compiling classes or deploying the site. If a feature is being used for the first time, the plug-in will be downloaded from a common repository; you no longer need to manually obtain all the parts before starting work.

- *Dependency management*: When dependencies are described in the Maven2 configuration file, they will be accessed from a local repository or downloaded to the local repository during the build process (just as the core Maven2 functionality is). As well as the explicitly configured dependency, the transitive dependencies are managed and downloaded as necessary.

- *Scope management*: The final distribution package contains only the elements required. Test code and dependencies that are not needed (or provided by application servers) in the final package are left out.

- *Archetypes*: The archetype plug-in allows developers to create a default implementation template for a project category. This is then used to quickly create a new project without the need for creating the common directory structure, creating the configuration files, and coding default classes and tests from scratch.

■**Note** More information on the many features of Maven2 is provided in the official document at `http://maven.apache.org`.

To build the project locally, you need to install Maven2 and learn about build life cycles.

COMPARING ANT AND MAVEN2

If you are familiar with Apache ANT build scripts, by now Maven2 may look a little overwhelming. The best example of the differences is comparing ANT vs. Maven2 to Struts2 vs. Ruby on Rails.

In Struts2, developers need to do a lot of work (although this is changing for the better), such as creating actions, mapping results, creating interceptors, and so on. Ruby on Rails abstracts away from the developer all possible configuration and common developer tasks and instead provides intelligent defaults (that can be modified if needed). Maven2 is the same. Instead of creating the same "clean," "compile," "test," and so on ANT tasks, these are handled by Maven2 by relying on a common directory structure. The order (Maven2 life cycle) that the tasks (Maven2 phases) are executed in is also handled automatically, as the common tasks are usually called in the same order for every ANT build file.

One of the most compelling reasons to use Maven2 is that project dependencies can be handled declaratively via the `pom.xml` configuration file. And, if the dependent libraries also use Maven2, transitive dependencies are resolved automatically (because they are defined in the dependent libraries configuration file, they can be automatically downloaded as well).

More information can be found at the Maven2 web site (`http://maven.apache.org`), including a complete list of features (`http://maven.apache.org/maven-features.html`).

Installing and Using Maven2

Installing Maven2 is easy; the project can be downloaded from the Apache project web site at `http://maven.apache.org/download.html`. Once downloaded, your development environment path needs to be modified to include the Maven2 `bin` directory. On a Linux or UNIX system, this is achieved by `export PATH=/usr/local/maven-2.0.6/bin:$PATH` (for Maven2 having been installed in the `/usr/localmaven-2.0.6` directory), and on a Windows system, with `set PATH=%PATH%; C:\maven-2.0.6\bin` (for Maven2 being installed in the `maven-2.0.6` directory).

■**Note** At the time of writing this book, the most recent version of Maven2 is 2.0.6. However, using any 2.0.x release should work without any significant issues. Version 1 of Maven uses a completely different configuration file and structure, and should be avoided.

Once installed, you can check whether the installation is correct by issuing the command `mvn -v`. If the installation is correct, you will get a response of `Maven version: 2.0.6`.

Using Maven2 to build a project is just as simple. First you need to create a Maven2 project configuration file. By convention, this file is called `pom.xml` and is located in the root directory of the project. To make it even easier, Maven2 provides an archetype feature that will create empty directory structures, the project's `pom.xml` file, and even configuration files and sample project files—all for a specific type of project.

After you have a `pom.xml` configuration file, you issue the `mvn` command in the directory that it is located, followed by one or many life cycle phases, for example, `mvn clean package`. Another option is to use a plug-in goal rather than a life cycle phase, for example, `mvn archetype:create`.

The Maven2 Life Cycle Phases

Unlike other build tools, Maven2 uses common life cycles for building a project. Each life cycle provides multiple phases, which are executed in a specific order to consistently generate the outcome expected for your project. The phases and the order cannot be modified; however, each plug-in (and remember everything in Maven2 is a plug-in) can bind a goal (which can be thought of as a target in ANT) to each and any phase. Because order is important, the following default life cycle phases for building a project are listed in the order that they are called:

- *validate*: Verifies that all needed resources are available.

- *compile*: Compiles the source code for the project.

- *test-compile*: Compiles the source code for any tests within the project.

- *test*: Runs unit tests from the project using an applicable testing framework. These tests should not require the code to be packaged or deployed.

- *package*: Packages the compiled code and resources into a distributable format.

- *integration-test*: Deploys the packaged project into an environment where any integration tests can be run and executes any integration tests.

- *install*: Installs the packaged project into a local repository so that other projects may use it.

- *deploy*: Deploys the package into a remote repository to share with other developers and projects.

■**Note** This is not a complete listing of all the life cycle phases that are available. If you are interested in learning more, the full life cycle phase list can be found at `http://maven.apache.org/guides/introduction/introduction-to-the-lifecycle.html`.

Two additional life cycles are available: *clean* and *site*.

The *clean* lifecyle removes the build directory, along with any other configured directories to restore the state of the project to a baseline.

The *site* life cycle has the following goals:

- *site*: Runs the reports configured for a project, rendering HTML documents.

- *site-deploy*: Deploys the HTML reports to a configured web server.

Similar to the *default* life cycle, both contain additional phases that are not listed.

The Struts2 Starter Application

The Struts2 project includes several Maven2 archetypes that can be used to kickstart project development. The full list of different archetypes can be found at `https://svn.apache.org/repos/asf/struts/maven/trunk`. Included are archetypes for portlet development, plug-in development, and Struts2 projects.

You will be using the *starter* project archetype, called `struts2-archetype-starter`. To generate the starter project, select the working directory, and issue the following command:

```
mvn archetype:create
  –DgroupId=com.fdar.apress.s2
  –DartifactId=app
  -DarchetypeGroupId=org.apache.struts
  -DarchetypeArtifactId=struts2-archetype-starter
  -DarchetypeVersion=2.0.9-SNAPSHOT
  -DremoteRepositories=http://people.apache.org/maven-snapshot-repository
```

This command has two parameters that can be varied. The `artifactId` property specifies the directory name to use as the base directory for the project (created in the working directory that you selected and in which you issued the Maven2 command to create the archetype) and is also used as the project's name. Into this directory, the project will be created with the common Maven2 directory structure. The `groupId` is the package name to use as the base class directory and the directory in which the starter classes will be located.

Now that the starter project has been created, you can see it working in a browser. The Maven2 command `mvn jetty:run` will start a servlet container with the application deployed, but remember to issue the command from the directory containing the `pom.xml` configuration file (the app directory). When this command is run for the first time, there will be many plug-ins and dependency artifacts to download, so it may take some time. After the artifacts are cached in your local repository, the startup time will improve. We will discuss how the servlet container is configured in the following chapters, but for now, you have a working application in only two steps.

The Maven2-Generated Directory and File Structure

After the Maven2 `struts2-archetype-starter` archetype has been run, many directories (in accordance with the Maven2 standard directory structure) and files are created. The complete directory structure follows.

```
app
  +- pom.xml
  +- src
      +- main
      |   +- java
      |   |   +- com
      |   |         +- fdar
      |   |               + apress
      |   |                    +- s2
```

```
|       +- resources
|       +- webapp
|           +- jsp
|           +- styles
|           +- WEB-INF
|               +- decorators
+- test
    +- java
    |   +- com
    |       +- fdar
    |           + apress
    |               +- s2
    +- resources
```

The standard directory structure goes like this: the src directory is the root for all code in the project, and within this directory, there is a main directory (for production code) and a test directory. Only the src directory's contents (after any processing/compiling is performed) go into the packaged artifact.

■**Note** For more detail on the standard directory structure, see the Maven2 documentation at http://maven.apache.org/guides/introduction/introduction-to-the-standard-directory-layout.html.

These two directories can contain many other directories, which are aligned with a plug-in or technology. The most common are the java and resource (containing property, XML, and other configuration files) directories—because Maven2 is a build tool for Java—but there are many more. When the AspectJ (AspectJ provides a way to weave additional code for cross-cutting concerns, with logging and transaction management being the commonly used examples, into existing compiled code) plug-in is included, an aspects directory contains the .aj files. The same goes for scripting, where a groovy directory contains the Groovy scripts that are to be executed. (Groovy is a dynamic scripting language with syntax similar to Java that can be executed on the fly or compiled down to byte code.) For a war packaged artifact, the main directory includes a webapp directory that contains the additional information for a WAR file that an EAR or JAR does not need.

The Maven2 Configuration File

As well as the starter program elements, the archetype will create a Maven2 pom.xml configuration file that is used to build the project. This file defines the project's dependencies, the packaging details, and the testing and reporting requirements.

The configuration file plays a central role, so let's take some time to understand its parts. The first part is the header information:

```
<project>
    <modelVersion>4.0.0</modelVersion>
    <groupId>com.fdar.apress.s2</groupId>
    <artifactId>app</artifactId>
    <packaging>war</packaging>
    <version>1.0-SNAPSHOT</version>
    <name>Struts 2 Starter</name>
    <url>http://www.myComp.com</url>
    <description>Struts 2 Starter</description>

    ...

</project>
```

The header of the configuration file contains information for the final packaging, and you should see several values that are familiar: the groupId and artifactId have the same values that were provided in the command to create the starter package.

Some information will remain constant; the modelVersion will always have a value of 4.0.0 (until a significant Maven2 configuration format revision occurs), which refers to the Maven2 model version. The packaging value for web applications is usually war. If this were a component of a larger application, the value would be jar; and if it were a J2EE application containing web components, EJB components, and other resources, it would be ear. The version value remains constant for the time being but will change over time. As this component becomes stable or goes into preview or testing phases, it may change. When the component is released for production use, it should be changed to 1.0. As further development starts, it may be changed to 1.1-SNAPSHOT (for enhancements) or 2.0-SNAPSHOT (for new major features).

Three elements—the name, url, and description tags—have a default value that you should change soon after the starter code has been generated. Each provides descriptive information to developers and consumers of the packaged artifact but is not utilized during building or packaging.

The next interesting part of the pom.xml file is the dependency section:

```
<project>

    ...

    <dependencies>
        <!-- Junit -->
        <dependency>
            <groupId>junit</groupId>
            <artifactId>junit</artifactId>
            <version>3.8.1</version>
            <scope>test</scope>
        </dependency>
```

```
<!-- Struts 2 -->
<dependency>
    <groupId>org.apache.struts</groupId>
    <artifactId>struts2-core</artifactId>
    <version>2.0.9</version>
</dependency>

...

<!-- Servlet & Jsp -->
<dependency>
    <groupId>javax.servlet</groupId>
    <artifactId>servlet-api</artifactId>
    <version>2.4</version>
    <scope>provided</scope>
</dependency>

...

</dependencies>

...

</project>
```

This part of the file describes the dependencies in the application, which will be downloaded from either a local or remote repository. Once downloaded, the dependency will be added to various classpaths to build the project and may be included in the final distribution package that is created (in this case, a WAR file). Each individual dependency includes several of the same tags as in the header: groupId, artifactId, and version. These three tags will become very familiar when working with Maven2 because they form the basis of describing the artifact or plug-in that you want to use.

The new element that has been introduced is the scope tag. It describes what the dependency is used for, how to find the dependency, and when it should be included in the classpath. There are five options for scope:

- *compile*: This is the default scope (the struts2-core artifact uses this scope because no other was provided), and these dependencies are available on all classpaths. Any dependency with compile scope will be packaged with the final artifact.

- *provided*: The dependency will be provided by the JDK or the application server at runtime. It is required for compilation but will not be packaged in the application.

- *runtime*: The dependency is not required for compilation but is required to run the application. It will be available only on the runtime classpath and the test classpath.

- *test*: The dependency is only required for testing and will be available on the test classpath and the runtime classpath.

- *system*: The dependency is always available (you need to provide the JAR file) and is not retrieved via a repository lookup.

The repositories section tells Maven2 the additional repositories that can be used to obtain the dependencies. Each repository has a name and url tag.

```
<project>

  ...

  <repositories>
    <repository>
      <id>Struts 2 Repository</id>
      <url>http://people.apache.org/builds/struts/2.0.9/m2-staging-repository/</url>
    </repository>
  </repositories>

  ...

</project>
```

Repositories can be set up for your organization, or they can be remote repositories. The repository defined in the preceding code is the official Apache staging repository. If this section is omitted, the official Maven2 central repository at http://repo1.maven.org/maven2 is used. This repository has been mirrored in many locations; one of the most popular is the Ibiblio mirror, which can be found at http://mirrors.ibiblio.org/pub/mirrors/maven2.

The final section in the generated pom.xml configuration file is the build section. This section contains specific information pertaining to the control of the build process, including nondefault configurations and plug-ins (that tie into one of the life cycle phases or can be invoked manually).

```
</project>

    ...

  <build>
      <finalName>app</finalName>
      <plugins>
          <plugin>
              <artifactId>maven-compiler-plugin</artifactId>
              <configuration>
                  <source>1.5</source>
                  <target>1.5</target>
              </configuration>
          </plugin>
```

```
        <plugin>
            <groupId>org.mortbay.jetty</groupId>
            <artifactId>maven-jetty-plugin</artifactId>
            <version>6.0.1</version>
            <configuration>
                <scanIntervalSeconds>10</scanIntervalSeconds>
            </configuration>
        </plugin>
    </plugins>
  </build>
</project>
```

The finalName tag provides an override mechanism for the name of the final artifact produced when building the application. By providing this tag, the final name will now be app.war. Without it, the name would be a combination of the artifactId and the version from the header section, hence app-1.0-SNAPSHOT.war. The generated file has a similar name, but this is not necessary, and the names could have been completely different.

Several plug-ins are configured next. The first plug-in configures the compiler for Java 5. The code is a simple template; if you want to know more about the configuration options, the plug-ins documentation can be found at http://maven.apache.org/plugins/maven-compiler-plugin/compile-mojo.html.

The next plug-in configures the Jetty servlet container. By configuring a servlet container in the build script, it will have access to the application's classpaths, it will know which directories are for the application, and it will know which files are to be deployed to run the application. One configuration parameter is provided—the scanIntervalSeconds parameter—which tells Jetty to check the WAR file periodically and, if it is changed, to reload the web application. By default, the server is bound to port 8080.

■Note More detailed information about the Jetty servlet container and the different configurations for the Jetty Maven2 plug-in can be found at http://www.mortbay.org/maven-plugin/.

The Jetty server is started by issuing the mvn jetty:run command. Once started, it will need to be explicitly stopped (via Ctrl+C). As the WAR file is checked for changes periodically, leaving the server running and building your application in another process will reduce the turnaround time from building to testing.

Starter Application Features

The starter Struts2 web application that was created by the Maven2 artifact includes all the basic elements, as well as common Struts2 plug-ins that most web applications will use. By examining this simple application, you will get a feel for how all the parts fit together. We will explore the classes, configuration files, and features as they are encountered from running the starter application.

Two plug-ins are utilized in the starter application: the SiteMesh and Spring Framework plug-ins. To enable plug-ins, the JAR file for the Struts2 plug-in needs to be included in the application. With Maven2, the following dependencies are added to the pom.xml configuration file in the dependency section. If you use another build technique, you want to ensure that the plug-in JAR files and all dependant SiteMesh and Spring JAR files are located in the /WEB-INF/lib directory of the final WAR file.

```
<dependency>
    <groupId>org.apache.struts</groupId>
    <artifactId>struts2-sitemesh-plugin</artifactId>
    <version>2.0.9</version>
</dependency>

<dependency>
    <groupId>org.apache.struts</groupId>
    <artifactId>struts2-spring-plugin</artifactId>
    <version>2.0.9</version>
</dependency>
```

When building the application with Maven2, the Struts2 plug-in JAR files (as well as any dependent JAR files) are downloaded and included in the final WAR packaging.

The web.xml configuration file also has to be modified to enable the plug-ins to work. Spring needs an initialization parameter to determine where the applicationContext.xml configuration file is located, and it needs a listener to allow Struts2 to access Spring's application context.

```
<context-param>
    <param-name>contextConfigLocation</param-name>
    <param-value>classpath*:applicationContext*.xml</param-value>
</context-param>

...

<listener>
    <listener-class>
        org.springframework.web.context.ContextLoaderListener
    </listener-class>
</listener>
```

SiteMesh needs additional filters to be defined and placed in the processing queue before the Struts2 filters. Here's what this configuration looks like.

```
<filter>
    <filter-name>action2-cleanup</filter-name>
    <filter-class>org.apache.struts2.dispatcher.ActionContextCleanUp</filter-class>
</filter>
```

```
<filter>
    <filter-name>sitemesh</filter-name>
    <filter-class>com.opensymphony.module.sitemesh.filter.PageFilter</filter-class>
</filter>
<filter>
    <filter-name>action2</filter-name>
    <filter-class>org.apache.struts2.dispatcher.FilterDispatcher</filter-class>
</filter>

<filter-mapping>
    <filter-name>action2-cleanup</filter-name>
    <url-pattern>/*</url-pattern>
</filter-mapping>
<filter-mapping>
    <filter-name>sitemesh</filter-name>
    <url-pattern>/*</url-pattern>
</filter-mapping>
<filter-mapping>
    <filter-name>action2</filter-name>
    <url-pattern>/*</url-pattern>
</filter-mapping>
```

The code example shows the Struts2 configuration as well as the SiteMesh configuration. In fact, for a bare minimum configuration, only the single Struts2 filter and filter mapping need to be configured.

Getting to the First Screen

After starting the Struts2 starter application with the mvn jetty:run command, you can point your browser to the URL http://localhost:8080/app. This will redirect you to the http://localhost:8080/app/index.action URL.

The struts.xml configuration file determines the mappings from the URL to the action class that is invoked. This file can be found in the src/main/resources directory. The following is the part of the file of interest at the moment for the index action:

```
<struts>
    <package name="myPackage" extends="struts-default">
        <action name="index" class="com.fdar.apress.s2.IndexAction">
            <result>/jsp/index.jsp</result>
        </action>
        ...
    </package>
</struts>
```

The default extension for a Struts2 application is .action. Combine this with the value of the name attribute of the action configuration (along with the web application's context), and you get the URL. If the package tag had a namespace attribute, it would be added between the web context and the action name; but in this case, the attribute is not provided.

■**Note** The `package` tag also has an `extends` attribute. This attribute acts similarly to class inheritance in Java, in that one package can extend another package, which in turn allows the extending package to get "something for nothing." In the case of packages, the extending package gets access to all the configurations that are in the parent package. Chapter 3 provides more information on this topic.

The `class` attribute provides the name of the action class that is invoked. For the index action, the class is `IndexAction`:

```
@Conversion()
public class IndexAction extends ActionSupport {

    private Date now = new Date(System.currentTimeMillis());

    @TypeConversion(converter = "com.fdar.apress.s2.DateConverter")
    public Date getDateNow() { return now; }

    public String execute() throws Exception {
        now = new Date(System.currentTimeMillis());
        return SUCCESS;
    }
}
```

If you are used to Struts actions, this is going to look a little strange. First, there is a class property now, with a getter `getDateNow()` that returns the value of the property. Unlike Struts actions, which can be reused between requests (and therefore need to be thread-safe), a new Struts2 action is created for each request. This allows Struts2 to use class properties instead of relying exclusively on method properties.

■**Note** Usually the JavaBean pattern of a property name of `now` having a getter of `getNow()` and setter of `setNow()` is used. In the `IndexAction` class, this is not the case. Although it is a little confusing at first, it does illustrate that any class property can be used in a getter or setter.

There are some similarities, too. The class extends an `ActionSupport` class and provides an `execute()` method, which is called to provide the action's processing logic. The return value is a `String`, and constant values are provided by the `ActionSupport` class. In this case, the `SUCCESS` constant returns a string value of `success`. This matches the `result` tag of the action configuration. When no `name` attribute on the `result` tag is provided, it is implicitly assigned to a value of `success`. Similarly, when no `type` attribute is provided, the result is expected to be a JSP, so the `/jsp/index.jsp` JSP is rendered to HTML for the user.

Note In this section, you will learn the basics of configuring actions. Actions can be configured in many ways, and you will learn about these in Chapter 3. For the time being, we will keep the options limited to focus on how all the elements interact.

Figure 2-1 shows the screen that is rendered from the following JSP code.

```
<%@taglib prefix="s" uri="/struts-tags" %>

<html xmlns="http://www.w3.org/1999/xhtml" xml:lang="en" lang="en">
<head>
    <title>Index</title>
    <s:head />
</head>
<body>
    <s:form action="helloWorld">
        <s:textfield label="What is your name?" name="name" />
        <s:textfield label="What is the date?" name="dateNow" />
        <s:submit />
    </s:form>
</body>
</html>
```

Comparing the screen and the code, two questions immediately spring to mind:

Where did all the extra user interface text come from? This is provided by SiteMesh. SiteMesh uses the filter that was previously configured to intercept and adds additional HTML to the Struts2 result. The WEB-INF/decorators.xml configuration file provides the information on which URL patterns map to which decorators. In the starter application, you have a single decorator file WEB-INF/decorators/main.jsp. There are three tags of interest: <decorator:title /> inserts the *title* of the original page into the decorator template; <decorator:head /> inserts the entire *head* tags' contents of the original page into the decorator template; and <decorator:body /> inserts the entire *body* tags' contents into the decorators template. As you can see, there is no reference from the original page to the decorator template file because it all happens behind the scenes, providing a loosely coupled option that allows the templates to be modified and reapplied across the entire web application very easily.

Where did the date come from? The action did not use the HttpServletRequest, HttpSession, or any other type of object, so how did it get rendered? The answer is that Struts2 is a pull-MVC (Model View Controller) framework. Instead of requiring that all model data be placed in a commonly accessible location, the custom tag libraries are able to access the action that just executed. Hence, the tag that displays the date called the getDateNow() method on the action. The name attribute on the <s:textfield … name="dateNow"/> tag uses the JavaBean specification for finding the correct getter (in this case, the getDateNow() getter).

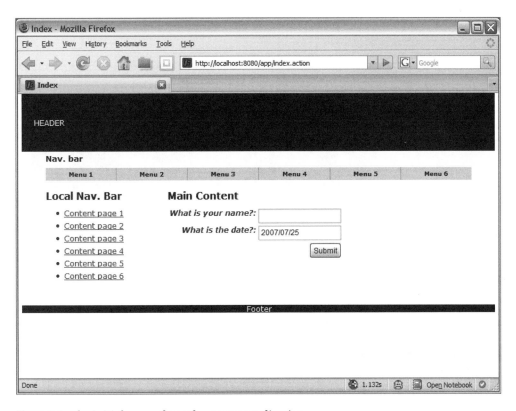

Figure 2-1. *The initial screen from the starter application*

■**Note** If you are interested in learning more about the features of SiteMesh, including the different tags and decorator mapping options, check out the project home page at `http://www.opensymphony.com/sitemesh`.

What should be familiar to you is the use of custom JSP tags. Most web application frameworks in Java provide wrappers around various HTML tags, as well as additional tags for logic functions, and Struts2 is no different. On the initial screen there are four tags:

- The `<s: head />` tag provides a single place for any additional JavaScript libraries needed by other tags to be specified and loaded.

- The `<s:form … />` tag is a body tag that encloses the field of the form that is to be submitted. The interesting thing here is that the `action` attribute is only a name value; there is no extension and no namespace. This is because the `form` tag will generate these for you, calling the action in the same namespace and adding an `.action` suffix.

- The `<s:submit />` and `<s:textfield … />` tags provide wrappers around the corresponding HTML form field tags. The `<s:textfield … />` tag has an additional attribute `label` that the HTML tag does not; this is used as the text to place in front of the input field. Each Struts2 tag that is a form field has this attribute, allowing the form to be formatted in a table with all the fields aligned.

That's it. The only thing left to do is enter a name and click the Submit button. Figure 2-2 shows the result of doing this.

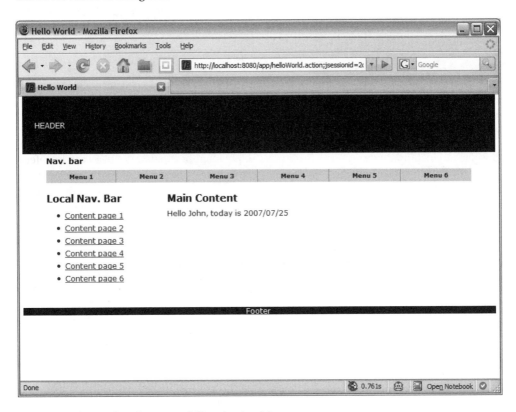

Figure 2-2. *The results of a successfully submitted form*

Submitting the Form

From the preceding discussion of the form tag, you know that the action being called is helloWorld, which results in a URL of http://localhost:8080/app/helloWorld.action. Going back to the struts.xml configuration file, you can see that the definition of this action is similar to the previous action, but a little different as well:

```
<struts>
    <package name="myPackage" extends="struts-default">
        …
        <action name="helloWorld" class="helloWorldAction">
            <result name="input">/jsp/index.jsp</result>
            <result>/jsp/helloWorld.jsp</result>
        </action>
    </package>
</struts>
```

The difference is that for the index action, Struts2 managed the creation of the action class. With helloWorld, this responsibility is delegated to the Spring Framework. The reference helloWorldAction corresponds to a bean defined in the applicationContext.xml configuration file, which is located in the src/main/resources directory with the struts.xml configuration file. The configuration for the action looks like this:

```
<beans>
    <bean id="helloWorldAction"
        class="com.fdar.apress.s2.HelloWorldAction" singleton="false" />
</beans>
```

It is very similar to what you would place in the struts.xml configuration file: a classname that is used to instantiate the action instance, a unique identifier so that the bean can be referenced from the struts.xml configuration file, and a property to ensure that Spring does not create a singleton. The last part is very important. To work correctly, Struts2 expects that each action is a new instance, so the Spring Framework needs to conform to this requirement.

With the additional configuration, why would you want to use Spring to manage the creating of the actions? The answer is that when defined in this manner, the actions can take advantage of the features provided by Spring, including declarative transaction management and aspect-oriented programming. Dependency injection is another feature that Spring provides, which is perhaps even the core advantage of choosing the framework, but it is not a reason to configure actions in this manner. Struts2 provides a Spring plug-in (the preferred way to create and manage business services) that provides Spring's dependency injection facility to actions configured in the struts.xml file without the need for additional configuration.

Let's take a look at the HelloWorldAction action:

```
@Validation()
@Conversion()
public class HelloWorldAction extends ActionSupport {

    private Date now;
    private String name;

    @TypeConversion(converter = "com.fdar.apress.s2.DateConverter")
    @RequiredFieldValidator(message = "Please enter the date")
    public void setDateNow(Date now) { this.now = now; }
    public Date getDateNow() { return now; }

    @RequiredStringValidator(message = "Please enter a name", trim = true)
    public void setName(String name) { this.name = name; }
    public String getName() { return this.name; }

    public String execute() throws Exception {
        return SUCCESS;
    }
```

This action has a lot more code than the index action but less internal functionality. The method that performs the business logic is the execute() method, and it simply returns SUCCESS. In fact, because the class extends ActionSupport, this method isn't necessary as ActionSupport provides the same implementation as a default.

This leaves you with getter and setter methods for two properties: a date property now and a string property name. So this action simply accepts a date and name, and then returns those to be displayed in the next page. You saw previously that the name attribute on the <s:textfield … name="dateNow"/> tag is used for finding the correct getter to display a value to the user; the same goes for providing data to the action. The same name attribute value tells Struts2 to use the setDateNow(…) method to transfer the value that the user entered in the HTML form to the action. Similarly, the <s:textfield … name="name" /> tag uses the setName(…) to provide the name value to the action.

To finish the cycle, here is the helloWorld.jsp code, which is the page to be rendered for a SUCCESS result:

```
<%@taglib prefix="s" uri="/struts-tags" %>

<html xmlns="http://www.w3.org/1999/xhtml" xml:lang="en" lang="en">
<head>
    <title>Hello World</title>
    <s:head />
</head>
<body>
    Hello <s:property value="name"/>,
    today is <s:property value="dateNow" /><br/>
</body>
</html>
```

This JSP introduces a new <s:property … /> tag. It looks and works very much like the <s:textfield … /> tag. The value attribute provides the name of the getter on the previously executed action that is called to provide the value to render to the user. Everything else in the JSP code should be familiar to you.

Validating the Form Field

In the previous explanation, you may have noticed that some of the code was skipped over. The omitted parts relate to validation and conversion of the values that the user entered in the HTML form. We'll now go back and explain how this works, starting with validation.

Validation has been configured via annotations. An @Validation class-level annotation tells Struts2 that this class is participating in validation. Once designated as having validation, method-level annotations can be applied to the setter methods. Here is the section of the action class that we are interested in:

```
@RequiredFieldValidator(message = "Please enter the date")
public void setDateNow(Date now) { this.now = now; }

@RequiredStringValidator(message = "Please enter a name", trim = true)
public void setName(String name) { this.name = name; }
```

As you will see in later chapters, many types of validators are available, and if none suit your requirements, you can easily define and configure your own. In this starter application, only two validators are used: the @RequiredFieldValidator and the @RequiredStringValidator. Both provide a check to ensure that a value for the field is present, and, if not, a message attribute provides an error message. For a String field validation, there is an additional attribute trim, which determines whether any whitespace should be removed from the beginning and end of the value before checking whether the value is empty.

Figure 2-3 shows the result of going back to the very first screen at the URL http://localhost:8080/app/index.action and submitting the form without a value for the name.

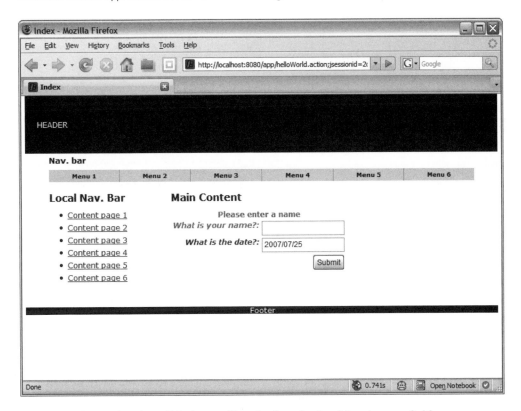

Figure 2-3. *The results of a validation problem in the submitted form's name field*

When validation errors occur, the screen rendered to the user is the same index.jsp that was just submitted. This is not automatic, and it doesn't even need to be the same HTML form that the user entered values into. The mapping of validation errors to the page viewed is made in the struts.xml configuration file. Here is the helloWorld action configuration again:

```
<action name="helloWorld" class="helloWorldAction">
    <result name="input">/jsp/index.jsp</result>
    <result>/jsp/helloWorld.jsp</result>
</action>
```

The element that we haven't discussed is the first result mapping for a `name` attribute value of `input`. This directs the user to the `index.jsp` page and is the behavior you just observed when the validation failed.

Note Actions are not restricted to only returning a single result value. In fact, actions usually return many different result values. Each value that can be returned by an action is mapped in the `struts.xml` configuration file to a different view with the `result` tag.

However, if you remember the `helloWorld` action, you will notice that it will only ever return SUCCESS. Validation in Struts2 works by intercepting values from the form as they are being applied to the action via the property setters. If all the validators pass, the method for processing the action's logic is called; otherwise, the action's method is short-circuited and the "input" result is used to determine the next view to be rendered.

Note This is a very simplistic representation of the actual validation process. In the next chapter, request processing will be discussed in much more detail, and, at that time, you will delve deeper into the "behind the scenes" processing that is involved.

When a validator is being processed and fails, the field's name and the message from the validator are entered into an error collection. The error collection allows information on whether there are errors, which fields failed, and the messages associated with particular fields to be determined. The `ActionSupport` class (that the `HelloWorldAction` action class extends) provides a default implementation of the error-management functions. You can provide your own implementation, but the default implementation is most likely going to provide everything that you need.

As you can see in Figure 2-4, the required field validation for generic objects as well as the string specialized validator present the same changes in the user interface to the user when a problem is found. The changes are an additional message (provided in the configuration for the validator) for the field, and both the message and the field name are highlighted.

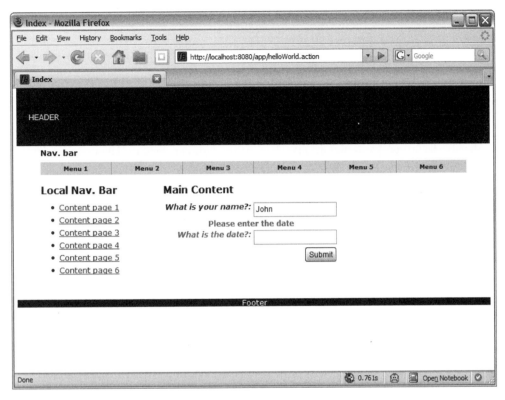

Figure 2-4. *The results of a validation problem in the submitted form's date field*

You have seen that the custom JSP tags provide additional layout for form fields using the `label` attribute. They also provide error-formatting functionality, including changing the CSS style to `errorLabel` (or `checkboxErrorLabel` if the element is a check box) for fields that have validation errors and adding an error message banner (if one is provided) above the field with a CSS style of `errorMessage`. Providing and applying common CSS styles for error-related formatting allows you to consistently change the format across all instances easily.

■Note Custom JSP tags have other features that make development easy. You will see how they work and what additional features are available in the next chapter.

The only changes you need to make to provide validation are to annotate the setter of the action and configure the page that the user is redirected to should there be validation errors. Struts2 handles everything else on your behalf.

Converting Data Types

By default, Struts2 automatically converts many common types between the String value received as a form field value and the object or primitive type that is to be set on the action. These include boolean, Boolean, char, Character, int, Integer, float, Float, long, Long, double, Double, and Date. If you have a special requirement or restriction for the conversion, then you need to implement a custom type converter.

In the starter application, a custom type converter has been supplied as an example. The configuration is similar to validation. An @Conversion annotation needs to be applied at the class level to let Struts2 know that the class has custom type conversions. Then method-level annotations are applied to the specific methods that require conversion.

In the HelloWorldAction class, the converter annotation is applied to the setter:

```
@TypeConversion(converter = "com.fdar.apress.s2.DateConverter")
public void setDateNow(Date now) { this.now = now; }
public Date getDateNow() { return now; }
```

On the IndexAction class, there is no setter, so the type converter is applied to the getter:

```
@TypeConversion(converter = "com.fdar.apress.s2.DateConverter")
public Date getDateNow() { return now; }
```

For the example, the only property for the annotation is the class name of the converter. This class is required to extend the StrutsTypeConverter class, and there are two methods that need to be implemented. The convertFromString(…) method is used to convert from a String to an Object, and the convertToString(…) method converts from an Object back to a String.

The example converter enforces a particular date format of year/month/date. Here's what the code looks like:

```
public class DateConverter extends StrutsTypeConverter {

    public Object convertFromString(Map context, String[] values, Class toClass) {

        if( values != null && values.length > 0 &&
                values[0] != null && values[0].length() > 0 ) {
            SimpleDateFormat sdf = new SimpleDateFormat("yyyy/MM/dd");
            try {
                return sdf.parse(values[0]);
            } catch(ParseException e) {
                throw new TypeConversionException(e);
            }
        }
        return null;
    }
```

```
public String convertToString(Map context, Object o) {
    if (o instanceof Date) {
        SimpleDateFormat sdf = new SimpleDateFormat("yyyy/MM/dd");
        return sdf.format((Date)o);
    }
    return "";
}
}
```

There are just a couple of things to point out about this code segment.

- The convertFromString(…) method has an array of strings as a parameter instead of a single String object. This allows one type converter to be used for HTML input, such as radio boxes or check lists that provide multiple values for a single form name.

- Along with the object, class, and string value, a context map is passed into both conversion methods. This provides additional environmental information that may be useful when converting the values.

- If there is a conversion error that cannot be handled, a TypeConversionException should be thrown. This allows the framework to manage the error consistently, as it would any other error. Figure 2-5 shows what the user would see when a value has been entered that could not be converted.

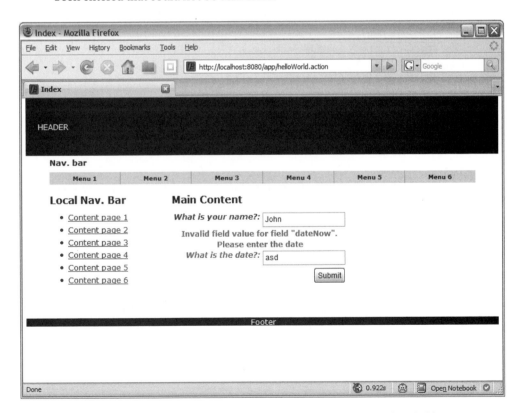

Figure 2-5. *The results of an unconvertible value in the submitted form's date field*

Configuring type conversion using annotations provides an unobtrusive mechanism for converting to and from the HTML user interface. Having an external converter, rather than manually performing the conversion in the setters and getters in the action, allows for greater reusability and less code.

Testing the Actions

Unit testing is an important part of all modern development, and Struts2 encourages unit testing with easily accessible application components. Actions are particularly easy to test because they are POJOs (Plain Old Java Objects). Test cases for action classes follow these simple steps:

1. Create an instance of the class.

2. Set any values on the action instance for the test case.

3. Call the method that processes the logic for the action, which in most cases is the execute() method.

4. Verify that the result from step 3 is what is expected; usually this will be SUCCESS.

5. Make sure that the state of the action is correct by verifying that values on the action are what you are expecting.

The starter application provides unit tests for both the IndexAction and the HelloWorldAction action classes. The actions are very simple, and so too are the test cases. Here is the test case for the IndexAction class:

```
public class IndexActionTest extends TestCase {

    public void testIndexAction() throws Exception {
        IndexAction action = new IndexAction();
        String result = action.execute();
        assertEquals(Action.SUCCESS, result);
    }
}
```

This test case skips steps 2 and 5 from the previous list. The action class is very simple, so this test case would do. However, to be complete, the following assertion would be added:

```
assertEquals( new Date(System.currentTimeMillis()), action.getDateNow() );
```

The new assertion provides 100% test coverage for the execute() method.

■**Caution** You should be aware that there is a slight chance that the unit test will fail. This is because the method call System.currentTimeMillis() used to create the date in the test may provide a different value than when it is called to create the date in the action. In most circumstances, you will not observe a failure because the execute() method executes quickly, it has only one method call (that creates the date), and the date assertion is made soon after the execute() method is called.

The unit test for the HelloWorldAction class is very similar to the IndexAction class's unit test. As the execute() method for the HelloWorldAction class only returns a value, it makes no sense to add additional assertions. You could add tests for the getters and setter but, in general, this level of coverage is unnecessary. Instead, leave this level of coverage until the setters or getters provide more than simple access to the class property. Here is the unit test for the HelloWorldAction class:

```
public class HelloWorldActionTest extends TestCase {

    public void testHelloWorldAction() throws Exception {
        HelloWorldAction action = new HelloWorldAction();
        String result = action.execute();
        assertEquals(Action.SUCCESS, result);
    }
}
```

Other Files

Three additional files are created with the starter application, which are all located in the src/main/resources directory. For completeness in describing the starter package, their purposes are described here briefly. In later chapters, you will learn about them in more detail.

- log4j.properties: This property file describes the logging properties for the application.

- struts.properties: This property file provides a mechanism to modify the internal configuration of the Struts2 framework.

- xwork-conversion.properties: Rather than using annotations, this property file is used to define application-level type converters.

Summary

In this chapter, you learned about the different elements that make up a Struts2 web application and generated a starter web application that you could test in the Jetty servlet container.

The chapter began by introducing the Maven2 build tool that will be used throughout this book to build, test, package, and deploy the projects created to a running servlet container. You learned how to install Maven2, what the life cycle phases are, and what types of functions each life cycle phase will perform. Using Maven2 and the Struts2 starter archetype, you generated a Struts2 starter web application. The different sections of the Maven2 pom.xml configuration file were described for a Struts2 web application, as well as the directory structure of the created project.

At the application level, the interactions among actions, configuration files, and JSP templates were explored. In a simple "hello world" example, you saw the how values entered by users get to the action and how the JSP accesses the data from the actions. To complete the application, you learned about validation and custom type conversion configurations.

At this point, you should have a good understanding of how to create and configure a basic web application. In the next chapter, we will take a closer look at each of the elements you were introduced to here. You will explore how the framework processes a user request, learn about framework elements that provide many of the features that you used in this chapter, and see that there are many different ways to provide configuration information.

CHAPTER 3

■■■

Framework Overview

In Chapter 2, you saw the elements that are needed for a basic web application. In this chapter, we will expand upon these to provide you with an understanding of the larger picture.

We will start by reviewing the architecture of Struts2 by walking through what happens during a user request—from when a user initiates a call to an action via a URL, all the way through to when the resulting JSP is rendered back to them in a browser.

Next we'll talk about the core elements that make up the Struts2 framework, the responsibilities of each element, the configuration details, and how the elements interact with each other. Finally, you will learn about the available extension points that allow you to modify the internal functionality and extend the framework.

Walking Through a Request-Response

In Chapter 2, we examined a working Struts2 application and discussed the role that actions and JSPs play in presenting information to and obtaining information from a user to perform application logic. Although simple, the example provided a complete life cycle from request through response. The deeper understanding of "how" the framework pieced everything together is the only thing missing.

In this section, we expand on the precursory introduction from the previous chapter and provide an in-depth understanding of how each of the elements interacts. To do this, we'll walk through the processing of a user request. In addition to the elements presented in Chapter 2, you will learn about other elements that work behind the scenes to provide the functionality present in Struts2.

Figure 3-1 shows the high-level components that participate in the request processing. Although this is a UML (Unified Modeling Language) sequence diagram, the actors are not classes; instead, they represent the user that initiated the request, components in the environment, some classes, and the more important elements of the Struts2 framework. For clarity, some of the components and calls have been excluded (helpers, such as the `Dispatcher` class; wrappers, such as the `ActionProxy`; and other low-level infrastructure classes, such as the `ConfigurationManager` and `ObjectFactory`).

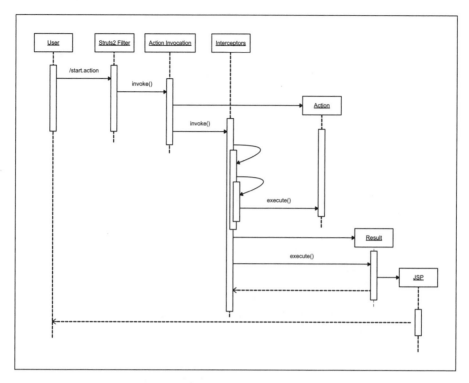

Figure 3-1. *An overview of the request walk-through*

The Request Initiation

The request-response cycle starts and finishes from the user's web browser. A URL that represents an action can be entered as a URL directly into the browser's address bar, or it can be generated by the framework when the user clicks on a link or submits a form. The URL will look something like `http://localhost:8080/app/index.action`.

Configuration files for the web application determine which URLs are handled by the Struts2 framework and which aren't. Usually, all requests for an entire web context or installed application are forwarded to the Struts2 servlet filter, and it makes the decision.

The Struts2 Servlet Filter

When requests are received at the servlet container, they are forwarded to either a servlet or a filter that will handle processing the request. In Struts2, a filter is used, and the class for handling the request is the `FilterDispatcher` class.

The filter and a `Dispatcher` class (to which many of the tasks are delegated) are the heart of the Struts2 framework. Together, they provide access to the infrastructure that will be needed to process the request. Upon startup, implementations of configurable elements in the framework, including `ConfigurationManager`, `ActionMapper`, and `ObjectFactory`, are loaded. With respect to processing the request, the Struts2 filter performs the following:

- *Serves static content*: Dojo content, JavaScript, and user configurable files can be served from the Struts2 or the web application's JAR file, allowing all the elements for a web application to be packaged together.

- *Determines the action configuration*: The filter uses the `ConfigurationManager` and the `ActionMapper` implementations to determine which action maps to the URL from the incoming request; by default, actions are determined by looking for a `.action` extension.

- *Creates the action context*: Because actions are generic and not specific to HTTP, the information contained in the web request needs to be converted to a protocol-independent format for the actions to use; this includes extracting data from the `HttpServletRequest` and the `HttpSession` objects.

- *Creates the action proxy*: There is an additional layer of indirection in the processing in the form of an `ActionProxy` class. This class contains all the configuration and context information to process the request and will contain the execution results after the request has been processed.

- *Performs cleanup*: To ensure that no memory leaks occur, the filter automatically performs cleanup of the `ActionContext` object.

When the `ActionProxy` class instance is created and configured, the `execute()` method is invoked. This signals that the preparation of the action is complete, and the real processing of the action is about to start.

The Action Invocation

The `ActionInvocation` object manages the execution environment and contains the conversational state of the action being processed. This class is the core of the `ActionProxy` class.

The execution environment is made up of three different components: actions, interceptors, and results. We'll discuss each of these next. In addition to these elements, actions can have methods configured as life cycle callbacks. The `ActionInvocation` class invokes these callback methods at the appropriate times.

The Action

One of the first tasks that the `ActionInvocation` performs is to consult the configuration being used and to create an instance of the action. Unlike Struts and other frameworks that reuse action instances, Struts2 creates a new action object instance for each and every request that is received. There is a slight performance overhead with this approach, but you gain the advantage that the object can behave as a Plain Old Java Object (POJO).

Interceptors

Interceptors provide a simple way to add processing logic around the method being called on the action. They allow for cross-functional features to be applied to actions in a convenient and consistent way, avoiding the need for adding code to each and every action that over time would create additional maintenance overhead. The functionality is similar to that provided by servlet filters and the JDK `Proxy` object.

Each action will have many interceptors configured. These interceptors are invoked in the order that they are configured. After they are all applied to the request, the actions method that processes the logic for the request is called. By convention, this is the `execute()` method; however, any no-argument method in the class that returns a `String` or a `Result` object may be used.

After the action logic is executed, the call returns through the configured interceptors in the reverse order, allowing for postprocessing of the action.

The Results

After the processing of the action is complete, it's time to turn your attention to the result. The method of the action class that processes the request returns a `String` as the result, which is mapped via configuration to an implementation of the `Result` interface, or the action can directly return a `Result` object instance.

The `Result` interface is very similar to an action class; it contains a single method that generates a response for the user. The response generated can vary dramatically between different concrete class implementations (know as result types). It could modify the HTTP response codes, generate a byte array for an image, or render a JSP. When returning a `String` as the result, the default configured `Result` implementation renders JSPs to the user.

The final step is to return the response (if one is generated) back to the user, which completes the current request processing cycle.

Exploring the Core Components

From reviewing the Struts2 starter application in Chapter 2 and the preceding request walkthrough, you may have noticed several components that are common: actions, result types (via configurations), and JSP results. Interceptors and non-JSP specific results are other components that you learned about in the previous section. You have not been exposed to one other component: the Value Stack. Together, these make up the core components of Struts2.

Figure 3-2 depicts the relationship between all the components under two circumstances. The first, shown by the wide arrows, are the components that a user request directly interacts with during the request processing. The secondary interaction is between the components (represented by the black lines) and primarily consists of interactions with the Value Stack.

In this section, we will explore each of the core components in much more detail. Instead of reviewing only what was needed to understand a specific task, we'll take a complete and comprehensive look at each one.

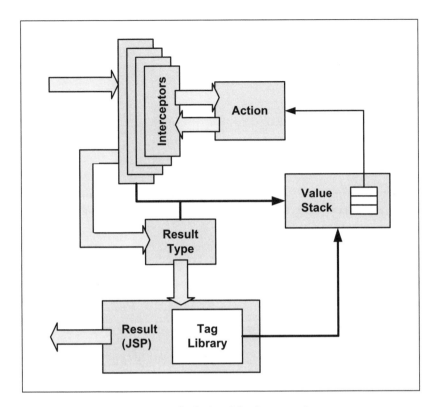

Figure 3-2. *The interactions and relationships between the core components*

Actions

Actions are the core of the Struts2 framework, as they are for any MVC (Model View Controller) framework. Each URL is mapped to a specific action, which provides the processing logic necessary to service the request from the user.

The only requirement for actions in Struts2 is that there must be one no-argument method that returns either a `String` or `Result` object. If the no-argument method is not specified, the default behavior is to use the `execute()` method. Otherwise, you will need additional configuration to specify the method name (configuration information about all the Struts2 elements is provided later in this chapter).

When the result is a `String` object, the corresponding `Result` is obtained from the action's configuration and instantiated. This is then used to generate a response for the user, the processing of which is covered in the following "Results and Result Types" section.

Even though there is no requirement that an action implements an interface or extends another class, sometimes it makes sense to extend helper classes or interfaces. Struts2 provides two such helpers that can be used. The first helper is the `Action` interface:

```
public interface Action {

    public static final String SUCCESS = "success";
    public static final String NONE = "none";
    public static final String ERROR = "error";
    public static final String INPUT = "input";
    public static final String LOGIN = "login";

    public String execute() throws Exception;
}
```

This interface does nothing more than supply the common string-based return values as constants and enforce that implementing classes provide the default execute() method.

■**Note** In the 2.0 version of WebWork (the framework from which Struts2 evolved), each action is required to implement the Action interface. In version 2.2 of WebWork, and hence Struts2, this restriction was removed and the interface remains as a helper class only.

The ActionSupport class is more interesting. It implements the Action interface and provides an implementation for the execute() method that returns the SUCCESS value.

Four other interfaces are also implemented. The Validateable and ValidationAware interfaces, as you would expect, provide support for validation. These allow the action to provide programmatic, annotation-based, and declarative XML-based validation. The TextProvider and LocaleProvide interfaces provide support for localization and internationalization. All these features are discussed further in later chapters.

```
public class ActionSupport
    implements Action, Validateable, ValidationAware,
    TextProvider, LocaleProvider, Serializable {

    …

    public String execute() throws Exception {
        return SUCCESS;
    }
}
```

Interceptors

Interceptors allow for crosscutting functionality to be implemented separately from the action as well as the framework. This makes the core framework code leaner than it may have originally been and able to adapt to new framework features much faster. In fact, the loose coupling means that users no longer have to wait for the framework to implement the new feature they require; instead, they can implement and apply the needed features themselves without modifying the underlying framework source code.

Using interceptors, the following can be achieved:

- Providing preprocessing logic before the action is called

- Interacting with the action, providing execution information, such as Spring-managed objects, and setting the request parameter on the action

- Providing postprocessing logic after the action is called

- Modifying the result being returned, hence changing what is rendered to the user

- Catching exceptions so that alternate processing can be performed or a different result can be returned

Many of the features of Struts2 are provided via interceptors. Table 3-1 lists the interceptors that come preconfigured and ready to use in Struts2.

Table 3-1. *Interceptors Provided with the Struts2 Framework*

Interceptor	Configured Name	Description
Alias Interceptor	alias	Allows parameters to have different name aliases across requests; this is particularly useful when chaining actions with different names for the same information.
Chaining Interceptor	chaining	Allows the previously executed action's properties to be available to the current action; usually this interceptor is used with the result type "chain."
Checkbox Interceptor	checkbox	Assists in managing check boxes by adding a parameter value of false for check boxes that are not checked (usually there would be no information in the HTTP request).
Conversion Error Interceptor	conversionError	Places error information from converting strings to parameter types into the action's field errors.
Create Session Interceptor	createSession	Automatically creates an HTTP session (if one does not already exist).
Debugging Interceptor	debugging	Provides several different debugging screens to the developer.
Execute and Wait Interceptor	execAndWait	Sends the user to an intermediary waiting page while the action executes in the background.
Exception Interceptor	exception	Maps exceptions that are thrown from an action to a result, allowing automatic exception handling via redirection.
File Upload Interceptor	fileUpload	Facilitates easy file uploading.
Internationalization Interceptor	i18n	Keeps track of the selected locale during a user's session.
Logging Interceptor	logger	Provides simple logging by outputting the name of the action being executed.

Continued

Table 3-1. *Continued*

Interceptor	Configured Name	Description
Message Store Interceptor	store	Stores and retrieves the messages, field errors, and action errors in the session for actions implementing the ValidationAware interface.
Model Driven Interceptor	modelDriven	Places the model object onto the stack for actions implementing the ModelDriven interface.
Scoped Model Driven Interceptor	scopedModelDriven	Stores and retrieves the model object from a configured scope for actions implementing the ScopedModelDriven interface.
Parameters Interceptor	params	Sets the request parameters on the action.
Parameter Filter Interceptor	n/a	Provides control over which parameters the action has access to (not configured by default).
Prepare Interceptor	prepare	Calls the prepare() method for actions implementing the Preparable interface.
Profiling Interceptor	profile	Allows simple profiling information to be logged for actions.
Scope Interceptor	scope	Stores and retrieves the action's state in the session or application scope.
Servlet Configuration Interceptor	servletConfig	Provides the action with access to various servlet-based information.
Static Parameters Interceptor	staticParams	Sets statically defined (param tags in the action's configuration) values on the action.
Roles Interceptor	roles	Allows the action to be executed only if the user is one of the configured roles.
Timer Interceptor	timer	Provides simple profiling information in the form of how long the action takes to execute.
Token Interceptor	token	Checks the action for a valid token to prevent duplicate form submission.
Token Session Interceptor	tokenSession	Same as token, but for invalid tokens, the submitted data is stored in the session.
Validation Interceptor	validation	Provides validation support for actions.
Workflow Interceptor	workflow	Redirects to an INPUT view without executing the action when validation fails.

Each interceptor provides a distinct feature to the action. As you can imagine, providing a fully equipped execution environment to an action requires more than one interceptor to be applied. Struts2 manages this by allowing interceptor stacks to be created and then referenced by actions, rather than needing each and every interceptor to be configured for each action. Table 3-2 lists the provided preconfigured stacks that are available and the interceptors that they contain. It is important to note that each interceptor is called in the order that it is configured.

Table 3-2. *Interceptor Stacks Provided with the Struts2 Framework*

Configured Stack Name	Included Interceptors	Description
basicStack	exception, servletConfig, prepare, checkbox, params, conversionError	The interceptors that are expected to be used in a minimal situation.
validationWorkflowStack	basicStack, validation, workflow	Adds validation and workflow to the basic stacks features.
fileUploadStack	fileUpload, basicStack	Adds file uploading to the basic stacks features.
modelDrivenStack	modelDriven, basicStack	Adds model functionality to the basic stacks features.
chainStack	chain, basicStack	Adds chaining to the basic stacks features.
i18nStack	i18n, basicStack	Adds locale persistence to the basic stacks features.
paramPrepareParamsStack	exception, alias, params, servletConfig, prepare, i18n, chain, modelDriven, fileUpload, checkbox, staticParams, params, conversionError, validation, workflow	Provides a complete stack including a pre-action method call. The params interceptor is applied twice: the first time to provide the parameters before the prepare() method is called, and a second time to reapply the parameters to objects that may have been retrieved during the prepare phase.
defaultStack	exception, alias, servletConfig, prepare, i18n, chain, debugging, profiling, scopedModelDriven, modelDriven, fileUpload, checkbox, staticParams, params, conversionError, validation, workflow	Provides a complete stack, including debugging and profiling.
executeAndWaitStack	execAndWait, defaultStack, execAndWait	Provides an execute and wait stack, which is useful for features such as file uploading where a waiting page is presented to the user.

Custom Interceptors

Creating a custom interceptor is easy; the interface that needs to be extended is the Interceptor interface.

```
public interface Interceptor extends Serializable {

    void init();

    void destroy();

    String intercept(ActionInvocation invocation) throws Exception;
}
```

As the names suggest, the init() method provides a way to initialize the interceptor, and the destroy() method provides a facility for interceptor cleanup. Unlike actions, interceptors are reused across requests and need to be thread-safe, especially the intercept() method. It is not as important for the init() method and the destroy() method because they are called only once when Struts2 is initializing and when the framework is shutting down, respectively.

If you have no need for initialization or cleanup code, the AbstractInterceptor class can be extended. This provides a default no-operation implementation of the init() and destroy() methods.

The Value Stack and OGNL

As you saw in Figure 3-2, the *Value Stack* is a central concept in the Struts2 framework. All of the core components interact with it in one way or another to provide access to context information as well as to elements of the execution environment.

Underneath, the Value Stack is exactly what it says—a stack implementation. However, there are differences between a traditional stack implementation and the Value Stack. The first difference is that the contents of the stack are made up of four levels:

- *Temporary objects*: These objects need temporary storage during the processing of a request, for example, the current element in a collection that is being iterated over.

- *Model object*: When the action implements the ModelDriven interface, the model object is placed on the stack in front of the action that is being executed; this level will not be present if the interface is not implemented by the action.

- *Action object*: This is the action that is currently being executed.

- *Named objects*: Any object can be assigned an identifier, making it a named object. Named objects can be developer created but also included are #application, #session, #request, #attr, and #parameters—each corresponding to an equivalent HTTP scoped object collection.

Another difference is how the stack is used. Traditionally, when using a stack, you would push objects on and pop objects off when you wanted to use them. With the Value Stack, you are searching for, or evaluating, a particular expression using OGNL (Object Graph Navigational Language) syntax.

Like other expression languages, such as JSTL (JSP Standard Tag Library) or MVEL (MVFLEX Expression Language), OGNL provides a mechanism to navigate object graphs using a dot notation and evaluate expressions, including calling methods on the objects being retrieved. Table 3-3 provides some concrete examples of what is possible in an OGNL expression.

Table 3-3. *Examples of OGNL Expressions*

OGNL Example	Description
address.postcode	Returns the value of calling getAddress().getPostcode(). This accessor pattern is known as dot notation in that each property name is separated by a period to provide navigation within an object graph.
#session['user']	Obtains the user object from the HTTP session.
!required	The expression returns true if the call to the isRequired() method returns false.
required && result.size()>1	Returns the result of performing a logical AND of the result of calling isRequired() and executing the logic to determine if the collection result has a size greater than 1.
hasActionErrors()	Returns the value from calling the hasActionErrors() method.
[2].id	Calls getId() on the third element of the Value Stack (index 0 is the top). This is most useful when you know the exact contents of the Value Stack, and the getId() method is present on objects higher than the index of the object you are after.
top	Returns the object on the top of the Value Stack.
results.{name}	Returns a collection consisting of calling getName() on each of the elements in the collection results. This is known as *projection*.
role in {'admin','user'} role not in {'admin','user'}	Determines whether the value returned from calling getRole() is either in, or not in, the collection of 'admin' and 'user'.
@com.static.Constants@getRoles()	Returns the value of calling the static method getRoles() on the class Constants.
@com.static.Constants@USER_NAME	Returns the static property value of USER_NAME on the class Constants.

■**Note** Although OGNL is the expression language for Struts2, work is underway to remove this dependency and allow different expression languages to be used. More information on OGNL can be found at http://www.ognl.org.

Searching is also not something that is generally associated with stacks. For the Value Stack, the OGNL expression is tested at each level, in the order they are listed at the start of the section. If the expression can be evaluated, the result is returned. Otherwise, the next level down is tested. When all the levels have been exhausted, and a result still cannot be evaluated, a null value is returned.

We'll cover many more features of OGNL as we develop the application.

Results and Result Types

After an action has been processed, it's time to send the resulting information back to the user. In Struts2, this task is split into two parts: the result type and the result itself.

The result type provides the implementation details for the type of information that is returned to the user. Result types are usually preconfigured in Struts2 (as shown in Table 3-4) or provided via plug-ins, but developers can provide custom result types as well. Configured as the default result type is the `dispatcher`, which uses a JSP to render the response to the user. After a result type is defined, it can be used many times by different action results.

Table 3-4. *Result Types Provided with the Struts2 Framework*

Configured Result Type Name	Class Name	Description
dispatcher	org.apache.struts2.dispatcher. ServletDispatcherResult	The default result type renders JSPs
chain	com.opensymphony.xwork2.ActionChainResult	Chains one action to another action
freemarker	org.apache.struts2.views.freemarker. FreemarkerResult	Renders Freemarker templates
httpheader	org.apache.struts2.dispatcher.HttpHeaderResult	Returns a configured HTTP header response
redirect	org.apache.struts2.dispatcher. ServletRedirectResult	Redirects the user to a configured URL
redirectAction	org.apache.struts2.dispatcher. ServletActionRedirectResult	Redirects the user to a configured action
stream	org.apache.struts2.dispatcher.StreamResult	Streams raw data back to the browser and is useful for downloadable content and images
velocity	org.apache.struts2.dispatcher.VelocityResult	Renders a Velocity template
xslt	org.apache.struts2.views.xslt.XSLTResult	Renders XML to the browser, which may also be transformed via an XSL template
plaintext	org.apache.struts2.dispatcher.PlainTextResult	Returns the content as plain text

To create your own result type, you need to implement the `Result` interface. This interface mimics the `Action` interface, with an `execute()` method that provides the implementation to generate the new result type's final response for the user. The `ActionInvocation` parameter provides everything the result needs to know about the action and the execution context.

```
public interface Result extends Serializable {

    public void execute(ActionInvocation invocation) throws Exception;
}
```

Results define what happens to the user's workflow in the Struts2 framework after the action has been executed—whether they go to a "success" view, an "error" view, or back to the "input" view (as some of the limitless options). If the action decides not to return a fully configured `Result` object, then it will return a `String` that is the unique identifier corresponding to a result configuration for the action or a globally configured result.

Each method on an action that is mapped to process a URL request needs to return a result, which includes specifying the result type (unless it is using the default result type) that it uses. Configuring the result is the most common configuration used; you'll learn about the configuration options later in this chapter.

Tag Libraries

Tag libraries provide the intersection between actions and views, allowing dynamic information from the actions to be rendered as well as making rendering decisions on the information to display at runtime. This is nothing unusual, and tag libraries in one form or another are available in most web application frameworks.

The difference between the Struts2 tag libraries and other tag libraries (such as JSTL) is that the Struts2 tag libraries have a tight integration with the framework. They take full advantage of the Value Stack to access action methods, and they take advantage of OGNL to evaluate expressions, project into collection properties, and perform on-the-fly object creation and collection generation.

The four different categories for tag libraries are listed here:

- *Control tags*: This group provides tags that control what information is rendered in the final view, as well as ways to manipulate collections of elements that can then be further utilized.

- *Data tags*: This group provides tags that render dynamically generated information (such as data) from the action that has just executed, internationalized text, and generated URLs and links. They can also provide debug information for the developer.

- *Form tags*: This group provides wrappers for HTML form tags, as well as additional user interface widgets. They include the option transfer group, date and time pickers, and check box lists.

- *Nonform tags*: The tags in this group are used in forms but are not directly form entry elements. They include error message displays, tabbed panels, and tree views.

▪**Tip** The full list of all the Struts2 tags can be found in the online documentation at `http://struts.apache.org/2.0.9/docs/tag-reference.html`.

The biggest difference between the Struts2 tag libraries and other tag libraries is in the architecture. Just as Struts2 is an MVC framework, so too are the tag libraries. Figure 3-3 shows the classes that make up the pattern and interaction between the elements.

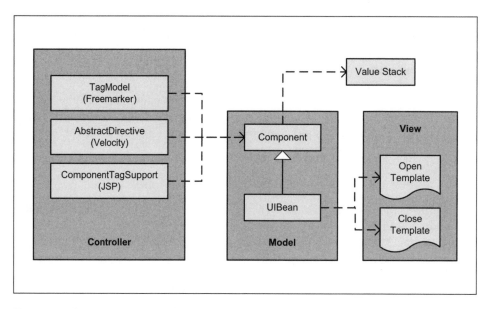

Figure 3-3. *The MVC structure of Struts2 tag libraries*

Following are the three main components that make up the Struts2 tag architecture:

Model: The model component in the diagram is the Component class. For tags that are form elements or those that provide a great deal of HTML, there is also the UIBean class. The UIBean class provides additional features to allow the tag's specific Freemarker rendering templates to be merged into the output stream. Each new tag requires a model class to be implemented that extends one of these two classes. The class is simple, providing the getters and setters for properties that are available to be used. The parent Component class has access to the Value Stack for retrieving extra parameters or for when OGNL expressions need to be evaluated.

View: The view consists of either one or two templates (by default, these are Freemarker templates); only one needs to be specified if the tag doesn't have enclosed tags. The templates provide a mechanism to keep formatting away from the logic and a way to change what is presented to the user on a per-project basis without recompiling the framework.

Controller: The controller allows tags to be accessed via JSP, Velocity, or Freemarker result templates. This is a major deviation from traditional tags. Normally, tag libraries are available to JSP templates but not to other view technologies. Struts2 fixes this by making tag library objects available in non-JSP templates. For each view technology that you want to support, a new subclass of TagModel, AbstractDirective, or ComponentTagSupport needs to be created. These classes provide a custom mechanism to populate the necessary fields in the model object.

Themes

As alluded to in the explanation of the view element of the tag libraries MVC pattern, the Freemarker templates can be easily modified. For out of the box functionality, the Freemarker templates are provided in the Struts2 JAR file but can be overridden by creating a new file with the same file name and in the same directory structure location (usually /template/xhtml) of the web application you are deploying. If you wanted to replace entire templates, this is the easiest way.

A more subtle method is to use themes. A *theme* is an additional directory that the tag can obtain the Freemarker template from. Struts2 provides four themes:

- `simple`: Provides the tag output with minimal decoration.

- `xhtml`: Provides formatting of form field elements in an HTML table and highlights and provides error message text next to the form field.

- `css_xhtml`: The same as the xhtml theme but uses CSS div tags instead of the table tags.

- `ajax`: Provides Ajax functionality to tags.

■**Caution** The `ajax` theme is marked to be removed and replaced by a tag library plug-in in version 2.1 of Struts.

To create a new theme, a new directory under the template directory needs to be created, for example, /template/mytheme. Each tag that you want to use the new theme will then use the value mytheme for the theme attribute on the tag. So, instead of using

```
<s:textfield name="name" />
```

you would use

```
<s:textfield name="name" theme="mytheme" />
```

When the theme of the form tag is modified, all enclosed elements will use the same theme. All four tags in the preceding code will use mytheme, either because the theme was explicitly specified or because it was inherited from the form tag. Even though the theme mytheme is inherited, it can be overridden in each enclosed tag.

```
<s:form action="helloWorld" theme="mytheme">
    <s:textfield label="What is your name?" name="name" />
    <s:textfield label="What is the date?" name="dateNow" />
    <s:submit />
</s:form>
```

The theme attribute is a common attribute provided on all tags.

Configuring the Elements of the Framework

Now that you are familiar with the elements of the framework, you will want to configure them to be used in your web application. We'll start with the web.xml configuration file. After that, we'll talk about the configuration of actions via annotations and XML.

The web.xml File

The web.xml configuration file is a J2EE configuration file that determines how elements of the HTTP request are processed by the servlet container. It is not strictly a Struts2 configuration file, but it is a file that needs to be configured for Struts2 to work. This is the first configuration file you'll need to configure if you are starting without the aid of a template or tool that generates it (such as Maven2).

In the previous chapter, there were multiple entries for this configuration file, each of which allowed for various plug-ins to be active. For just the Struts2 framework, without any plug-ins, the following is all that is required to be present in the web.xml configuration file:

```
<filter>
    <filter-name>action2</filter-name>
    <filter-class>org.apache.struts2.dispatcher.FilterDispatcher</filter-class>
</filter>
<filter-mapping>
    <filter-name>action2</filter-name>
    <url-pattern>/*</url-pattern>
</filter-mapping>
```

As plug-ins are enabled, additional configuration will be required. Any additional configuration will be introduced as the plug-ins are introduced.

Zero Configuration Annotations

Struts2 has a prerequirement of Java 5 and can therefore take advantage of annotations as a configuration mechanism. The *Zero Configuration* terminology is used to describe the departure from a pure XML-based configuration to an annotation-based configuration. Using annotations, the struts.xml configuration can be completely avoided in most situations.

■**Note** Although there is a prerequirement of Java 5 to use Struts2, there is also another option. For those projects that cannot move away from Java 1.4, a compatible version can be generated using the retrotranslator library (http://retrotranslator.sourceforge.net). Retrotranslator transforms Java 5 byte code so that it can be run on a Java 1.4 JVM and supports all the Java 5 features used in Struts2. To build Struts2 for Java 1.4, the Maven2 command is mvn clean install -Papps,j4 -Djava14.jar="$JAVA_HOME/jre/lib/rt.jar".

To enable Zero Configuration, you first need to tell Struts2 which packages have actions that are using annotations by adding an `init-param` called `actionPackages` to the filter configuration in the `web.xml` configuration file. The value that the parameter takes is a comma-delimited list of package names. The following example shows two packages enabled:

```
<filter>
    <filter-name>struts2</filter-name>
    <filter-class>org.apache.struts2.dispatcher.FilterDispatcher</filter-class>
    <init-param>
        <param-name>actionPackages</param-name>
        <param-value>com.fdar.apress.s2,com.apress.s2</param-value>
    </init-param>
</filter>
```

After the packages that have actions using Zero Configuration have been configured, it is time to add annotations to the action. The first example is very simple. The `ZCAction`, shown next, uses the default `execute()` method for processing the request that always returns the "success" string as a result.

To configure a result for the return value, you add the `@Result` annotation at the class level. There are three parameters for configuring the annotation:

- `name`: The string value that is being returned from the methods that process the request.

- `value`: A value that the result type uses. For JSP, Freemarker, and Velocity results, this is the name of the template to render.

- `type`: The class of the result type. These can be found in Table 3-4 shown earlier. (Note that in the annotation, the class is used, and not a string value, so no quotes are needed around the value in the annotation.)

Here's what the class looks like with code and annotations:

```
package com.fdar.apress.s2;

@Result(name="success", value="/jsp/success.jsp",
        type= ServletDispatcherResult.class)
public class ZCAction {

    public String execute() {
        return "success";
    }
}
```

■Caution Remember that the `@Result` and `@Results` annotations are class level and not method level. The configuration will not work correctly if defined at the method level.

Configuring multiple results is just as easy. You use the @Results annotation, placing each individual @Result annotation within it. Expanding upon the last example, this next action class provides two results; the selection of which result to use is made randomly.

```
package com.fdar.apress.s2;

@Results({
    @Result(name="success", value="/jsp/success.jsp",
            type= ServletDispatcherResult.class),
    @Result(name="input", value="/jsp/input.jsp",
            type= ServletDispatcherResult.class)
})
public class ZC2Action {

    public String execute() {
        return new Random().nextBoolean() ? "success" : "input";
    }
}
```

The relationship between the packages configured in the web.xml configuration file and the packages that the actions are located in is important. You have configured the results, but how is the action invoked? The rules for determining this URL are easy:

1. The name of the action is the action's class name (the first letter in lowercase) where the suffix "Action" has been removed; so the ZCAction class would become zC.action in the URL.

2. The URL path is the action's package path (with the periods replaced with path separators) from the package level configured in the web.xml configuration file. By using the web.xml configured value com.fdar.apress.s2 that you configured previously and by placing the ZCAction action in the same com.fdar.apress.s2 package, there would be no additional namespace, and the URL would be http://localhost:8080/app/zC.action. However, if the action was in the com.fdar.apress.s2.book.test package, the URL would become http://localhost:8080/app/book/test/zC.action.

Following these rules, the preceding action examples would be invoked using the URLs http://localhost:8080/app/zC.action and http://localhost:8080/app/zC2.action.

Two other annotations assist in configuring the action, and both contain a single parameter. The first is the @Namespace annotation. In the preceding rules for determining URLs, it was stated that the URL will match a part of the action's package name, but this is not always the case. The @Namespace annotation allows you to modify the namespace to any value. Following is the ZC3Action, which is located in the com.fdar.apress.s2.book.test package. Without the annotation, the URL is http://localhost:8080/app/book/test/zC3.action, but with the annotation, it becomes http://localhost:8080/app/testing/zC.action.

```
package com.fdar.apress.s2.book.test;

@Result(name="success", value="/jsp/success.jsp",
        type= ServletDispatcherResult.class)
@Namespace("/testing")
@ParentPackage("struts-default")
public class ZC3Action {

    public String execute() {
        return "success";
    }
}
```

The final annotation is the @ParentPackage annotation. As you will see in the next section, packages provide a mechanism to manage configuration groupings. A default-configured package (the struts-default package) is provided by Struts2; others can be provided by plug-ins or developed specifically for deployable web applications. The @ParentPackage annotation provides a way to allow the action to take advantage of the package mechanism. In ZC3Action, we are using the struts-default package.

■**Caution** When you use an @ParentPackage that is not deployed in the Struts2 JAR or a plug-in, you need to provide a struts.xml configuration file with its definition and configuration. This is a useful technique but does move the application away from being configured strictly by annotations.

The struts.xml File

The struts.xml configuration file is the core configuration file for Struts2 web applications. The Zero Configuration option is fairly new and a great way to keep the actions code and configuration together to handle some of the configuration features. However, if you want fine-grained control over all the configuration options, you need to know your way around struts.xml. Most likely, you will want to use these two options in parallel. In this section, we'll point out when this method makes sense.

■**Note** In the struts.xml configuration file, there are configuration options specific to plug-ins and extending the framework. We'll postpone the discussion of these elements until the next section, which exclusively talks about extending the framework.

The entire definition of the struts.xml configuration file (excluding configuration elements under the struts tag) is given here:

```
<?xml version="1.0" encoding="UTF-8" ?>

<!DOCTYPE struts PUBLIC
    "-//Apache Software Foundation//DTD Struts Configuration 2.0//EN"
    "http://struts.apache.org/dtds/struts-2.0.dtd">

<struts>

…

</struts>
```

At the top level, under the `struts` tag, there are four elements: `include`, `package`, `constant`, and `bean`. The `constant` and `bean` tags will be explained in the next section on extending the framework.

Include Files

The `struts.xml` configuration file can be divided into many smaller pieces enabling manageability and modularity in configuration. There is no difference structurally between the parent file and those being included; they follow the same DTD (Document Type Definition), and thus have exactly the same elements. Files are included by using the `include` tag at the top level.

```
<struts>

    <include file="struts-module1.xml" />
    <include file="struts-module2.xml" />

…

</struts>
```

When including files, the order is very important. Dependencies between include files are not automatically determined and resolved, so if `struts-module1.xml` is dependent on the configuration provided in `struts-module2.xml` (and `struts-module2.xml` is configured after `struts-module1.xml`), an exception is thrown. The solution is to change the file that the dependent configuration is contained within or to change the order of the include files.

Three files follow the `struts.xml` structure and are loaded in the order shown by the Struts2 framework during startup:

- `struts-default.xml`: The default `struts.xml` configuration file that comes with the Struts2 framework and proves many configurations for result types, interceptors, and interceptor stacks.

- `struts-plugin.xml`: If plug-in JAR files are located on the classpath, the `struts-plugin.xml` file from each of the plug-ins will be loaded.

- `struts.xml`: The file you provide to configure your web application.

Packages

Splitting configurations into different files is one way to achieve modularization, and packages is the other. *Packages* provide a container to hold mapping and execution type configuration. The tags configuration is straightforward:

```
<package name="test" extends="struts-default" abstract="false" namespace="/tests" >

    ...

</package>
```

The package tag is directly underneath the struts tag and contains four attributes:

- name: This is a unique name for the package that is provided by the developer.

- extends: Packages can extend each other, allowing the extending package to access all the extended package's configurations, including action configuration in the extending package's namespace.

- abstract: If abstract, the package's actions are not available via a URL, and the package is purely for configuration modularization.

- namespace: The URL path that the actions configured in this package will be accessible under.

■**Caution** The name attribute as well as the namespace attribute needs to be unique. If not, Struts2 will not start up correctly.

The struts-default.xml configuration file contains the struts-default package, which contains all the result types, interceptors, and interceptor stacks that were discussed earlier. Whenever you create your own packages, it is good practice to extend struts-default. The only time this is not the case is when you are using a plug-in that provides another package that is more applicable; for example, with the tiles plug-in, you would extend the tiles-default package. In most cases, plug-in packages will extend the struts-default package.

The elements contained within the package tag are result-types, interceptors, default-interceptor-ref, default-action-ref, global-results, global-exception-mappings, and action.

■**Tip** Using the @Namespace annotation on action classes allows each action to be placed in a different namespace. When placing actions in package configurations defined in the struts.xml configuration file, each namespace needs to be a separate package configuration, all of which should extend from a common package (containing the common configuration).

Result Types

Before Struts2 can use results, they need to be configured by using the `result-types` and `result-type` tags:

```
<package name="test" extends="struts-default" abstract="false" namespace="/tests" >

    <result-types>
        <result-type name="apress" default="false"
            class="com.fdar.apress.s2.ApressResult" />
        <result-type name="fdar" class="com.fdar.apress.s2.FdarResult" />
    </result-types>

    …

</package>
```

The `result-types` tag can contain many `result-type` tags. Each `result-type` tag has three attributes:

- `name`: The unique, developer-provided name for the result type.

- `class`: The package and class name of the result type implementation.

- `default`: Determines if this is the default result type (meaning that the type does not need to be specified for each configuration; instead, it is assumed); this attribute is not required and defaults to `false`.

Once configured, the result types are available to be used in action configurations in the `struts.xml` configuration file or via annotations.

Interceptors

Like result types, interceptors have a very simple configuration: a developer-provided unique `name` attribute, and the `class` attribute, which provides the package and class name of the interceptor's implementation class:

```
<interceptor name="apress" class="com.fdar.apress.s2.ApressInterceptor" />
```

Things become more interesting as single interceptors are combined into stacks of interceptors. The configuration structure for interceptors and interceptor stacks is given here:

```
<package name="test" extends="struts-default" abstract="false" namespace="/tests" >

    …
```

```
<interceptors>
    <interceptor name="apress" class="com.fdar.apress.s2.ApressInterceptor" />
    <interceptor-stack name="apressStack">
        <interceptor-ref name="basicStack" />
        <interceptor-ref name="apress" />
    </interceptor-stack>
</interceptors>

<default-interceptor-ref name="apressStack" />

...

</package>
```

When configuring interceptors and interceptor stacks:

- The `interceptors` tag can contain any number of `interceptor` and `interceptor-stack` tags.

- The developer-provided `name` attribute value needs to be unique across both the `interceptor` and `interceptor-stack` tags.

- The `interceptor-ref` and `default-interceptor-ref` tags' `name` attribute value can represent either an interceptor or interceptor stack.

- The `interceptor-stack` tag can contain any number of `interceptor-ref` tags, and each interceptor will be called in the order it was configured.

The `default-interceptor-ref` tag allows for either an interceptor or interceptor stack to be configured as the default and be applied to all the action being executed in this package.

Tip Being able to configure custom interceptors and custom interceptor stacks is the primary reason to combine annotation-based action configuration with the `struts.xml` configuration file. Create a custom package with the interceptor and interceptor stack configurations, and then use the `@ParentPackage` annotation to reference the package from actions.

For the `interceptor` and `interceptor-ref` tags, there is an additional configuration parameter. To demonstrate the usage, we'll use the `interceptor-ref` tag. Here is an example from the `struts-default.xml` configuration file:

```
<interceptor-ref name="validation">
    <param name="excludeMethods">input,back,cancel,browse</param>
</interceptor-ref>
```

By using a `param` tag, a value from the configuration file can be applied to the interceptor. In the example, the validation interceptor is having `input,back,cancel,browse` set to the `excludeMethods` property (via a setter). Any property on the interceptor class that has an exposed setter can have a value applied using this method. The `name` attribute provides the property name, and the body value of the tag provides the property value.

For the case when you want to override the values passed to the interceptor, two options are available. The first is to reconfigure the interceptor or the entire interceptor stack, providing the new `param` tag value. Alternatively, when applying the stack to an action, you can provide only `param` tags for values that need to be changed. Prefix the property in the `name` attribute with the `name` of the interceptor; that is, to change the validation interceptor's `excludeMethods` property, you would use the value `validation.excludeMethods` as shown here:

```
<action name="testMe" class="com.fdar.apress.s2.MyAction">
    <interceptor-ref name="defaultStack">
        <param name="validation.excludeMethods">prepare,findById</param>
    </interceptor-ref>
</action>
```

Global Results

When common results are used across many actions, it makes sense to configure them once rather than for each action. Examples of results that benefit from this configuration are viewing module home pages or dashboards, login and logout, errors and exceptions, and security authorization failures. Some of these results can be returned from the action itself, but more commonly, an interceptor provides the result.

```
<package name="test" extends="struts-default" abstract="false" namespace="/tests" >

    ...

    <global-results>
        <result name="logout" type="dispatcher">/index.jsp</result>
        <result name="error" type="freemarker">/error.ftl</result>
    </global-results>

    ...

</package>
```

The `global-results` tag can contain many `result` tags. The `result` tag looks very similar to the `@Result` annotation you saw earlier and will be exactly the same as the `result` tag in the action configuration. The following are the attributes:

- `name`: A unique, developer-provided name, which must be unique throughout the current package as well as any packages that extend the package in which the result is configured. This attribute should always be specified.

- `type`: The configured result type name value (refer to Table 3-4).

A value to be passed to the result type is provided as the body to the `result` tag. Usually this is the name and location of the template to be rendered.

Global results work closely with global exception handling.

Global Exception Handling

Global exception handling works by declaratively describing which exceptions (and subclasses of the exception) are expected, and which results should be invoked when such an exception occurs.

```
<package name="test" extends="struts-default" abstract="false" namespace="/tests" >

    ...

    <global-exception-mappings>
        <exception-mapping exception="java.sql.SQLException"
                           result="error1" />
        <exception-mapping exception="java.lang.Exception"
                           result="error2" name="error" />
        <exception-mapping exception="java.lang.RuntimeException"
                           result="error3" />
    </global-exception-mappings>


    ...

</package>
```

The `global-exception-mappings` tag can contain many `exception-mapping` tags. The attributes for the `exception-mapping` tag are provided here:

- `exception`: The exception that will be acted upon.

- `result`: The name of the configured global result to use (bypassing what the action may have returned).

- `name`: The unique name of the exception mapping; this attribute is not required, doesn't make much sense, and should be avoided. (Unlike other configurations, the `name` attribute in the `exception-mapping` tag is not referenced and provided for consistency. When specified, it may confuse developers into thinking that it is referenced from somewhere else.)

When a subclass of the declared exceptions is thrown, the closest (in class hierarchy depth) declared exception mapping is invoked. Let's say a `ClassCastException` for the preceding configuration is thrown. Both the `Exception` and `RuntimeException` classes are super classes of this exception. However, because `RuntimeException` is one step closer to `ClassCastException` in class depth, its configured result will be invoked.

LOGGING EXCEPTIONS IN THE GLOBAL EXCEPTION HANDLING

Global exception handling is a great service, but it can also cause problems depending on the exception-handling strategy of your application. If you are logging exceptions when they occur, you should not have any issues, but if you are using the application server for logging, the exceptions are no longer available because the `exception` interceptor consumes the exception during processing.

To avoid this issue, the `exception` interceptor can be configured with additional properties to log error messages to an application-specific log file. The attributes (all of which are optional) include the following:

- `logEnabled`: `true` or `false`, determines whether the exception is logged.

- `logLevel`: The priority level for the exception being logged (common levels include `trace`, `debug`, `info`, `warn`, `error`, `fatal`).

- `logCategory`: The category to log the exception.

Here is an example of a fully configured `exception` interceptor:

```
<interceptors>

    <interceptor-stack name="exceptionMappingStack">
        <interceptor-ref name="exception">
            <param name="logEnabled">true</param>
            <param name="logCategory">com.fdar.apress.s2</param>
            <param name="logLevel">WARN</param>
        </interceptor-ref>

    </interceptor-stack>
    ...

</interceptors>
```

The `exception` interceptor uses the Apache Commons Logging project (`http://commons.apache.org/logging`), which is an implementation-agnostic API. This means that it can be configured to use a number of different logging implementations "behind the scenes." The `logCategory` and `logLevel` properties in the `exception` interceptor configuration should match those from the logging implementation that you are using.

■Note Global exception handling is an unusual configuration. It is not actually part of the core functionally; instead, the feature is provided by the "exception" interceptor that must be part of the interceptor stack for this feature to work. However, unlike other interceptors, it has custom XML configuration in the `struts.xml` configuration file.

Actions

The configuration for actions is similar to the information provided for the annotations; however, the XML configuration is much richer in the configuration options available.

■**Caution** Be careful when configuring the same action class using XML and annotations. If referenced in the XML with the same namespace and action name as the annotations use, the annotation will prevail, and the XML configuration will be ignored. This may lead to confusing error messages.

One difference from the annotation configuration is that with XML, an action can be designated as the default action for a package. When a URL is entered by a user and has no action mapped, the servlet engine will return an HTTP 404 error. To avoid this outcome, an action can be specified as the default using the `default-action-ref` tag to be executed when no other mapping is present. In the following example action mapping, the default action is `testMe`:

```
<package name="test" extends="struts-default" abstract="false" namespace="/tests" >

    ...

    <default-action-ref name="testMe" />

    ...

    <action name="testMe" class="com.fdar.apress.s2.MyAction" method="findValue" >
        <result name="success" type="dispatcher">/jsp/found.jsp</result>
        <result name="exception" type="dispatcher">/jsp/found.jsp</result>
        <interceptor-ref name="apressStack" />
        <exception-mapping exception="java.lang.Exception" result="exception" />
        <param name="version">2.0.9</param>
    </action>

</package>
```

Unlike the Zero Configuration option, when using XML configuration, the action's namespace is specified by the namespace of the package that it is contained in. Additional configuration elements are needed to specify the name of the class that implements the action (via the `class` attribute) as well as the name of the action (via the `name` attribute). Being able to provide the name of the action is a level of flexibility that the annotations currently do not allow. Another such level is the `method` attribute, which specifies the method on the action that contains the processing logic for the request and allows a single action class to have different action configurations that each call a different method.

We have already explained the tags, which are configured in exactly the same manner:

- *result tag*: Under the action, there can be many result tags, each providing a configuration for a different outcome of the request. The name attribute can be omitted for a value of success, and the type attribute can be omitted if the value is the default result type (unless changed, this is dispatcher).

- *interceptor-ref tag*: Replaces the package configured default interceptor reference with one specific to the current action.

- *exception-mapping tag*: You can provide localized exception mapping at the action level (that is handled before the global exception mapping), and the result attribute value can be either a result from the current action or a global result.

- *param tag*: Sets static values onto the action via the XML configuration.

■**Tip** The action, interceptor, and interceptor-ref tags are not the only elements that the param tag can be applied to. The result-type, default-interceptor-ref, default-action-ref, result, and exception-mapping can all use the tag in their bodies. In most circumstances, the tag is most useful when applied to actions and interceptors.

Wildcard Configuration

As your application develops, you will most likely start to see patterns in the configuration, for example, when the package names start to match the URLs used to invoke the action (such as /app/admin/user/add.action and /app/sales/user/edit.action), or when the action name includes a domain name or method on the action class that is invoked (such as /app/addUser.action and /app/editUser.action).

When patterns such as these start emerging, there is an alternative. Instead of explicitly defining each and every action configuration, which for large applications could become very time consuming, the configuration can be consolidated into a single action configuration using wildcards. An asterisk is used in the action's name attribute to specify a wildcard token, and then each token can be retrieved individually using a number (starting from index 1) surrounded by curly brackets.

As an example, let's say that the URLs for a web application have the standard form of web context, followed by an entity object name, and ending with an action. Examples of this pattern are /app/user/add.action; /app/user/edit.action; /app/project/add.action; and /app/project/edit.action. The standard is also to have a single action class per entity object (i.e., UserAction and ProjectAction) with multiple methods to handle the user interface interactions (edit() and add() methods).

Using wildcards, this pattern can be realized with a single configuration for all entity objects:

```
<action name="*/*" class="com.fdar.apress.s2.{1}Action" method="{2}" >
    <result name="success">/{1}/{2}.jsp</result>
    <result name="input">/{1}/edit.jsp</result>
    <result name="home">/{1}/home.jsp</result>
</action>
```

The name of the class and the name of the method are specified using parts of the incoming URL. When the URL is /app/user/add.action, the class name will be "com.fdar.apress.s2.userAction", and the method will be "add" (note that the case of the URL and class name will be the same).

Wildcard support also extends to the result tag. For the URL /app/user/add.action, the view /user/add.jsp would be rendered for a "success" result, /user/edit.jsp for "input", and /user/home.jsp for "home".

The only restriction when using wildcards in the action's name attribute is not to place two asterisks together without a separating character. In this case, the framework will not know how to separate the action name. Instead, a separator can be used, such as the "/" character (shown previously) or an "_" character for a URL of /app/user_edit.action.

If the entire untokenized URL is required, the special accessor {0} can be used.

■**Caution** If you do use slashes in the action name, such as name="*/*", you need to set the environmental property struts.enable.SlashesInActionNames to true.

Configuring the Execution Environment

The default.properties configuration file contains the execution environment configuration properties for Struts2. It is packaged in the Struts2-core JAR file and provides the default values for all properties (the primary properties are shown in Table 3-5).

Developers can override these values in two ways. The first is by providing a struts.properties configuration file in the classpath root directory. Any property that is supplied in this file is used in preference to the same property value in the default.properties file.

The preferred method is to use the constant tag from within the struts.xml configuration file. To enable developer mode, the following configuration is added directly under the struts top level tag:

```
<constant name="struts.devMode" value="true" />
```

where the name attribute is a known property from the default.properties file, and value attribute is the new value to assign to the property.

Table 3-5. *Environmental Properties from the* default.properties *File*

Property Name	Default Value	Description
struts.locale	en_US	The locale to use.
struts.i18n.encoding	UTF-8	The encoding scheme to use.
struts.objectFactory	spring	The factory that is configured to create object instances.
struts.objectFactory. spring.autoWire	name	How to wire up the Spring objects; valid values are name, type, auto, and constructor.
struts.objectFactory. spring.useClassCache	true	Indicates to Spring that class instances should be cached.
struts.multipart.parser	jakarta	The MIME multipart/form-data to use for file uploads; valid options are cos, pell, and jakarta.
struts.multipart.saveDir	n/a	The directory to save uploaded form data to.
struts.multiart.maxSize	~2MB	The maximum size of uploaded files.
struts.custom.properties	n/a	Comma-delimited list of additional property files to load.
struts.mapper.class	org.apache. struts2. dispatcher. mapper. DefaultAction Mapper	The class that maps the URL to and from actions.
struts.action.extension	action	The extension for action names in the URL.
struts.server.static	true	Whether to serve static content from the Struts2 filter.
struts.server.static. browserCache	true	Determines whether HTTP headers should be written so that browsers cache static content.
struts.enable. SlashesInActionName	false	Whether to allow slashes in the action names.
struts.devMode	false	Provides a developer-friendly mode by reloading internationalization files and XML configuration, raising debug or less important issues to errors, and failing on errors faster.
struts.i18n.reload	false	Whether to reload resource bundles on every request.
struts.ui.theme	xhtml	The interface theme to use as the default.
struts.ui.templateDir	template	The base directory that theme templates are stored in.
struts.ui.templateSuffix	ftl	The suffix of the template view technology.
struts.configuration. xml.reload	false	Whether the struts.xml configuration file should be reloaded when it is modified.
struts.url.http.port	80	The HTTP port used by the application.
struts.url.https.port	443	The HTTPS port used by the application.
struts.url.includeParams	get	Parameters to use when building URLs; available options are none, get, or all.
struts.custom.i18n. resources	n/a	Custom internationalization resource bundles to be loaded.

Property Name	Default Value	Description
struts.dispatcher. parametersWorkaround	false	A workaround for application servers that don't handle getParameterMap() from the servlet request.
struts.xslt.nocache	false	Whether to cache the style sheets from an XSLT result.
struts.configuration. files	struts-default.xml, struts-plugin. xml, struts.xml	The configuration names to load automatically.
struts.mapper.always SelectFullNamespace	false	Whether the namespace is everything before the last slash or not.

Extending the Framework

For the most common scenarios, we've already discussed how to extend the Struts2 framework. You saw the interfaces that need to be implemented to create custom result types and interceptors, what interceptors look like, and how to write actions and configure them. The only decision left is how to deploy the extensions. For this, there are two approaches:

Use the new features directly in your web applications: The first way to use the extension mechanisms is to configure them from your web application and use them directly. This avoids some additional configuration but limits the use to only one web application. When you decide that the new features are generic enough to share with other applications, you can create a plug-in.

Bundle the new features into a plug-in: Creating a plug-in is only slightly more complex than using the features directly in your web application. A plug-in is basically a web application, as the structure and content are exactly the same as a web application. Instead of struts.xml, the configuration file is called struts-plugin.xml; the deployment file is a JAR and not a WAR; and most of the time, the plug-in will not have view templates.

Note The *config-browser* plug-in is interesting because it provides a complete add-on to your web application (including interceptor stacks, global results, and actions) and, like all plug-ins, is enabled by including the JAR file in the /WEB-INF/lib directory of the final WAR file. This means that plug-ins can provide not only framework extensions and new features, but they can also act as separately deployable modules. The trick is to use a view technology other than JSP; in this plug-in's case, Freemarker is used. Both Freemarker and Velocity can have their view templates deployed in any directory.

You can also change the internal behavior of Struts2 at strategic extension points. Like result types and interceptors, modifying the behavior involves implementing a specific interface. After the new implementation has been created, it is installed in the execution environment using the constant tag.

Table 3-6 lists the available extension points to change the default internal implementation. The table includes the property name that you will use to configure the new implementation, the interface class that needs to be implemented, and the scope that the new implementation should use.

Table 3-6. *Available Framework Extension Points*

Property Name	Interface/Class Name	Scope	Description
struts.objectFactory	com.opensymphony. xwork2.ObjectFactory	Singleton	The factory that is responsible for creating all objects within the framework
struts.actionProxyFactory	com.opensympony. xwork2.ActionProxy Factory	Singleton	Creates the ActionProxy class instance
struts.objectTypeDeterminer	com.opensymphony. xwork2.util. ObjectType Determiner	Singleton	Determines what the key and element from a map or collection are
struts.mapper.class	org.apache.struts2. dispatcher.mapper. ActionMapper	Singleton	Determines how a URL maps to an action class and how an action call maps back to a request
struts.multipart.parser	org.apache.struts2. dispatcher.multipart. MultiPartRequest	Per request	Parses and manages the data for a multipart request (file upload)
struts.freemarker.manager. classname	org.apache.struts2. views.freemarker. FreemarkerManager	Singleton	Responsible for loading and processing the Freemarker templates
struts.velocity.manager. classname	org.apache.struts2. views.velocity. VelocityManager	Singleton	Responsible for loading and processing the Velocity templates

When you are using the new feature directly in your web application, configuring the class to be used is the same as modifying any property. The name is the property being modified, and the value is the package and class name of the new class:

```
<constant name="struts.mapper.class"
    value="com.fdar.apress.s2.MyCoolActionMapper" />
```

Another option involves two configuration elements:

```
<bean type="org.apache.struts2.dispatcher.mapper.ActionMapper"
    class="com.fdar.apress.s2.MyCoolActionMapper"
    name="apressMapper" scope="singleton" optional="true" />

<constant name="struts.mapper.class" value="apressMapper" />
```

The difference between the two configurations is that the second has an implementation definition separate from the assignment. As for the direct-use scenario, the constant tag is provided with a value attribute that has been assigned implementation information via a bean tag. This allows your web application to include many different implementation options that are already configured. You just need to decide which you want to use.

The other properties of the bean tag include the following:

- `type`: The interface that the new class implements, from Table 3-6.

- `class`: The name of the class implementing the new features that is being configured.

- `name`: A developer-provided, unique name.

- `scope`: The scope that the object instance exists within. The values can be `default`, `request`, `session`, `singleton`, or `thread`.

- `optional`: Usually an exception during instantiation prohibits the web application from starting; by configuring a bean as optional, exceptions are not thrown and loading continues.

There is an additional attribute to the `bean` tag:

```
<bean class="com.fdar.apress.s2.MyCoolActionMapper" static="true" />
```

When configured with a `static` value of "true", the class specified in the configuration has static properties from the `StrutsConstants` class injected into properties. The property setter in your new class must also be annotated with the `@Inject` annotation to receive the value. If the class `MyCoolActionMapper` had the following setter, the `httpPort` property would be injected with the value `StrutsConstants.STRUTS_URL_HTTP_PORT`.

```
@Inject(StrutsConstants.STRUTS_URL_HTTP_PORT)
public static void setHttpPort(String val) {
    httpPort = Integer.parseInt(val);
}
```

Summary

We have covered a lot of material in this chapter. The request walk-through expanded upon the starter application in Chapter 2, providing more detail on how Struts2 processes the request internally. From there, we reviewed the core elements that make up Struts2, and you saw the different options for configurations: annotation based or XML-based. Finally, you saw the different extension points that Struts2 provides to modify its internal behavior.

This completes the overview chapters. Next, you will be introduced to the application that will be built within the remainder of the book. We'll review the use cases, discuss technologies, and introduce some of the business service classes. After you understand the common elements, implementing the Struts2 application implementation will be much quicker and easier.

CHAPTER 4

■■■

Application Overview

To illustrate how to develop Web 2.0 applications using Struts2, we first need an application to build. This chapter focuses on providing an overview of the application, technologies, and development process that will be used throughout the remainder of the book.

For context, the first topic to be covered is a high-level review of the features that will be developed. Next, we'll cover the technologies that will be integrated and the domain model. As well as the features of the application itself, the process of developing the application is important. You'll see how agile development and continuous integration are used in the development of the application.

To wrap up, you'll explore the persistence infrastructure for the application. With an understanding of how the persistence is configured and achieved, each chapter can focus on the task at hand—developing the web application—and avoid confusion by introducing too many new elements concurrently.

Finally, this chapter is meant as an introduction. If you are more interested in jumping directly to the features, feel free to skip this chapter.

The Application

When assessing an application to be showcased, there are many considerations. First and foremost, the application needs to be a Web 2.0 web application. As such, the application should follow the values and attributes that make an application Web 2.0. But this in itself is difficult. Many of the features that make up a Web 2.0 application are not necessarily specific to any technology, and many use the same underlying framework or technology for implementation.

As well as being a Web 2.0 application, the application and the features that the application provides should be easily understood by a wide audience and be able to keep the reader's interest. The Sun pet store is a great example of an application that is well known and understood. The Sun pet store application isn't a particularly good example for a Web 2.0 application because it has been overused, both by Sun and the development community at large. Any mention of the Sun pet store at conferences is usually followed by a groan from the crowd. In addition to this, the Sun pet store is an e-commerce application.

There are many elements to a Web 2.0 application (including clean user interfaces that are useable, highly interactive site, etc.), but a true Web 2.0 application needs to have community aspects. As an example, think of Google. Google Mail is a great looking and performing application, but it's still a fancy Web 1.0 application with a single task of checking your e-mail.

Google Maps, on the other hand, has crossed the chasm from a Web 1.0 application that has a single task (to look up information geographically) to a Web 2.0 application that has a community aspect of embedding maps into other applications and providing maps that can aggregate information from multiple sources.

The application we'll develop is a community entertainment service that allows users to vote for contestants in events. Whether it's a local talent show or this week's episode of *American Idol* (which allows viewers to vote on who they think is best), you can use this application to register the event, and then vote on the contestants with your friends. When the event is over, everyone can view the voting results. Given the popularity of *American Idol* and the swarm of other television programs that use this format, most people should be familiar with the features that need to be developed.

When interacting with the application, there will be very specific usage patterns. The first is when a user wants to register a new, previously unknown event. In this scenario, the following steps are taken:

1. Existing events are searched to see if the event already exists (this is optional, and the user may just decide to go ahead without this step).

2. The user needs to log on (and register if not already registered).

3. An event is created that has a name, start time, end time, voting duration, and time zone offset.

4. The contestants are added to the event.

After an event exists, it is visible for all users to view, and any user can vote on the event. To vote on an event, the user follows these steps:

1. Log on (and register if they have not already).

2. Enroll in the event the user wants to vote on.

3. Vote for a contestant in the event.

When the event concludes, the results are made available, and all users (whether they are logged on or not) can view the results.

Use Cases

The use cases are derived from the user scenarios or usage patterns. For the user to be able to achieve each task, several low-level features need to be available. Table 4-1 shows the use cases that need to be implemented to provide the user scenarios that were previously mentioned. As a roadmap, Table 4-1 also provides the chapter in which the use case will be implemented.

Table 4-1. *The Use Cases As They Will Be Introduced*

Chapter	Use Cases
Chapter 5	Register Update Profile Upload Portrait to Profile
Chapter 6	Create Event
Chapter 7	Logon User Logoff User
Chapter 8	Search for Events by Name Search for Events by Location Search for Events by Contestant
Chapter 9	Publish Event Information
Chapter 10	Enroll in an Event Vote for a Contestant in an Event Find Event Results

In each chapter, we will be adding to the features of the application a couple of use cases at a time. Step by step, the application will be built up in an order that allows you to review the progress and test the application. If this were a real project, changes to the priority of any unbuilt use cases could be made at any time, as well as adding additional use cases or removing use cases that are no longer required.

Note In agile methodology, this is known as "responding to change over following a plan" and allows an organization to be ready and flexible knowing that requirements will always change.

Integration Technologies

To provide a useful application, and not just sample code, Struts2 needs to be integrated with several other technologies. We'll focus on the following technologies:

- *Hibernate*: Used to provide the object-relational mapping for persistence via the Java Persistence API (JPA).

- *Spring Framework*: Used to provide business services, this is an architectural layer that separates the Struts2 action and the persistence layer.

- *Acegi*: Used as one of the options to provide authorization and authentication services.

- *Rome*: Used to generate RSS feeds for sharing data.

- *Google Web Toolkit (GWT) and the Dojo Toolkit*: Used to provide Ajax user interfaces.

More details on the technology and the integration techniques are provided in the subsequent chapters.

■Note As well as providing information on the features of Struts2, the other goal of this book is to provide the know-how to integrate not only these technologies but also any other technology you want with Struts2. When discussing the specific integration of the preceding technologies, these techniques are provided for you.

The Domain Model

Every application needs classes that represent the core concepts of the application being developed. As well as concepts, these classes contain and manage the various relationships between the core concepts. Together, this forms the domain model for the application. The domain model for the application we are developing, as a UML (Unified Modeling Language) diagram, is shown in Figure 4-1.

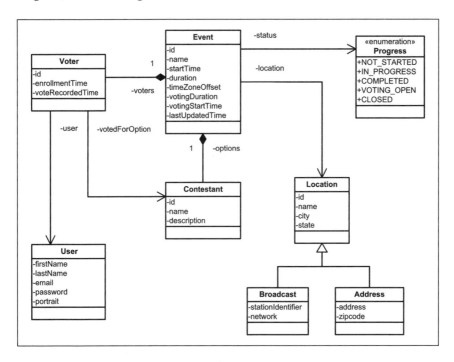

Figure 4-1. *The application domain model*

The domain model in Figure 4-1 contains the following classes:

Event: The Event class is the central domain object in the model, which provides properties for all the basic information of the event. Information that can be reused by multiple Event class instances has been broken out into the Progress enumeration and the Location, Address, and Broadcast classes.

Progress: The Progress enumeration provides life cycle states that the event can exist as. Each state allows users to perform specific tasks, that is, no one can vote when the event is CLOSED or NOT_STARTED.

Location: The Location class provides information on where the event will take place and has two subclasses: the Address class for events that have a physical address, and the Broadcast class for events that are broadcast on television networks.

User: The User class describes the current user of the web application. In this application, the application user cannot also be a contestant.

Contestant: The Contestant class contains information about a contestant in an Event. A contestant is defined as a person that is competing in an event and can be voted on by users that are enrolled to vote on an event.

Voter: The Voter class is a relationship between an event and a user. When a user enrolls to vote, a Voter class instance is created. When the user votes, the contestant selected for an event is recorded.

Because we are using an agile process for the development of the application, and the application is brand new with no preexisting code, the model could have evolved during the development. This may not always be the case, and another common scenario is that existing code needs to be used—perhaps Java code or database structures that provide persistence.

The approach taken is to provide a domain model ahead of developing the application, although it could have been evolved. This was done to allow you to become familiar with the core classes and relationships before they are used in a Struts2-specific context. It also allows us to discuss the infrastructure and configuration needed to persist the domain model now, rather than in each chapter as the model changes.

An Agile Development Process

The *agile development* techniques for developing software have been evolving since the mid 1990s. They focus on activities that provide direct benefits to delivering working software and limits those that are supplemental. Of the many benefits and characteristics, iterative development and responding quickly to change are the ones most closely associated with agile development. Many processes can be categorized as agile, including Extreme Programming, Crystal Methodologies, Agile Unified Process, Scrum, and Feature Driven Design.

The *Agile Manifesto*, which can be found at http://agilemanifesto.org, provides a list of core beliefs that unifies many of the agile processes. Essentially the manifesto states that for the most effective environment to create software in today's ever-changing and complex environment, the following principles should be observed:

- Individuals and interactions over processes and tools

- Working software over comprehensive documentation

- Customer collaboration over contract negotiation

- Responding to change over following a plan

The items on the right in those statements are no less essential than those on the left, but given the choice, those on the left provide more direct benefits to the end goal of working software.

With the user interaction, dynamic environment, and ever-changing nature of Web 2.0 applications, agile processes provide a great fit. The product development phase is broken into many small iterations (between two and six weeks on average). During each of the iterations, the features that will be completed are selected, planned, implemented, tested, and signed-off by a client or product manager. After each iteration, a review is conducted to determine what improvements (implementation based, managerial based, or process based) can be made. An additional benefit of implementing small pieces of functionality in this manner is that the entire application will evolve, keeping it fresh and avoiding dead code.

As much as possible, the example application will be developed using agile development processes. Keep in mind that there will be minimal iteration management because the features being developed are the objectives for a chapter, and therefore priority and implementation durations will not be discussed. The focus will be on the following:

- Performing iterative development with each chapter being a single iteration

- Creating a simple design that provides only what is required and no more

- Providing the know-how to unit test framework elements

- Refactoring code when and as needed

Continuous Integration

Another important characteristic of modern software development is continuous integration. The idea follows the Extreme Programming ideals—if there is a good practice (testing, for example), then performing that practice more often is better than performing it less often.

Building the project is a good practice. You can overcome problems such as determining whether code is properly integrated, errors with executing the build scripts, and benefits from showing the end users the result earlier. By building the project more often, you can resolve the issues and take advantage of the benefits more often. In the demo application, you are the only developer, but you will still work as if a continuous integration environment is being used.

The build process introduced in Chapter 2 uses Maven2. This in itself is not continuous integration, but it does facilitate continuous integration. It provides a *pushbutton* mechanism (using the command mvn install) that anyone can use to create the project. Maven2 can be used by many different continuous integration servers, such as Apache Continuum, to provide a complete continuous integration environment. Building a project (scheduled or built on demand) requires the following steps:

1. Remove all files from the working directory.

2. Check out the code from the source repository.

3. Issue the command to build the project (in this case, using Maven2).

4. Send notification for either a successful or erroneous build.

Depending on the continuous integration server, there may be more or less functionality, but these steps constitute what is usually the bare minimum functionality. The goal is to provide a clean, isolated environment where the project can be built independently to exclude any developer-workstation irregularities.

ADVANCED CONTINUOUS INTEGRATION SERVER FEATURES

Good continuous integration servers provide many more features than simply building the project. The following are some of the available features:

- Viewing files that were checked out from the source repository

- Accessing build artifacts

- Viewing reports generated during the build

- Viewing historical reports on build activity and success rates

- Automatically providing additional reporting features (not included in the build script)

- Parallel processing to concurrently build multiple projects or to concurrently process a single project

- Allowing operating system-specific elements in build scripts to be processed correctly (on the machine with the correct operating system)

- Searching capabilities across build activity as well as reports created during the build process

   Each of these features can make the regular building of the project much more than just checking that each developer's code integrates correctly. They can help manage the quality of the project from a much higher level with guiding metrics.

Because there is only one developer, less can go wrong. Also, you only need to perform step three from the earlier list: issue the Maven2 command to build the project. Having said that, checking out the project and building the project on a different workstation from the one being developed (or in a different directory) is always a good idea. It lets you know quickly whether all the files necessary are checked into the source repository.

Integrating the Persistence Layer

Hibernate will be used to provide the object-relational mapping layer for the application, allowing the model to be persisted to a database. Additionally, instead of using the custom Hibernate mapping mechanism, you'll use the Hibernate-provided JPA extensions. JPA is a J2EE standard for mapping and persisting data to a database.

■**Note** If you are planning to only review the Struts2 code, you have used Hibernate/JPA extensively, or you are not planning to run the examples from the book, you can skip the remainder of this chapter.

By using Maven2 and Hibernate, the mundane tasks of downloading dependencies and issuing SQL to create the correct database structure can be avoided. In fact, only three steps are needed to provide a complete and working development environment:

1. Configure Maven2 with new repositories and new artifacts in the pom.xml configuration file.

2. Download and install MySQL, and then create a new database called s2app.

3. Run mvn test to check the configurations; this command creates the necessary tables and tests that the database integration is configured correctly.

Each of these steps will now be covered in more detail.

■**Note** MySQL is not the only database option. If you have another Hibernate-supported database (and most databases are supported; see http://www.hibernate.org/80.html for the complete list), you just need to create a database or schema called s2app and then change the Hibernate configuration to the correct database dialect (more information is presented on the properties later in the chapter). Also remember to add a dependency to the pom.xml configuration file for the database driver class being used. With this in place, you can skip step 2.

Configuring the Dependencies

Until now, there has been no configuration for repositories in the pom.xml configuration file because there is a built-in default repository (pointing to http://repo1.maven.org/maven2). Most of the time, open source projects will publish artifacts to the central repository, but they can also host their own repositories. Hibernate, which is now under the JBoss umbrella of projects, is such an example.

To integrate Hibernate into the web application, two different types of dependencies are required: for the Hibernate code itself, and for the JPA and transactional APIs that are implemented. The JBoss repository contains both of these types, so configuring the pom.xml configuration file is easy. A new repositories tag is added under the top-level project tag, which in turn contains a repository tag with an id tag (providing a unique identifier) and a url tag (that supplies the URL of the repository).

```
<project>

    …

    <repositories>
        <repository>
            <id>jboss</id>
            <url>http://repository.jboss.com/maven2</url>
        </repository>
    </repositories>

<project>
```

Tip As well as the common repositories outside your organization, you can also create repositories inside your organization—all you need is an HTTP server. This is a great strategy because developers know that if an artifact is installed in the organization's repository, it can be used. Along with external artifacts, this repository can host internal projects and libraries to provide a central access point.

INSTALLING NEW ARTIFACTS IN THE MAVEN2 REPOSITORY

When dealing with a build tool that automates dependency management (especially downloading the libraries for you) such as Maven2, the artifact or library that you require may not be available.

The following are two scenarios when JAR files are not automatically retrieved and installed:

- The distributing organization does not publish the JAR files to the standard remote repositories (such as `ibiblio.com`).

- A legal restriction such as a user acknowledgment or license agreement needs to be accepted before using the files.

In either of these cases, additional steps are required before the JAR file can be configured in the `pom.xml` configure file and utilized in your application:

1. Locate the download location for the libraries that are needed.

2. Accept the license agreement (if applicable), and download the file.

3. If the files are downloaded as archives (other than JAR files), expand the archive into a working directory.

4. Install the required libraries into your local Maven2 repository.

Once downloaded, Maven2 provides a command to install the library into the correct local repository location and to create the necessary metadata files within the repository. The command has the following form:

```
mvn install:install-file -DgroupId=<groupId> ➥
    -DartifactId=<artifactId> ➥
    -Dversion=<version>➥
    -Dpackaging=jar -Dfile=</path/to/file>
```

For an example, let's take the Hibernate annotations file (remember this is an example and this step doesn't need to be performed). Following is the dependency configuration that will be added into the web application's `pom.xml` configuration file:

```
<dependency>
    <groupId>org.hibernate</groupId>
    <artifactId>hibernate-annotations</artifactId>
    <version>3.2.1.ga</version>
</dependency>
```

> This provides all the information needed to issue the install command from earlier. By substituting the groupId, artifactId, and version information, and issuing the command from the directory that the hibernate-annotations.jar (the name of the file that was downloaded) is located, the Maven2 command to install the library becomes the following:
>
> ```
> mvn install:install-file -DgroupId=org.hibernate ➡
>     -DartifactId=hibernate-annotations➡
>     -Dversion=3.2.1.ga -Dpackaging=jar -Dfile=hibernate-annotations.jar
> ```
>
> The preceding pom.xml configuration is now able to access the dependency from your local development environment.

The next step is to configure Maven2 so that the application can access the Hibernate dependencies. In Chapter 2, you saw that this is achieved by adding the dependency file information to the dependencies node of the pom.xml configure file. When configured in this manner, Maven2 goes out and retrieves the JAR files from either a local repository or the newly configured remote repository.

```
<dependency>
    <groupId>org.hibernate</groupId>
    <artifactId>hibernate</artifactId>
    <version>3.2.1.ga</version>
</dependency>
<dependency>
    <groupId>org.hibernate</groupId>
    <artifactId>hibernate-annotations</artifactId>
    <version>3.2.1.ga</version>
</dependency>
<dependency>
    <groupId>org.hibernate</groupId>
    <artifactId>hibernate-entitymanager</artifactId>
    <version>3.2.1.ga</version>
</dependency>
```

■**Note** Each Hibernate dependency also has its own dependencies, known as *transitive dependencies*. When the project you are using is built for Maven2, the transitive dependencies are configured and downloaded automatically with the dependency that you have configured. But occasionally, you will encounter a project that has not been built for Maven2. In this case, you need to add each of the transitive dependencies individually to the pom.xml configuration file manually.

As MySQL is going to be used as the database, an additional dependency is needed that provides the database driver class as well as additional supporting classes. If you are using a database other than MySQL, you need to substitute this dependency for that of the database that you are using.

```
<dependency>
    <groupId>mysql</groupId>
    <artifactId>mysql-connector-java</artifactId>
    <version>3.1.14</version>
</dependency>
```

Several Java APIs are also needed. These fall into the second category and usually need to be downloaded from http://developers.sun.com/downloads/ and installed. Luckily for you, the JBoss repository provides access to the dependencies without needing to install them locally. All that is needed is to add the following to your pom.xml configuration file:

```
<dependency>
    <groupId>javax.persistence</groupId>
    <artifactId>persistence-api</artifactId>
    <version>1.0</version>
</dependency>
<dependency>
    <groupId>javax.transaction</groupId>
    <artifactId>jta</artifactId>
    <version>1.0.1B</version>
</dependency>
```

Installing MySQL

MySQL 4.1 was used to develop the example in this book. To install MySQL, download the installer from http://dev.mysql.com/downloads/mysql/4.1.html, and then follow the provided instructions.

Installation is straightforward and wizard driven. If possible, you want to use the default port provided for the server. Also remember to make note of the root password that you entered because this will be needed to create the database for the web application.

After the installation is complete, the database that the web application uses needs to be created. To interact with the database server, you use the MySQL Command Line Client, which on Microsoft Windows XP is created as a menu item under the MySQL group. When starting the application, you are prompted for the root password, which you made note of during the installation (see Figure 4-2). After logging in, the command to create the database is

```
create database s2app;
```

```
MySQL Command Line Client                                              - □ ×
Enter password: ********
Welcome to the MySQL monitor.  Commands end with ; or \g.
Your MySQL connection id is 7 to server version: 4.1.16-nt

Type 'help;' or '\h' for help. Type '\c' to clear the buffer.

mysql> create database s2app;
Query OK, 1 row affected (0.02 sec)

mysql>
```

Figure 4-2. *The command-line interface to MySQL*

At this point, everything that is needed to run the application is configured. All that is left to do is issue the Maven2 command that downloads the dependencies, compiles the code, and runs the tests to check the configuration. The command to do this follows:

```
mvn test
```

When complete (this step may take up to two minutes to complete), everything is set up and configured, and the application is ready to use. The database structure created is shown in Figure 4-3.

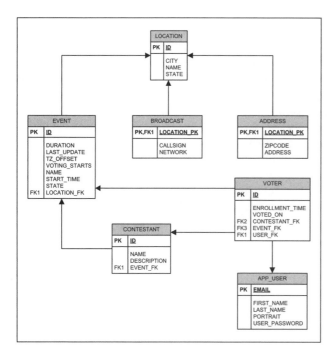

Figure 4-3. *The ER (Entity-Relationship) diagram representing the domain model*

At this point, you are ready to move on to the next chapter. For those that are interested, or if you are not using the MySQL database, the next sections talk about the Hibernate configuration.

Configuring Hibernate

To configure JPA, a `persistence.xml` configuration file must be located in the `META-INF` directory of the deployment module. Because Maven2 is being used to build the project, the corresponding project location for the configuration file is `/src/main/resources/META-INF`.

The following is the configuration file provided for the web application:

```
<persistence>
    <persistence-unit name="s2app">
        <provider>org.hibernate.ejb.HibernatePersistence</provider>
        <properties>
            <property name="hibernate.dialect"
              value="org.hibernate.dialect.MySQLDialect"/>
            <property name="hibernate.connection.driver_class"
              value="com.mysql.jdbc.jdbc2.optional.MysqlConnectionPoolDataSource" />
            <property name="hibernate.connection.url"
              value="jdbc:mysql://localhost/s2app" />
            <property name="hibernate.connection.username" value="root" />
            <property name="hibernate.connection.password" value="password" />
            <property name="hibernate.hbm2ddl.auto" value="update"/>
            <property name="hibernate.archive.autodetection" value="class"/>
            <property name="hibernate.show_sql" value="true"/>
            <property name="hibernate.format_sql" value="true"/>
        </properties>
    </persistence-unit>
</persistence>
```

As this book is on Struts2 and not Hibernate/JPA, we won't focus on the configuration in detail; however, you need to be aware of some properties from the configuration.

The first is the `name` attribute from the `persistence-unit` tag, which has a value of `s2app`. This value could be anything you like, but as the database that was created is called `s2app`, using the same name helps to associate the persistence unit to the database. It's especially important to create this association because the `persistence.xml` configuration file may contain multiple persistence unit (which are similar to database connections) definitions, and the application developer must specify which one to use.

Next is the `provider` tag. The value of the tag is the class name of the JPA provider's implementation. In our case, this is the Hibernate implementation, but it could have been a Top Link or IBM implementation.

To configure a specific JPA implementation, vendor-specific properties must be configured. These are provided as `property` tags. The assumption is that MySQL 4.1 is being used, and the preceding configuration values reflect the correct values for this database. If you are using a different database server, these values need to be updated. The database-specific properties that need to be changed are outlined in Table 4-2.

Table 4-2. *Database-Specific Properties of the* persistence.xml *Configuration File*

Property Name	Description
hibernate.dialect	The dialect tells Hibernate how to construct SQL and DDL (Data Definition Language) statements for a specific database server.
hibernate.connection.driver_class	This is the JDBC (Java Database Connectivity) driver class that is used to connect to the database server.
hibernate.connection.url	The URL that provides the location of the specific database or schema for the application.
hibernate.connection.username	The username that the application will connect to the database server as.
hibernate.connection.password	The password of the user that the application will connect to the database server as.

Other configuration properties are specific to the JPA provider, in this case, Hibernate. These provide additional functionality and features useful in developing applications. From a developer's perspective, one of the most useful is to view the SQL being generated, which can be enabled by using the hibernate.show_sql property. The properties configured for the application are described in Table 4-3.

Table 4-3. *The Hibernate-Specific Properties of the* persistence.xml *Configuration File*

Property Name	Description
hibernate.archive.autodetection	Informs Hibernate how to discover the classes that are persistent. The value class tells Hibernate that annotations are being used; the other possible value is hbm, which tells Hibernate that the older XML configure file style is being used.
hibernate.hbm2ddl.auto	Determines whether Hibernate will issue DDL commands to the database server to manage data structures. The values can be validate—the structures are only validated; create—the structures are created; update—the database is updated to match the model; and create-drop—the data structures are created when the session factory is created and dropped when the session factory is destroyed.
hibernate.show_sql	Logs the SQL being issued to the database.
hibernate.format_sql	Formats the SQL being logged into a format that is easier to read.

■**Tip** For a list of all the possible configuration options, see the Hibernate documentation at http://www.hibernate.org/hib_docs/reference/en/html/session-configuration.html.

The most controversial property is hibernate.hbm2ddl.auto. Using this Hibernate feature, the database structure can be created or updated during the application startup phase. This is a great time saver when working on the initial data structures, however, problems can occur when integration test data needs to be managed, or migration from one version of the data structures to another needs to be performed. Under these circumstances, a better approach is to automatically generate the data structures and then codify the resulting information into DDL scripts. Of course, this approach may also be completely off-limits if you have a strict DBA.

Caution Sometimes tables and table columns will not be modified correctly (due to existing constraints), so when using `hibernate.hbm2ddl.auto` with a value of `update`, you may need to drop the entire database or schema regularly. Alternatively, the `create-drop` option can be used.

This is the feature that was used to create the data structures in the database. Because the value of `hibernate.hbm2ddl.auto` is `update`, it generates any necessary changes to the database, including creating the initial structure, when Hibernate persistence is first used. The first use of the persistence code should be when the unit tests are initially executed.

Using Hibernate to Create Data Access Objects

With Hibernate configured, the last step is to implement the domain model (shown earlier in Figure 4-1). The class being implemented is the User class, and the domain object with Hibernate/JPA persistence annotations looks like this:

```
@Entity @Table(name="APP_USER", schema="S2APP")
public class User implements Serializable {

    ...

    @Id @Column(name="EMAIL")
    public String getEmail() { return email; }

    public void setEmail(String email) { this.email = email; }

    @Column(name="FIRST_NAME")
    public String getFirstName() { return firstName; }

    public void setFirstName(String firstName) { this.firstName = firstName; }

    @Column(name="LAST_NAME")
    public String getLastName() { return lastName; }

    public void setLastName(String lastName) { this.lastName = lastName; }

    @Column(name="USER_PASSWORD")
    public String getPassword() { return password; }

    public void setPassword(String password) { this.password = password; }
}
```

The following are the annotations used in the User class:

- @Entity: Defines the class as being an entity that is mapped to a database.

- @Table: Provides additional information on how to map this class to a database table, in this case, using the table APP_USER in the schema S2APP.

- @Id: Signifies the column as being the primary key for the table.

- @Column: Provides additional information on how to map this property to a table column in the preceding examples using a specific column name.

Many more options are available for the annotations used in this class, and many more annotations are also available.

■**Note** Because this book is focused on Struts2 and not Hibernate or JPA, this example will be the limit of code examples with explanation. The mapping annotations for all the remaining domain classes can be found in the Source Code/Download area of the Apress web site (http://www.apress.com). Further information on Hibernate's annotations for mapping domain classes along with Hibernate's support of JPA can be found at http://annotations.hibernate.org.

After the domain classes are implemented, they can be used. To ensure that everything is working as expected, unit tests are developed along with each of the domain classes.

Each unit test that is testing persistent domain objects will have common functionality: to obtain the entity manager factory instance, to create the entity manager instance, and to manage transactions. A base test class, shown next, encapsulates these services so each individual test case only needs to be concerned with a specific domain object.

```
public class PersistenceBaseClass extends TestCase {

    private EntityManagerFactory emf;
    protected EntityManager entityMgr;
    protected EntityTransaction tx;

    public PersistenceBaseClass() {
        super();
        emf = Persistence.createEntityManagerFactory("s2app");
    }

    protected void setUp() throws Exception {
        super.setUp();
        entityMgr = emf.createEntityManager();
        tx = entityMgr.getTransaction();
        tx.begin();
    }
```

```
    protected void tearDown() throws Exception {
        super.tearDown();
        tx.rollback();
    }
}
```

If you have worked with databases before, much of this code should look familiar. The entity manager factory is obtained in the constructor. This method call requires a preconfigured JPA context as a parameter. The context value s2app matches the name attribute of the persistence-unit node in the persistence.xml configuration file.

```
Persistence.createEntityManagerFactory("s2app");
```

The setup() method is called before each test method and creates an entity manager from the factory, obtains a transaction, and starts the transaction. After the test method has completed, the tearDown() method is called. This method rolls back the transaction to ensure that no data is persisted to the database.

To test the User class, a UserTestCase class is created that creates a new user, persists the user, finds the user by the primary key, and then tests that the found instance is the same as the instance persisted. By using the common functionality provided in the preceding PersistenceBaseClass, the UserTestCase can focus on only the User class-specific testing functionality:

```
public class UserTestCase extends PersistenceBaseClass {

    public void testCreateFind() throws Exception {

        User u = new User();
        u.setEmail("test@test.com");
        u.setFirstName("mr");
        u.setLastName("test");
        u.setPassword("pw");
        entityMgr.persist(u);
        entityMgr.flush();

        User test = entityMgr.find(User.class,u.getEmail());
        assertNotNull(test);
        assertEquals(u.getEmail(),test.getEmail());
        assertEquals(u.getFirstName(),test.getFirstName());
        assertEquals(u.getLastName(),test.getLastName());
        assertEquals(u.getPassword(),test.getPassword());
    }
}
```

The PersistenceBaseClass base class manages the transactions, rolling each back after the test case has been executed. This way, the database is always left in the same state as it started, which is exactly what you want from a unit test.

To run the unit tests with Maven2, issue the mvn test command.

Summary

You should now have everything needed to start application development: you know what the application does and which development process will be followed; you have a list of use cases (that will be expanded upon as they are developed in each chapter); and you've seen the domain model.

The development infrastructure should also be in place. From Chapter 2, the libraries for Struts2 have been downloaded and installed in your local Maven2 repository. In this chapter, you have installed a database server and executed the unit tests to test the persistence of the model. Executing the tests resulted in the downloading and installation of additional libraries for persisting the domain model and creating the necessary database structures in the database.

You are now ready to dive into the application's development.

CHAPTER 5

■■■

Data Manipulation

To provide interactivity, web applications need to provide the basic functionality of entering, editing, viewing, or deleting user provided data, that is, CRUD (Create Read Update Delete) functionality. That functionality is the focus of this chapter.

In this chapter, you will learn about developing actions, including an overview of the different styles that are available. You will learn how actions interact with existing domain objects, how to access Spring business services, how to access information from the action in the user interface, and how to add internationalization, validation, and exception handling. Finally, you will learn how to add file uploading and downloading into an application.

There's a lot to cover, so let's get started.

The Use Case

In this chapter, you will be developing three use cases. The use cases are focused around the user of the web application, allowing for the registration and updating of their personal information.

The other common use cases that usually go along with providing registration are logging on to and logging off the application. These will be handled in Chapter 7 with the discussion on security. The three use cases are described here:

Register: Before users can create an event, enroll in an event, vote on an event, or perform a number of other tasks, they need to register. To register, users enter several pieces of information, including an e-mail address and a selected password. After users register, they can log on to the application. And, once logged in to the application, they can perform features that are not available to unregistered users. Once registered, a user will have a profile.

Update Profile: When users get their profile, they are allowed to edit it. Users are only allowed to edit their own profile, and they may only edit their profile after they have logged in to the application.

Upload Portrait to Profile: To make Web 2.0 applications more personable, they usually provide a way to upload an image that is then associated with and commonly substituted for the user. This use case performs this action. After users register (or during registration) and have a profile, they are allowed to upload an image that will be associated with their online presence. A user can change the image any number of times. Similar to the Update Profile use case, users can only make changes after they have logged in to the application.

CRUD Functionality

All the use cases that are to be developed in this chapter are user related. In Chapter 4, you were introduced to the domain model, in which the class that represents the user is the User class. This class is the focus of the discussion of CRUD functionality.

There are a few different ways that the required features could be implemented. To guide you in determining which methods to use in developing the use cases, let's first review the characteristics of this particular problem. Here's what we know:

- We already have a domain model class available.

- Some of the features need setup or prepopulation code.

- Many of the features being implemented share a similar configuration.

- To support the use cases, there will be more than one function implemented per domain model class.

- We want to make configuration as easy as possible for developers.

Let's see how much we can achieve.

The Domain Model

In Chapter 4, we discussed the infrastructure classes that would be used in the application. For the use cases in this chapter, you need only one of these: the User class. Without the persistence annotations, the User class is

```
public class User implements Serializable {

    private String firstName;
    private String lastName;
    private String email;
    private String password;
    private byte[] portrait;

    public String getEmail() { return email; }

    public void setEmail(String email) { this.email = email; }

    public String getFirstName() { return firstName; }

    public void setFirstName(String firstName) { this.firstName = firstName; }

    public String getLastName() { return lastName; }

    public void setLastName(String lastName) { this.lastName = lastName; }

    public String getPassword() { return password; }
```

```
    public void setPassword(String password) { this.password = password; }

    public byte[] getPortrait() { return portrait; }

    public void setPortrait(byte[] portrait) { this.portrait = portrait; }
}
```

In Chapter 2, you saw that if there is a property with a setter on the action, Struts2 can manage the access to this property from the action, along with all data conversions between primitive Java types. For example,

```
public void setAge( int age ) { .. }
```

can be accessed by a Struts2 `textfield` tag using the `name` attribute value of age:

```
<s:textfield label="What is your age?" name="age" />
```

This functionality is handled by the `params` interceptor, which is standard in most of the interceptor stacks. As well as performing the assignment, the interceptor will perform any necessary data conversion.

As the domain object provides getters and setters for its properties, providing the same getters and setters on the action violates the DRY (Don't Repeat Yourself) principle. It also incurs an overhead of more code to provide the mapping to and from the domain object, in turn adding more work in maintenance cycles. The solution is to provide access to the domain object's properties from the action, as if they were the action's own.

Model-Driven Actions

Providing access to the domain object is achieved by creating a *model driven* action. There are two steps to enable this process. The first step is to have the action extend the `ModelDriven` interface. The `ModelDriven` interface is a simple interface that consists of a single method:

```
public interface ModelDriven<T> {

    T getModel();
}
```

The action implementing this method decides what to return. The options available are to return either a new instance or a prepopulated instance of a domain object that is ready to use.

The second step is to ensure that the `modelDriven` interceptor is being applied to the action implementing the `ModelDriven` interface. The interceptor retrieves the domain model for the action and places it on the Value Stack ahead of the action. With the domain model placed on the stack ahead of the action, the Struts2 tags can be more generalized. They can reference only the property name that they are interested in, without needing to worry about the object. With only the property name (and not including the domain object) referenced, the same JSP could be reused in different contexts with different domain objects—assuming they have the same properties.

For a concrete example in the current context, the following is the JSP tag referencing the e-mail property of an action (where the domain object is called model with an appropriate getter method):

```
<s:textfield label="Email Address" name="model.email" />
```

Using an action implementing the ModelDriven interface, the tag becomes

```
<s:textfield label="Email Address" name="email" />
```

With the knowledge that you can reuse the domain object properties as if they belong to the action, it's time to start developing the code the action needs for the use cases. The name chosen for the action is UserAction, and it will implement the Struts2 provided ActionSupport base class. For the model driven implementation, the action becomes the following:

```
public class UserAction extends ActionSupport
        implements ModelDriven<User> {

    private User user;

    public User getModel() {
        return user;
    }

}
```

The next problem is how to prepopulate the User domain object or provide setup code for the action.

Setup Code and Data Prepopulation

In the use cases being implemented, the setup code consists of prepopulating the domain object. For this scenario, the setup is performed using an interface and interceptor combination, just as it was previously for the model driven action.

The Preparable interface provides a callback into the action, allowing logic to be executed before the method that provides the processing logic for the action (for example, the execute() method). The interface has only one method:

```
public interface Preparable {

    void prepare() throws Exception;
}
```

The prepare interceptor uses this interface, making the call into the action implementing the interface. Ensure that the interceptor is configured and available on the interceptor stack for all actions that implement the Preparable interface. This interceptor is configured and available when using any of the interceptor stacks from the Struts2 distribution.

For the use cases, there will be two uses for the prepare() method:

- In the Register use case, a new instance of the domain object needs to be created; user entered data is then assigned to the object and persisted.

- In the Update Profile use case, an existing instance needs to be retrieved from the database; the information is then viewed and modified by the user and finally persisted back to the database.

Depending on how the action is implemented, the prepare() method may need to perform one of these functions or possibly both. The action could be implemented with the logic for all the use cases on a single class or split up over several action classes. By implementing the prepare() method once with the necessary logic for all use cases, the method can be reused for any implementation that is chosen.

There are a couple of other pieces needed before you get to the action implementation. The first is how the User instance is retrieved. As a business tier, we are using the Spring Framework; Spring is used as the default dependency injection provider. For user functionality, we have defined the following interface:

```
public interface UserService {

    public User findByEmail( String email );

    public void persist( User user, String emailId );

}
```

Note Although Spring is the default dependency injection provider, it isn't the only option. Guice and Plexus plug-ins are also available. You can also enable a custom provider; the configuration to enable a custom provider was shown in Chapter 3.

Along with the interface, a UserServiceImpl class has been created. This class uses the JPA (Java Persistence API) mappings on the domain object to persist the object instance to the database. To use the UserServiceImpl class as the UserService interfaces implementation, you configure it in the applicationContext.xml file.

```
<?xml version="1.0" encoding="UTF-8"?>

<beans xmlns="http://www.springframework.org/schema/beans"
       xmlns:xsi="http://www.w3.org/2001/XMLSchema-instance"
       xsi:schemaLocation="http://www.springframework.org/schema/beans
       http://www.springframework.org/schema/beans/spring-beans-2.0.xsd">

    <bean id="userService" class="com.fdar.apress.s2.services.UserServiceImpl" />

</beans>
```

If you've used Spring before, this should be nothing new (and if Spring is new to you, don't worry, it should make sense after the following explanation). The real magic is how the object defined in the Spring configuration gets injected into the action. Without delving into the implementation, the answer is to write a setter for the property on the action class. The setter must conform to JavaBean properties, with the name of the property being the value of the id attribute in the Spring configuration. So for a value of userService, you need a setter:

```
public void setUserService(UserService service) {
    this.service = service;
}
```

The longer answer is that the action is wired by Spring using the name of the setter. There are other options available, they are type, auto, constructor, and name (the default). There are two options to change the method being used. Add the property to the struts.properties configuration file as follows:

```
struts.objectFactory.spring.autoWire = type
```

or add assign the property in the struts.xml file:

```
<constant name="struts.objectFactory.spring.autoWire" value="type" />
```

■Caution Loosely coupled systems provide a lot of flexibility, but it comes at a price. In the case of Struts2, the price for loosely coupling Spring by wiring business objects by name is in debugging. If the name of the business service in the Spring configuration file is accidentally spelled wrong (or the setter is named incorrectly), no match will be found, and the business service required by the action will not be injected. With no object being injected, the action property will be null, and any methods called against a null value object with throw a NullPointerException. When debugging this scenario, most developers jump immediately to the implementation of the business service's method rather than checking that the action's property was properly set, sometimes spending minutes to hours trying to determine why there is a NullPointerException being thrown from an action. If this happens to you, the first thing you should check is that the names of the setters for Spring-managed objects match the IDs provided in Spring's applicationContext.xml configuration file.

There is one last problem to solve. To use the UserService business object method to find a User, an e-mail address is needed as a parameter. As it currently stands, the e-mail property is on the User object. So the first option is to use the e-mail address from the domain object:

```
private User user = new User();

public void prepare() throws Exception {
    user = service.findById(user.getEmail());
}
```

In this example, you need to have a form field or request parameter supplying the e-mail address, that is, `http://localhost/findUser.action?email=ian@test.com`.

I like to place all the setup code in the `prepare()` method, whether it is the instantiation of a new object or retrieving an existing instance. So instead of using a property on the domain object, a new property (along with a setter) is created on the action, for example, `emailId`. The URL then becomes `http://localhost/findUser.action?emailId=ian@test.com`. Using a different property name provides separation between the property used as the lookup key and the property on the domain object instance, doesn't require the domain object to be created, and makes the URL a little more descriptive for the user.

Tip Just because an action is model driven doesn't mean that all the properties must be on the domain model. If the property setter doesn't exist on the model (which is on the top of the Value Stack), searching continues down the Value Stack to determine if the value can be assigned to another object (this pass-through feature, which you have also seen working in reverse to obtain property values, cannot be turned off). Next in line after the domain model is the action. So if the property is not available on the domain object, but it is available on the action, it will be applied correctly. This also means that when you choose property names, you should make sure that they are different between the domain model and action.

Let's put together the action with everything you've learned from this section. The action class implementation now becomes

```
public class UserAction extends ActionSupport
        implements ModelDriven<User>, Preparable {

    private User user;
    private String emailId;
    private UserService service;

    public User getModel() {
        return user;
    }

    public void setUserService(UserService service) {
        this.service = service;
    }

    public void setEmailId(String emailId) {
        this. emailId = emailId;
    }

    public String getEmailId() {
        return emailId;
    }
```

```
public void prepare() throws Exception {
    if( emailId==null || "".equals(emailId) ) {
        user = new User();
    } else {
        user = service.findByEmail(emailId);
    }
}

…

}
```

This implementation should be just as you expect.

Configuration

Interceptors have been discussed in the past two sections, but you must understand the importance of the ordering of the interceptors. For the action class to be configured and data prepopulated as needed, the following steps need to occur in the following order:

1. The emailId parameter needs to be set on the action class (params interceptor).

2. The prepare() method needs to be called (prepare interceptor).

3. The domain model needs to be placed onto the Value Stack (modelDriven interceptor).

4. Now that the model is available (possibly retrieved from the database), values can be assigned to it (params interceptor).

The paramsPrepareParamsStack interceptor stack performs these steps in this order and has already been created. For all actions that perform similar steps, you'll want to ensure that this interceptor is being used.

What happens if these steps are not performed in the correct order? Most likely it will be a strange bug that doesn't seem possible. Here are some examples:

- If the params interceptor is not called before the prepare interceptor, the value of emailId will always be null, and the domain object will never be loaded from the database.

- If the modelDriven interceptor is not applied to the action, the domain model will not be on the Value Stack, hence modified or new values will not be assigned to the domain object, and it will seem like data never made it to the action, or the values did not change.

- If the params interceptor is not called twice, the data will not be assigned to the domain object and the result mimics the preceding issue.

- If the prepare interceptor is not called, a NullPointerException is thrown, or the data of the domain object will not be updated.

THE PARAMS-PREPARE-PARAMS PATTERN

This particular interaction between the Struts2 interceptors and the action is known as the *params-prepare-params* pattern (named for the interactions that are invoked):

- *The first params stage*: Parameters from the request (form fields or request parameters) are set on the action.

- *The prepare stage*: The prepare() method is invoked to provide a hook for the action to perform lookup logic (i.e., find the domain object using a primary key) using data from the first step that has been set on the action.

- *The last params stage*: The parameters from the request are reapplied to the action (or model if one now exists), which overwrites some of the data initialized during the prepare stage.

The key to the pattern is in the final step: data that is loaded in the prepare() method is overwritten by request parameters. By allowing the framework to do this work, the execute() method becomes very simple. When performing a differential update on a domain object (as is being done in the Update Profile use case), the execute() method becomes a one-line method call to persist the object. Without the params-prepare-params pattern, the execute() method would need to load the domain object; check whether each request parameter needed to be updated on the model; perform the update of the value if needed; and finally persist the domain object.

One concern that developers have when first learning about this pattern is that it is not a pattern at all; instead, it is a code smell that should be avoided. The reality is that to avoid the framework performing the same work twice, you would need to write the code manually; with the options being to collect and apply the domain object values to the domain object after it has been retrieved, or if the values are applied to the domain object in the action, to retrieve a new domain object instance and then to compare and update those fields with values that have changed. For me, using the framework is always the better option, even though there may be a very slight performance overhead in doing so (as the framework needs to generically determine and assign values from form fields or request parameters, where developer-provided code acts only on those fields required).

Although this pattern is particularly helpful when performing differential updates on domain objects, you will find it useful in other scenarios as well.

Note It isn't necessary to have an interceptor to assign Spring-managed objects to an action. This is handled at a higher level of abstraction in the ObjectFactory. As the action class instance is created, it is checked to determine whether there is a dependency on any other managed objects. If there are dependencies, the dependent objects are created (if necessary) and injected into the action class.

A good rule of thumb is to use the provided interceptor stacks or create your own interceptor stacks, applying the stacks consistently across all the actions. Configuring packages to
use a default interceptor stack is the best way to achieve this:

```
<package name="user" extends="struts-default" namespace="/user" >
    <default-interceptor-ref name="paramsPrepareParamsStack" />
    ...
</package>
```

Tip If there is a strange bug, a `NullPointerException`, or data not present on a property that should have
an assigned value, there is a good chance that it may have something to do with interceptors. Interceptors in
the wrong order or missing interceptors are problems that can have consequences that do not point immediately to interceptors. The good news is that spelling mistakes in the `interceptor` or `interceptor-ref`
attributes names will cause the initialization of Struts2 to be aborted, and the problem can be quickly rectified.

The Action Class

The action is the mechanism for implementing web application features in Struts2 and is
where we'll start looking at specific use case implementations.

When implementing actions, there are two approaches:

- Each action provides a single unit of work (which could be a use case or a URL invoked
  from a web page), and a single web page may use many action classes to implement all
  the features present.

- An action provides implementations for all the features that a single web page requires.

The implementations of these two main categories of actions are discussed separately.
You can choose which to use on your projects.

Single Unit of Work

The first scenario is when an action provides a single unit of work. By default, the method of
the class performing the work is the execute( ) method, but it doesn't need to be. Any method
of the action class can be used, as long as it returns a `String` and has no arguments.

Note Returning a `String` is the most common scenario, but you can also return a `Result`. This is useful
for advanced uses, especially when building complex applications, but in general is unnecessary because
the result needs to be programmatically configured rather than using the more simple case of XML or annotation-based configuration. Examples of returning a `Result` rather than a `String` are when the location of
the JSP template is dynamically determined by the action code and cannot be statically placed in configuration files, and when the action logic needs to determine the type of result to return.

Optionally, the method signature may define that the method throws an `Exception` or a subclass of `Exception`.

```
public String something() throws Exception {
    …
    return SUCCESS;
}
```

If the `execute()` method is not used, the method needs to be configured in the `struts.xml` configuration file.

```
<action name="index" method="something" class="TestAction" >
    <result name="success">showSomething.jsp</result>
</action>
```

The advantage to this approach is that it's simple, and you have most likely seen the same approach in other web frameworks. Each task is separate, with the action class named according to the task that is being performed (i.e., the `FindUserAction` action class retrieves a user from the database). Further separation can be achieved using package names.

One of the first issues with this implementation is that even though there are more action classes, a lot of commonality still exists between the classes. In Struts2, classes are not reused and thus are allowed to contain class-level properties. This allows for flexibility in what can be provided in base classes.

To avoid code duplication, the first step in implementing the action is to take the common code and push it into a base class that each action can extend. The common code for user functionality has to do with making actions model driven and providing a `prepare()` method that creates or finds the required domain model instance. Here is the resulting `BaseUserAction` action that contains the common code:

```
public abstract class BaseUserAction extends ActionSupport
        implements ModelDriven<User>, Preparable {

    protected User user;
    private String emailId;
    protected UserService service;

    public User getModel() {
        return user;
    }

    public void setEmailId(String emailId) {
        this.emailId = emailId;
    }

    public String getEmailId() {
        return emailId;
    }
```

```
    public void setUserService(UserService service) {
        this.service = service;
    }

    public void prepare() throws Exception {
        if( emailId==null || "".equals(emailId) ) {
            user = new User();
        } else {
            user = service.findByEmail(emailId);
        }
    }
}
```

This makes each action's implementation very simple. The FindUserAction retrieves a user via an e-mail address, and its implementation is now one line of code.

```
public class FindUserAction extends BaseUserAction {

    public String execute() throws Exception {
        return SUCCESS;
    }
}
```

■Tip In fact, this implementation could be even simpler. If the BaseUserAction was not abstract, this class would not be needed. The BaseUserAction extends the ActionSupport action class, and the ActionSupport class provides a default implementation of an execute() method that returns SUCCESS (the same as FindUserAction does). To avoid implementing FindUserAction, you could just use BaseUserAction rather than FindUserAction in the struts.xml configuration file.

Zero Configuration

The real advantage of this approach is that you can reduce the XML configuration in favor of annotation-based configuration. Although it wasn't shown previously, each individual action in the application needs to have its own configuration information in struts.xml. Using annotations, the information relating to the class configuration is right in the source file along with the logic. Let's take a look at the FindUserAction action class with annotations:

```
@ParentPackage("base-package")
@Results({
    @Result(name="success",
            type=ServletDispatcherResult.class,
            value="/WEB-INF/jsp/user/user.jsp")
})
public class FindUserAction extends BaseUserAction {
```

```
    public String execute() throws Exception {
        return SUCCESS;
    }
}
```

The new elements to this action are the @ParentPackage, @Results, and @Result annotations. These annotations make up a feature know as *zero configuration*.

■**Note** You can find more information on zero configuration in the Apache Struts documentation at
http://struts.apache.org/2.x/docs/zero-configuration.html.

XML AND ANNOTATIONS WORKING TOGETHER

With a limited set of annotation-based configurations available (work is going on to improve the available annotations), you can't achieve all the configuration in a web application using annotations, unless you have a very simple web application. Instead, you'll end up with a combination of XML and annotation-based configuration. The good news is that annotation-based and XML-based configuration of actions can coexist.

The way I like to conceptualize the problem is that the annotations provide the default configuration. For alternative configurations, I use XML. This may be when a different result type needs to be used or different interceptor stacks need to be applied to the processing.

A benefit of using XML over annotations is being able to change the configuration of a running system. When dev mode is enabled, changes to the struts.xml configuration file are reloaded into the runtime configuration, allowing you to make configuration changes to deployed applications. Having said this, it's not a practice that I would recommend because there will be a performance penalty as the timestamp on the configuration file is continually checked to determine whether it has been updated, and a live production system is not the place to be making untested changes to configuration.

To enable zero configuration, you first need to configure the dispatcher with which package the actions are contained in. This is achieved by adding a new parameter to the web.xml configuration file with a name of actionPackages:

```
<filter>
    <filter-name>action2</filter-name>
    <filter-class>org.apache.struts2.dispatcher.FilterDispatcher</filter-class>
    <init-param>
        <param-name>actionPackages</param-name>
        <param-value>com.fdar.apress.s2.actions</param-value>
    </init-param>
</filter>
```

The value of the parameter contains a list of comma-delimited package names that contain actions. Action classes do not need to be in the listed packages and can instead be contained within subpackages. In our application, the action classes are in the com.fdar.apress.s2.actions.user package, but as we expect more actions to be added in other package names, we have selected a common root and used it in the configuration. For multiple action packages, the configuration takes the following form:

```
<init-param>
    <param-name>actionPackages</param-name>
    <param-value>com.fdar.admin.actions,com.fdar.app.actions</param-value>
</init-param>
```

With the additional configuration in place, the packages and all their subpackages are scanned when Struts2 starts up. Any class found that provides configuration annotations will have a configuration object created and added to the configuration manager.

Selecting which packages are defined in the configuration is also important because they provide the namespace for the actions. The namespace is determined by the relative location of the action class from the package defined in the actionPackages configuration value. As an example, the FindUserAction action class from earlier is placed in the com.fdar.apress.s2.actions.user package. The value configured in the parameter actionPackages is com.fdar.apress.s2.actions, and so the relative package path from the configured package to our action is user, and the namespace is /user. If the action had been in the package com.fdar.apress.s2.actions.search.user, the namespace would have been /search/user.

Tip An @Namespace annotation also can be used to specify the namespace to use for the action. However, most of the time, the actions you develop will be placed into packages with names that provide the correct namespaces.

Knowing the name of the action to invoke in the URL is also important. Converting the action class name to the URL action takes three steps:

1. Make the first character of the class name lowercase.

2. Drop the "Action" suffix (if it exists).

3. Add the action extension, which is usually .action.

So the FindUserAction action class will be invoked as /app/user/findUser.action (remember the package name and web context prefix).

The first annotation in the action class is the @ParentPackage annotation. This annotation is important because it provides the only way to specify the interceptors to use for the action. The value provided in the annotation needs to specify a valid package that is configured in the struts.xml configuration file. In the FindUserAction action, we specified a value of "base-package". Following is the package's XML configuration:

```
<package name="base-package" extends="struts-default" >
    <default-interceptor-ref name="paramsPrepareParamsStack" />
</package>
```

Earlier, you saw how important assigning the correct interceptors (in the correct order) is to the action behaving as expected. For zero configuration actions, it's important to have a different package configured for each combination of interceptors that are needed.

To configure the results of executing the action, the @Results and @Result annotations are used. When the action returns only a single result, the @Result annotation can be used alone:

```
@Result(name="success",
        type=ServletDispatcherResult.class,
        value="/WEB-INF/jsp/user/user.jsp")
public class FindUserAction extends BaseUserAction {

    public String execute() throws Exception {
        return SUCCESS;
    }
}
```

When multiple results are returned, the @Result annotations need to be enclosed by the @Results annotation:

```
@Results({
    @Result(name="success",
            type=ServletDispatcherResult.class,
            value="/WEB-INF/jsp/user/user.jsp"),
    @Result(name="error",
            type=ServletDispatcherResult.class,
            value="/WEB-INF/jsp/user/error.jsp")
})
public class FindUserAction extends BaseUserAction {

    public String execute() throws Exception {
        return SUCCESS;
    }
}
```

■**Caution** Even though the @Results and @Result annotations are used to determine the results for a method, the annotations themselves are class-level annotations. A common mistake when starting out is to place the annotations on the execute() method rather than at the class definition. Also, due to the lack of action configuration, the @Results and @Result annotations can only be used when the action class uses the execute() method (and not a different method name for the business logic).

The @Result annotation duplicates the information provided in the XML result configuration and has three attributes:

- name: A String value (unique between result annotations for the current action class), which selects this result as the one to be used for rendering the result of the action; this is one of the possible values that the execute() method could return.

- type: The class that performs the work of rendering the result (see Table 5-1).

- value: Configuration information for the result type; for JSP, Velocity, and Freemarker, this value is the path and name of the result template to be rendered.

Table 5-1. *Result Type Classes That Can Be Assigned in the* @Result *Annotation*

Class	Description
ServletDispatcherResult.class	Renders the configured JSP template
ServletRedirectResult.class	Redirects to the configured URL
ServletActionRedirectResult.class	Redirects to the configured action
ActionChainResult.class	Chains the current action to the configured action
FreemarkerResult.class	Renders the configured Freemarker template
VelocityResult.class	Renders the configured Velocity template
XSLTResult.class	Returns a property (possibly transformed via XSLT) as XML
PlainTextResult.class	Displays the raw content of the configured resource (JSP, HTML, etc.)
HttpHeaderResult.class	Returns an HTTP header as a result
StreamResult.class	Returns a data stream (for downloading files or images)

In this section, you've seen a lot of different code for the same example. In summing up this section, here is the final (and actual) code for the FindUserAction action class:

```
@ParentPackage("base-package")
@Result(name="success",
        type= ServletDispatcherResult.class,
        value="/WEB-INF/jsp/user/user.jsp")
public class FindUserAction extends BaseUserAction {

    public String execute() throws Exception {
        return SUCCESS;
    }
}
```

The Codebehind Plug-In

We can make another simplification to the FindUserAction action class. When the result renders a JSP, Freemarker template, or Velocity template, the codebehind plug-in can be used to eliminate the need to specify a result altogether.

When the codebehind plug-in is enabled and no existing result is configured (annotation-based or XML-based), a template name is constructed using a convention and searched for. If the template is found, it is rendered. The template name is constructed by appending the following:

- A path prefix (if configured)

- The URL action name

- A "-" character

- The value of the execute() method's result

- Each template extension in turn until a match is found: .jsp for JSP, .ftl for Freemarker, and .vm for Velocity

An example will make this easier to understand. For the FindUserAction action class, which is invoked via the URL /app/user/findUser.action, and a result of success, the JSP /user/findUser-success.jsp, Freemarker template JSP /user/findUser-success.ftl, and Velocity template JSP /user/findUser-success.vm are constructed, and the templates are searched for. If the result was input the templates would be /user/findUser-input.jsp, /user/findUser-input.ftl, and /user/findUser-input.vm.

Tip Another benefit of this approach (apart from configuration reduction) is that when prototyping an application, "throw away" developer templates can be developed. As the properly designed and formatted templates are created, they can either replace the codebehind template name, or they can be configured for the action. When there is a configured result, the codebehind template is never used.

In the struts.xml configuration file, there are two new constants to be configured. The first provides the package name (or a parent package name) for the actions that are to use the codebehind functionality:

```
<constant name="struts.codebehind.defaultPackage" value="base-package" />
```

Additionally, a path prefix can be specified. This is particularly useful when the templates are not in the web application's context root directory, a common practice for web applications where Java code needs to be executed and the resulting object values rendered in the template. A common location is under the /WEB-INF directory, where they cannot be invoked directly by a browser. To duplicate the JSP directory location of the earlier @Result annotation, the following path prefix value is used:

```
<constant name="struts.codebehind.pathPrefix" value="/WEB-INF/jsp/"/>
```

Returning once again to the FindUserAction action class, we now have

```
@ParentPackage("base-package")
public class FindUserAction extends BaseUserAction {

    public String execute() throws Exception {
        return SUCCESS;
    }
}
```

The codebehind plug-in is enabled by placing the JAR file in the /WEB-INF/lib directory, or because we are using Maven2, by including the following configuration in the dependencies section:

```
<dependency>
    <groupId>org.apache.struts</groupId>
    <artifactId>struts2-codebehind-plugin</artifactId>
    <version>2.0.9</version>
</dependency>
```

Note More information on the codebehind plug-in can be found at the plug-ins home page in the Apache Struts documentation at http://struts.apache.org/2.x/docs/codebehind-plugin.html.

Finishing Up

As well as the FindUserAction, which has been showcased heavily, there is a second action: the UpdateUserAction action class. This action has a dual role of creating new users (the Register use case) and updating user information (the Update Profile use case).

```
@ParentPackage("base-package")
@Result(name="success",value="index",type=ServletActionRedirectResult.class)
public class UpdateUserAction extends BaseUserAction {

    public String execute() throws Exception {
        service.persist(user,emailId);
        return SUCCESS;
    }
}
```

In this case, rather than using the codebehind plug-in, the result is explicitly configured. This is because after creating or updating the user information, there is nothing more to do, so the user is redirected back to a common home page. If the codebehind plug-in was used, many JSPs would either be duplicates of each other or would forward the HTTP request to a single common action. Configuring the result directly in the action avoids all this duplication. Figure 5-1 shows how the actions, JSPs, and URLs interact.

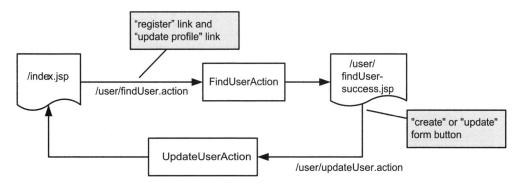

Figure 5-1. *The action and JSP workflow for the Register and Update Profile use cases*

■**Caution** The `codebehind` plug-in uses the `ServletDispatcherResult` type. When performing the logic after submitting a form, this plug-in should not be used because if the user clicks the Refresh button on the browser, the form is resubmitted. Instead, and as shown in the preceding `UpdateUserAction`, a redirecting result should be used.

As the target index action isn't providing any functionality, a new action class doesn't need to be created. Instead, the `ActionSupport` class is used (that already provides an `execute()` method that returns a `SUCCESS` result) to configure the index action in the XML configuration. Following is the complete `struts.xml` configuration file:

```
<struts>

    <constant name="struts.codebehind.defaultPackage" value="base-package" />
    <constant name="struts.codebehind.pathPrefix" value="/WEB-INF/jsp/"/>

    <package name="base-package" extends="struts-default" >

        <default-interceptor-ref name="paramsPrepareParamsStack" />

        <action name="index" class="com.opensymphony.xwork2.ActionSupport" >
            <result name="success">/WEB-INF/jsp/index.jsp</result>
        </action>

    </package>
</struts>
```

> **Note** In the case of the successful completion of the UpdateUserAction, you will notice that the user is redirected to an action rather than rendering a JSP. This is a common web application pattern called *redirect-after-post.* The pattern is used when a user-initiated request can be repeated by clicking the browser's Refresh button, and the result of the request is some type of unwanted state change; that is, the user gets frustrated waiting for a delete request, clicks the Refresh button, and deletes two records instead of one. To avoid the request being performed twice, a redirect to a lookup action is performed. Once that is done, if the user clicks the Refresh button, multiple lookups are performed and not multiple deletes.

Multiple Units of Work

The other option for implementing actions is to implement a single action class with a different method for each unit of work. In effect, all the action classes from the previous section are being consolidated into a single action class. Instead of a single execute() method, the action has many methods that are invoked by different URLs.

A similar feature was available in Struts 1.x using the DispatchAction action, although the implementation is slightly different. The DispatchAction action provides a method that, when called, provides additional information to dispatch the request to other methods on the same class. As you have seen in Chapter 2 and Chapter 3, in Struts2 there is no central method that actions implement; instead, the invoked method can have any name. This provides a much greater level of flexibility by allowing the method that is being invoked to be determined by convention or configuration, or to be specified when the URL is invoked.

The new action class being created is called UserAction and resides in the com.fdar.apress.s2.actions.user package. This class contains all the code from the BaseUserAction, a method to represent the FindUserAction (called find()), and a method to represent the UpdateUserAction (called update()).

```
public class UserAction extends ActionSupport
        implements ModelDriven<User>, Preparable {

    private User user;
    private String emailId;
    private UserService service;

    public User getModel() {
        return user;
    }

    public void setEmailId(String emailId) {
        this.emailId = emailId;
    }
```

```
    public String getEmailId() {
        return emailId;
    }

    public void setUserService(UserService service) {
        this.service = service;
    }

    public void prepare() throws Exception {
        if( emailId==null || "".equals(emailId) ) {
            user = new User();
        } else {
            user = service.findByEmail(emailId);
        }
    }

    public String find() {
        return INPUT;
    }

    public String update() {
        service.persist(user,emailId);
        return SUCCESS;
    }
}
```

To be invoked as actions, the find() and update() methods must duplicate the method signature of the default execute() method. This means it is public, returns a String, has no arguments, and can optionally throw Exception or a subclass of Exception. Along with the names of the methods changing, the only other difference is the return value: INPUT for the find() method, and SUCCESS for the update() method. If the resulting JSP templates were the same, the return values could have also been the same. But, in this case, you want to show the screen to edit the user's information after the find() method and return to the home screen after the update() method, so different return values are needed to forward to the correct JSP template.

The major change comes when it's time to configure the action. Constructing the action class in this fashion means that you can no longer use zero configuration annotations and must fall back to XML configuration (remember that the @Result annotation is a class-level annotation, not method level). You have fewer action classes, but just as many lines of configuration—perhaps more code because the method attribute is added so that the correct method on the action class is called. Here's what the configuration looks like:

```
<struts>

    <package name="user" extends="struts-default" namespace="/user" >

        <default-interceptor-ref name="paramsPrepareParamsStack" />

        <action name="index" class="com.opensymphony.xwork2.ActionSupport" >
            <result name="success">/WEB-INF/jsp/index.jsp</result>
        </action>

        <action name="findUser" method="find"
            class="com.fdar.apress.s2.actions.user.UserAction" >
            <result name="input">/WEB-INF/jsp/user/findUser-success.jsp</result>
        </action>

        <action name="updateUser" method="update"
            class="com.fdar.apress.s2.actions.user.UserAction" >
            <result name="success" type="redirectAction">index</result>
        </action>

    </package>
</struts>
```

■**Note** The action name and JSP names have been selected so that one set of JSPs can be developed and reused for both styles of writing action classes. These names could be anything, although following a convention for naming always makes it easier for you as a developer and for those that follow you.

Wildcard Configuration Mappings

In a simple example of a single class, the XML configuration isn't too concerning. When the application being developed has many domain objects (each with CRUD functionality), entering and maintaining the configuration becomes a problem.

For the User domain object, there are two configurations and limited logic in the methods that implement the action logic. For more complex domain objects, there could be create, update, delete, and several different find methods.

```
<action name="findUser" method="find"
    class="com.fdar.apress.s2.actions.user.UserAction" >
    <result name="input">/WEB-INF/jsp/user/findUser-success.jsp</result>
</action>
```

```
<action name="updateUser" method="update"
    class="com.fdar.apress.s2.actions.user.UserAction" >
    <result name="success" type="redirectAction">index</result>
</action>
```

When comparing these two action configurations, you'll notice that there are similarities. The prefix of the action name matches both the method name and the prefix of the "input" result mapping.

Wildcard configuration mapping allows you to take advantage of these patterns to reduce the number of action configurations that need to be specified. An asterisk is used to replace a series of text in the action's name, and many asterisks can be used as long as there is known text between them to act as a delimiter. Each asterisk can then be referenced in any part of the action configuration by specifying the asterisk index (starting from 1) and enclosing the index number in curly braces.

This can be a little confusing, so let's see what will change when you apply these rules to the user action configurations:

```
<action name="*User" method="{1}"
    class="com.fdar.apress.s2.actions.user.UserAction" >
    <result name="input">/WEB-INF/jsp/user/{1}User-success.jsp</result>
    <result name="success" type="redirectAction">index</result>
</action>
```

You end up with a configuration that is specific to one type of domain object, in this case, the User domain object. When the URL is /app/user/findUser.action, the asterisk matches the value "find", and this value is substituted for any occurrence of {1} in the configuration. For /app/user/updateUser.action, the value "update" is used.

If a new use case is needed for the UserAction, say a delete feature, no more configuration is needed. Instead, you just add a verifyDelete() method that returns INPUT (to return a page to verify the deletion) and a delete() method that returns SUCCESS (to perform the actual deletion) to the UserAction class. The URLs that call these methods (/app/user/verifyDeleteUser.action and /app/user/deleteUser.action) and the JSP that is rendered for verifyDelete() (/WEB-INF/jsp/user/verifyDeleteUser-success.jsp) are automatically available via the existing wildcard configuration.

You can also provide a single configuration for multiple domain objects. In this case, the domain object and the action name need to be part of the action's name. The names also need to be separated by characters. In the following example, the URL /app/User_find.action invokes the find() method on the UserAction, and if a result of INPUT is returned, the JSP template /WEB-INF/jsp/updateUser.jsp is rendered.

```
<action name="*_*" method="{2}"
    class="com.fdar.apress.s2.actions.{1}Action" >
    <result name="input">/WEB-INF/jsp/{2}{1}.jsp</result>
    <result name="success" type="redirectAction">index</result>
</action>
```

> **■Caution** When using wildcard mapping with class names, case is extremely important. The class `userAction` is not the same as the class `UserAction`, and so the URL invoked needs to be `/app/User_find.action` and not `/app/user_find.action`.

Finally, there are some things to remember regarding wildcard mapping:

- There is a limit of nine text groups, {1} through {9}.

- The token {0} is special and contains the entire URL requested.

- The * token will match 0 or more characters, *excluding* the "/" character.

- The ** token will match 0 or more characters, *including* the "/" character.

- The "\" character is used as an escape sequence to punctuation characters, thus \\ matches the "\" character, and * matches the "*" character.

Unit Testing

Testing should be an integral part of any development effort, and Struts2 makes it easy to test action classes in an isolated environment. A key to making testing easy is to ensure that any object that the action interacts with is injected into the class via a setter.

The interaction so far has been limited to a Spring-managed business service. To replicate the services of this object, you'll use a mock object. A *mock* object provides the same methods as the real object but allows you to set what the expected method calls are going to be. Then, after the method being tested is run, the mock object can verify that the methods were called correctly, all the expected methods were called, and no additional methods were called. Usually a library is used, and, in this case, you'll use the jMock library (http://www.jmock.org).

> **■Note** Testing, including the use of mock objects, is a very large topic. This book points out the areas that are testable and provides samples where possible, but it's not feasible to provide tests for all the code being developed.

Only one library file is required for jMock. This is added to the Maven2 `pom.xml` as the following dependency:

```
<dependency>
    <groupId>jmock</groupId>
    <artifactId>jmock</artifactId>
    <version>1.0.1</version>
    <scope>test</scope>
</dependency>
```

It's now time to work on the tests themselves. So far there are three classes (the fourth, UserAction, provides the same logic as these three and is left as an exercise for you to test): BaseUserAction, FindUserAction, and UpdateUserAction. An element of testing that is over-looked is what to test. Very rarely do you have the opportunity to test every line of code because of time constraints, poorly integrated code, or development patterns that are test-ing antipatterns. Therefore, selecting the method or blocks of code to test is important.

TESTING TO SIMPLIFY DESIGN

When developing test code together with production code (or before the production code when using test-driven development), the production code will evolve much differently than if there was no testing.

In particular, methods are more concise, constructors are simpler (with a preference for using factory or builder patterns), and dependency injection is preferred over creating a new instance of an object. Each of these techniques allows for easier testing but, more importantly, a better design of the production code.

Testing anti-patterns are development techniques that inhibit testing (or at the very least make testing very complex). A good example is static methods. Testing a static method of the class that it belongs to is easy, but testing the interaction of a class with a static method is not. Especially when the static method returns state or object instances that are then used by the calling object (and need to be replaced by different objects for testing). When providing test coverage for a class becomes complex, a judgment call needs to be made on whether it is better to provide the test coverage or to move on to the next task.

Two of the classes, FindUserAction and UpdateUserAction, extend the BaseUserAction class. Therefore, BaseUserAction does not need to be tested individually. When examining the code, the FindUserAction class is extremely small. In fact, it is used mostly for annotation-based configuration, and all the logic of the class is contained in the BaseUserClass class. So the only class that needs to be tested is the UpdateUserAction class.

Following is the pattern for testing action classes:

1. Create the mock objects, and set expectations.

2. Create the action instance.

3. Set test data on the action instance, including dependent objects (and the mock objects).

4. Execute the method that is being tested.

5. Assert that the results are correct, including that methods on the mock object were called as expected.

Logically there are two test cases for the UpdateUserAction class: creating a new user and updating an existing user. The first test case will be for creating a new user.

```
public void testPersistNewUser() throws Exception {

    Mock service = new Mock(UserService.class);
    service.expects(once()).method("persist")
        .with(isA(User.class),eq(null));

    UpdateUserAction action = new UpdateUserAction();
    action.setUserService((UserService)service.proxy());

    action.prepare();
    assertEquals(Action.SUCCESS,action.execute());
    service.verify();
}
```

The syntax for jMock may not be familiar, but it should be readable. A mock object is created by passing in the UserService interface. The expectation is that the persist() method will be called once, with a User class as the first parameter and null as the second parameter. Because a new User instance is created, the test is limited to checking for a type.

Before calling the execute() method, there is a call to the action's prepare() method. This wasn't one of the steps in the preceding list, but it is required because some of the functionality the test depends on is performed externally to the action by the Struts2 framework. To be duplicated, the method prepare() is called before continuing. The alternative is to set up a configuration and action execution environment and then execute the test. For most action tests, this is overkill, and simply making the necessary method calls (duplicating those the interceptors would make) is enough.

The next test case is for updating an existing user.

```
public void testPersistExistingUser() throws Exception {

    User user = new User();

    Mock service = new Mock(UserService.class);
    service.expects(once()).method("findByEmail")
        .with(eq("bob@test.com"))
        .will(returnValue(user));
    service.expects(once()).method("persist")
        .with(same(user),eq("bob@test.com"));

    UpdateUserAction action = new UpdateUserAction();
    action.setUserService((UserService)service.proxy());
    action.setEmailId("bob@test.com");

    action.prepare();
    assertEquals(Action.SUCCESS,action.execute());
    service.verify();
}
```

JUNIT

The unit testing library being used in this chapter is JUnit (http://www.junit.org). JUnit was developed by Kent Beck and Erich Gamma and is the Java port of SUnit (the original of all the xUnit testing frameworks built in Smalltalk).

Following is an example JUnit test class, using version 3.8 of JUnit. This version is the older but more commonly used version. It uses naming conventions to determine the methods of the test class that are test cases (methods starts with "test"), and those that are called before each test case (the setUp() method) and after each test case is executed (the tearDown() method). Test classes are also required to extend the JUnit-provided TestCase class:

```java
public class UpdateUserTestCase extends TestCase {

    protected void setUp() throws Exception {
        // called before each test case method
    }

    protected void tearDown() throws Exception {
        // called after each test case method
    }

    public void testPersistUser() throws Exception {
        // the unit test code
    }
}
```

Each test case (the testPersistUser() method in the previous example) will follow a common pattern: create the object being tested, call methods on the object to perform the logic being tested, and then assert that the results are those that you are expecting. The first two steps are straightforward. By extending the TestCase class, the test class method is provided with access to a full complement of helper methods for the last step, provided by the JUnit Assert class (more information on the available methods can be found at http://junit.sourceforge.net/javadoc/junit/framework/Assert.html). All of the examples in this book follow this pattern and use JUnit or JUnit in combination with jMock.

Recently there has been a resurgence in JUnit, with a long overdue update (version 4). Instead of using naming conventions, annotations are used to signify the test methods, as well as the method to invoke before and after each test case (rather than using the setUp() and tearDown() methods). Additionally, annotations provide advanced features such as ignoring test cases, running a method once before all test cases start and once after all test cases have been completed, providing timeouts for test cases, and parameterizing test cases. More information can be found at http://www.junit.org.

As well as JUnit, there are other options for unit testing. TestNG (http://testng.org) is one such option, which is mature, annotation based, integrated into IDEs, and provides many of the same features as JUnit 4, as well as some that JUnit does not.

Much of the code is the same; the only difference is in setting the expectations and assigning an e-mail address to the action before calling the method being tested.

The first expectation configured is that the findByEmail() method is called once using the e-mail address "bob@test.com"—the same as we later set on the action. When this method is called on the mock object, it returns the user object that was created earlier. The second expectation is that the persist() method is called once, with the same user instance that was returned in the first expectation and the e-mail address "bob@test.com."

If you think about how the UpdateUserAction class works, this is exactly what the code is doing. Always think about the problem you are testing!

■Note Along with unit testing, all web applications should incorporate some type of automated user interface tests. This type of testing can catch issues that unit tests can't, including internationalization issues, layout problems, and cross-browser incompatibilities. Check out *WebTest* (http://webtest.canoo.com), *Selenium* (http://www.openqa.org/selenium/), and *HttpUnit* (http://httpunit.sourceforge.net/) to get you started.

JSP Templates

Now that the action classes and their configurations have been developed, we need to focus our attention on the user interface. Because of its popularity and the fact that it's a standard technology on the J2EE stack, the focus throughout this book is on JSP.

For both styles of action class construction, the action URLs and the JSPs needed are the same. To start, let's take a look at the /user/findUser-success.jsp file. This JSP is used in two scenarios: for creating a new user in the Register use case and for updating the user information in the Update Profile use case.

```
<%@ taglib uri="/struts-tags" prefix="s" %>

<head>
    <title>User Information</title>
</head>
<body>

<s:form namespace="/user" action="updateUser" method="post" >

    <s:textfield label="First Name" name="firstName" />
    <s:textfield label="Last Name" name="lastName" />
    <s:textfield label="Email Address" name="email" />
    <s:password label="Password" name="password" />

    <s:hidden name="emailId" />
```

```
        <s:if test="email==null">
            <s:submit value="Register" />
        </s:if>
        <s:else>
            <s:submit value="Update" />
        </s:else>

</s:form>

</body>
</html>
```

If you are familiar with building JSPs, or even HTML pages for that matter, this code should hold no surprises. It consists of an HTML form (as shown in Figure 5-2), with a logic section to determine whether the text on the submit button is for registering or for updating existing information.

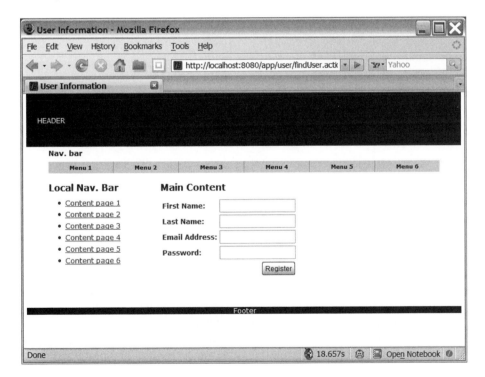

Figure 5-2. *The form fields empty and ready to register a new user*

The page relies heavily on custom tags provided by the Struts2 framework. To use the Struts2 tag libraries, they first need to be defined. The first line in most Struts2 JSP files performs the definition:

```
<%@ taglib uri="/struts-tags" prefix="s" %>
```

Next is the form. The form takes a very similar format to that of an HTML form. There is an enclosing `<s:form … />` tag, which surrounds a number of form field tags. The `form` tag shares the `method` attribute and the `action` attribute with its HTML counterpart, although in the Struts2 case, the `action` attribute is the name of the action (without the extension). The URL that the form calls is generated by concatenation of the web application context, the `namespace` attribute value, the `action` attribute value, and the action extension (retrieved from configuration). Thus, the URL for the action generated in the following JSP template is `/app/user/updateUser.action`.

```
<s:form namespace="/user" action="updateUser" method="post" >

    <s:textfield label="First Name" name="firstName" />
    <s:textfield label="Last Name" name="lastName" />
    <s:textfield label="Email Address" name="email" />
    <s:password label="Password" name="password" />

    <s:hidden name="emailId" />

    …

</s:form>
```

Within the form are three different types of tags: the `textfield` tag, the `password` tag, and the `hidden` tag. These are some of the many different form field tags available, and similarly to the `form` tag, they duplicate the features provided by the form field tags available in HTML. As well, the Struts2 tags provide enhancements that the HTML versions are not capable of, the features being supplied by the integration with Struts2. Following are the enhanced features in the preceding form:

Grouping field description and input: Tags in Struts2 are rendered by templates (specified using the `theme` or `template` attribute), which provide layout and formatting. By providing a `label` attribute, the form field description can be grouped together with the field input control.

Retrieving data from the action: When an action has been invoked, it is available on the Value Stack (as well as the model object if the action is model driven). The `name` attribute on form fields is used to retrieve a data value and render it for the user to modify by searching for a getter on the action or model, that is, `fieldName` will look for a `getFieldName()` method. If no matching method can be found, no value is rendered. This feature allows the same JSP to be used for entering a new user and modifying an existing user's information.

Submitting data to the action: When submitting the form, the `name` attribute is used to search for a setter on the action being invoked, that is, `fieldName` will look for a `setFieldName()` method on the action or model.

A couple of other features are available, and they will be further explained in upcoming sections and chapters.

▮Note There are many more attributes to the Struts2 tags than covered here. See the Struts2 documentation at `http://struts.apache.org/2.x/docs/tag-reference.html` for the complete list of tags and their attributes.

The last element in the form is the submit button. Just like the other form fields, the HTML `input` tag of type `submit` has a corresponding Struts2 version. It's actually a little easier than the other tags, as the only attribute we are concerned with is the `value` attribute, which behaves exactly the same as the HTML submit button.

As the same JSP is used for creating a new user and modifying existing users, the issue now is rendering the correct text on the submit button depending on what function the user is performing. In Figure 5-3, user information has been retrieved from the database, and the submit button has the text "Update" rather than "Register".

Let's consider the application for a moment. When creating a user, the e-mail address is used as the primary key. This means that when user data is being modified, the e-mail address is present, and when this is a new user, the e-mail address is `null`. Conditional logic tags are used to wrap and select the correct version of the submit tag to render: the `if` tag provides a `test` attribute containing an OGNL expression to evaluate (which must evaluate to a boolean result); the `else` tag provides a catch-all for when the expression evaluates as `false`.

```
<s:if test="email==null">
    <s:submit value="Register" />
</s:if>
<s:else>
    <s:submit value="Update" />
</s:else>
```

This completes all the JSPs that are needed to add, edit, and view `User` domain objects.

What's left are the links to initiate the action that renders the `/user/findUser-success.jsp` template. For now, we'll place these in `/index.jsp`. There will be two links on this page:

- A link for registering

- A link to edit the current user's profile

The other requirement is that only one of these links will be displayed at any time: the user needs to be registered to modify his profile; if the user has not yet registered, he won't have a profile to edit.

Chapter 7 addresses security, including the Logon User and Logoff User use cases. Before then, you need to know how to determine whether a user has logged into the web application. The assumption is that when a user is logged in, the user's `User` domain object is placed in the HTTP Session under a key of `user`.

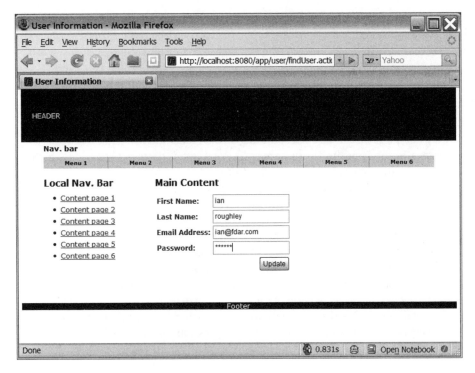

Figure 5-3. *The form preloaded with user information*

The `if` tag can then be used to determine whether the user has logged in, using the expression `#session['user']==null`. In Chapter 3, you saw how the Value Stack contains various objects, including the HTTP Session, which can be referenced using the `#session` identifier. In this expression, you are selecting the attribute with the name of "user" and testing to determine whether it has a `null` value. If it does, you render the link.

```
<s:if test="#session['user']==null">
    <s:url id="register" action="findUser" namespace="/user" />
    <s:a href="%{register}">Register</s:a>
</s:if>
```

To render the link, two more Struts2 tags are used. The first is the `url` tag. Like the `form` tag, it uses an `action` attribute and a `namespace` attribute to generate a correct URL, which is then placed on the Value Stack under the lookup value of the `id` attribute. The a tag then uses this value (notice the `%{register}` value, so that the URL is rendered and not simply the text "register" rendered). Figure 5-4 shows the starting page with the `Register` link visible.

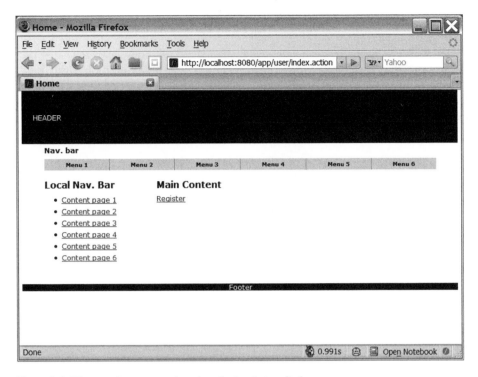

Figure 5-4. *The starting screen showing the* Register *link*

Tip Alternatively, the url tag could have been omitted and the a tag's href attribute assigned a value of /app/user/findUser.action. Two tags are used here instead of one for consistency, and it doesn't make a lot of sense (it would assist if the action extension or URL format changed, but this very rarely happens). When URL parameters need to be assigned with values from the Value Stack, this form of constructing the URL provides better readability and a simpler way to describe the dynamic values.

If the HTTP Session attribute is not empty, the update link needs to be rendered. The prepare() method of the action class uses the emailId property to lookup the User domain object, so you need to find the e-mail address of the user that is currently logged in and supply this as a request attribute on the URL.

The else tag works in partnership with the if tag from the Register link, so that the Update link is only rendered when an HTTP Session object is available. Generating and displaying the link is exactly the same as shown previously. The only addition being the param tag, which is used within the url tag to provide request attributes. In the code example, the param tag is used to provide the e-mail name/value pair. Because we need to provide the e-mail address, and we know that the HTTP Session object for the key "user" is not null, we can assign the email property directly from the session's object.

```
<s:else>
    <s:url id="update" action="findUser" namespace="/user" >
        <s:param name="emailId" value="#session['user'].email" />
    </s:url>
    <s:a href="%{update}">Update Profile</s:a>
</s:else>
```

The complete page becomes

```
<%@ taglib uri="/struts-tags" prefix="s" %>

<head>
    <title>Home</title>
</head>
<body>

<s:if test="#session['user']==null">
    <s:url id="register" action="findUser" namespace="/user" />
    <s:a href="%{register}">Register</s:a>
</s:if>
<s:else>
    <s:url id="update" action="findUser" namespace="/user" >
        <s:param name="emailId" value="#session['user'].email" />
    </s:url>
    <s:a href="%{update}">Update Profile</s:a>
</s:else>

</body>
</html>
```

VERIFYING THE GENERATED LINK

Until the Logon User use case is implemented, you need a way to check that the Update link is working correctly. One way is to modify the execute() method of the FindUserAction so that whenever it finds a user, it places the user into the HTTP Session.

Before the HTTP Request object can be used to access the HTTP Session and store the User, the action class needs to be able to access it. By implementing the ServletRequestAware interface, the current HTTP Request object is assigned to the action for use.

```
@ParentPackage("base-package")
public class FindUserAction extends BaseUserAction
        implements ServletRequestAware {

    private HttpServletRequest request;

    public void setServletRequest(HttpServletRequest httpServletRequest) {
        request = httpServletRequest;
    }

    public String execute() throws Exception {
        if( user!=null ) {
            request.getSession(true).setAttribute("user",user);
        }
        return SUCCESS;
    }
}
```

With this action in place, you can load a user by executing the action /app/user/findUser. action?emailId=email@test.com (assuming that a user with an e-mail address of "email@test.com" has already been created). To create the user, simply use the URL /app/user/findUser.action, and enter the new user's information.

Internationalization

For the pages that have been developed, there are only a few places that internationalization needs to be applied. In fact, this represents the majority of the internationalization that will occur in the web application. Internationalization needs to be applied to the following:

- Pure text elements of the page, including HTML tags (such as the title tag) and value of the Struts2 tags (such as the a tag)

- Attribute values of the Struts2 tags (such as the label attribute of the textfield tag)

As these are the only elements, we will look at each in turn but only for the findUser-success.jsp template.

Internationalized Text Resources

Before getting to the specific JSP changes, you need to know where the internationalized text comes from. The short answer is a Java properties file with the name and package/directory location being the same as that of the action class that is using it.

Practically, this solution leads to a lot of duplication, so a multitiered search was developed so that properties can be placed in a number of different files (in different locations). Here are the steps, and each is performed until a value for the key being searched on is found:

1. A file with the same name and in the same package/directory as the action class is searched for, that is, com/fdar/apress/s2/actions/user/FindUserAction.properties.

2. The class hierarchy is searched (using the same name mapping from the class name and package/directory as earlier) all the way back to Object, that is, com/fdar/apress/s2/actions/user/BaseUserAction.properties, com/opensymphony/xwork2/ActionSupport.properties, and java/lang/Object.properties.

3. Every implemented interface (using the same name mapping from the class name and package/directory as earlier) and subinterface is searched.

4. If the action is model driven, a properties file for the model class (using the model name, class hierarchy, and interfaces as in steps 1, 2, and 3) is searched for.

5. The file package.properties is searched for in the action class's directory and every parent directory up to the class root directory.

6. The global resource property file is searched (specified using the struts.custom.i18n.resources configuration property).

Tip In most applications, the number of property files is limited. This reduces the number of locations that a developer needs to look (when searching for a key's value to change) and reduces the number of files that need to be converted into each supported language.

The name of the properties file also varies. For the action class FindUserAction, the properties file FindUserAction.properties represents the default locale. The default locale is configured using the property struts.locale (either in the struts.properties or the struts.xml configurations files).

For each supported language, and language/locale pair, a new file is created. For German, the file FindUserAction_de.properties would need to be created, and for an Australian locale, the file FindUserAction_en_Au.properties would need to be created. Each file contains the same key, with the text value representing what is to be displayed to the user for the language and locale that the file represents.

Tip If you need to modify how the encoding is performed, you can modify the configuration property struts.i18n.encoding. By default, encoding is set to UTF-8.

Because the example web application is small, the internationalization file configuration chosen is to provide a `com/fdar/apress/s2/actions/package.properties` resource file that contains all the key/value pairs for all the actions and then individual resource files for each domain object. At the moment, we have only the `User` object, so the `com/fdar/apress/s2/domain/User.properties` resource file is added.

After converting both the `findUser-success.jsp` template and the `index.jsp` template, the `package.properties` file becomes

```
# COMMON ELEMENTS

# Buttons
button.register=Register
button.update=Update

# Links
link.register=Register
link.updateProfile=Update Profile

# SPECIFIC TEMPLATES

# index.jsp
home.title=Home

# findUser-success.jsp
user.findUser.title=User Information
```

and the `User.properties` file becomes

```
user.firstname=First Name
user.lastname=Last Name
user.email=Email Address
user.password=Password
```

Tip When creating keys for internationalization text, it's a good idea to determine a common naming pattern. The pattern can be rigorously defined or be ad hoc—the important thing is that everyone knows what it is and knows how to use it. In the preceding `package.properties` file, there are two patterns. The first is that for common elements, the type is a prefix to the definition, that is, `button.register` and `link.register`. The other pattern is building up key names for template: first the module name, then the page name, and finally the element definition, that is, `user.findUser.title`.

If you've been paying attention, you know this isn't going to work for the code that has been developed so far. The `index.jsp` template is returned by the `/index.action` URL, whose logic is provided by the `ActionSupport` class. Because the `ActionSupport` class is in the `com.opensymphony.xwork2` package, it will not use the `package.properties` resource file from the `com/fdar/apress/s2/actions` package.

■Note Another option is to configure a global properties file using the `struts.custom.i18n.resources` property in the `struts.xml` or `struts.properties` configuration file. This removes the need to have all action classes extend from a common base class, as long as all the classes implement the `TextProvider` and `LocaleProvider` interfaces (needed to provide internationalization support).

To rectify this and consolidate all the action internationalization resources under one file, you need to make two changes. The first is to create a new `BaseAction` class, in the `com.fdar.apress.s2.actions` package. This is nothing more than a placeholder and extends the `ActionSupport` class as follows:

```
public class BaseAction extends ActionSupport {
}
```

Next, you need to modify the `/index.action` configuration to use the newly created class:

```
<action name="index" class="com.fdar.apress.s2.actions.BaseAction" >
    <result name="success">/WEB-INF/jsp/index.jsp</result>
</action>
```

■Caution All the action classes in the application extend the `ActionSupport` class provided by Struts2. This class implements two important interfaces: the `TextProvider` interface that provides access to the properties files and their text messages; and the `LocaleProvider` interface that provides the locale for the current user. Both these interfaces need to be implemented if internationalization is needed and `ActionSupport` is not extended.

Now that the resources are defined, they can be used in the JSP templates.

Text Elements

To internationalize text in the JSP template, Struts2 provides the `text` tag. The tag has only one attribute, the `name` attribute, which specifies the key for the text value. An example in the `findUser-success.jsp` template is the `title` HTML tag:

```
<head>
    <title>User Information</title>
</head>
```

As the key `user.findUser.title` is already defined in the `package.properties` resource file, it's a simple matter of adding it as a `text` tag attribute:

```
<head>
    <title><s:text name="user.findUser.title" /></title>
</head>
```

Any text in a JSP template can be replaced in this manner.

Attributes and Labels

The other time when text needs to be internationalized is for the labels of the form fields. Rather than using the label attribute, the key attribute is used.

```
<s:form namespace="/user" action="updateUser" method="post" >

    <s:textfield key="user.firstname" name="firstName" />
    <s:textfield key="user.lastname" name="lastName" />
    <s:textfield key="user.email" name="email" />
    <s:password key="user.password" name="password" />

    <s:hidden name="emailId" />

    <s:if test="email==null">
        <s:submit key="button.register" />
    </s:if>
    <s:else>
        <s:submit key="button.update" />
    </s:else>

</s:form>
```

When internationalized text is required within an attribute of a Struts2 tag but not as the label, a different strategy is needed. The property tag is used to obtain a value from the Value Stack by providing an expression in the value attribute. Instead of the text tag to display the title of the page

```
<s:text name="user.findUser.title" />
```

a property tag could have been used:

```
<s:property value="getText('user.findUser.title')" />
```

Of course, this is a trivial example, and for this case, the text tag makes more sense to use. But in more complex scenarios, you may need to obtain internationalized text in this way.

Input Validation

Having user-entered information saved to the database is one thing, but having information that is valid and useable throughout the application is an entirely separate problem. Struts2 provides a robust validation framework that is powerful and easy to work with.

Annotation-based validation is the quickest and easiest way to apply validation to your actions. Following are the requirements for the action classes:

- The class needs to have a class-level @Validate annotation.

- A result must be configured for a return value of INPUT. This is the result that the validation framework returns when validation fails.

- The validation interceptor (that performs the validation) and the workflow interceptor (to return the INPUT result) must be applied to the action. They are part of the preconfigured validationWorkflowStack, paramsPrepareParamsStack, and defaultStack interceptor stacks.

■**Note** As well as annotations, XML can be used to configure validation. This style of validation is not covered in this book (as annotations provide the same functionality and without additional configuration files—at least one per action class), but if you are interested, all the information you will need is in the Struts2 documentation at http://struts.apache.org/2.x/docs/validation.html.

Validation only needs to be performed by those actions that are creating or saving data, so for the zero configuration classes, only the UpdateUserAction needs to be modified. Applying the rules listed previously and the required validations, the class becomes the following:

```
@Results({
    @Result(name="success", value="index", type=ServletActionRedirectResult.class),
    @Result(name="input",type=ServletDispatcherResult.class,
        value="/WEB-INF/jsp/user/findUser-success.jsp")
})
@Validation
public class UpdateUserAction extends BaseUserAction {

    @Validations( visitorFields = {
            @VisitorFieldValidator(
                    message="Default message",
                    fieldName="model", appendPrefix=false) }
    )
    public String execute() throws Exception {
        ...
    }
}
```

There are two ways to apply validations to an action class:

- Apply a specific validation annotation to the setter method of the property to validate.

- List all the validations to apply for the action class on the execute() method.

In the `UpdateUserAction` class, the second method is used because `UpdateUserAction` extends a base class (that many actions use), and the property is not readily available.

The `@Validations` annotation allows you to group together multiple instances of any (or all) type of validation annotation. In this case, there is only one instance of one validator, the `@VisitorFieldValidator`.

The `@VisitorFieldValidator` is one of the more complex validators available and one of the most powerful. It implements the visitor pattern and allows each property object in the action to potentially provide its own validation information. This makes sense. Why would you want to provide the same validation configuration for the same `User` object over multiple actions? Follow the DRY principle, and place all the validation configuration in one place—on the object itself—and reuse that configuration over multiple actions.

Three attributes are used:

- `message`: A required field that provides a description to the user of the problem; this attribute provides only a default fallback message when obtaining an internationalized text value using the key attribute (not shown as the model object never directly displays a validation error).

- `fieldname`: This is the name of the property of the object to validate.

- `appendPrefix`: Determines whether a prefix should be added when storing the name of the field with a validation issue; that is, for a `true` value, an object property of `"model"`, and field `"email"`, the error would be stored under the key `"model.email"`; for a value of `false`, the error would be stored under a key of "email". Because the form fields are named `"email"` and not `"model.email"`, a value of `false` is needed.

When an `@VisitorFieldValidator` annotation is encountered, the validation framework steps into the object class to search for additional validations. Here are the validation annotations that have been added to the `User` class:

```
public class User implements Serializable {

    @EmailValidator(message="Validation Error", key="validate.email")
    public void setEmail(String email) { … }
    public String getEmail() { … }

    @RequiredStringValidator(
        message="Validation Error", key="validate.notEmpty", trim=true)
    public void setFirstName(String firstName) { … }
    public String getFirstName() { … }

    @RequiredStringValidator(
        message="Validation Error", key="validate.notEmpty", trim=true)
    public void setLastName(String lastName) { … }
    public String getLastName() { … }
```

```
@RequiredStringValidator(
    message="Validation Error", key="validate.notEmpty",
    trim=true, shortCircuit=true)
@StringLengthFieldValidator(
    message="Length too short", key="validate.minLength.6",
    trim=true, minLength="6")
public void setPassword(String password) { … }
public String getPassword() { … }


}
```

This probably looks more like the configuration that you were expecting, and the same validations could have been added to the action class if it used properties rather than being model driven and exposing a domain model.

Each validation has a message (providing a default description) and key (allowing the internationalized text to be looked up from the key) attribute. Validators that work with strings have a trim attribute, which removes whitespace before running the validation logic. Validators that are length-based or range-based have a minimum and maximum attribute. An interesting optional attribute that all validators have is the shortCircuit attribute. In the case of multiple validators on the same field, this attribute determines on a failure whether validators after it should be executed (possibly providing multiple errors for a single field) or whether to stop with only one error for the field. This is the case for the password. If the string is empty, it will also be less than six characters, so the second message is not needed.

■**Tip** The full list of validation annotations can be found on the Struts2 documentation web site at http://struts.apache.org/2.x/docs/annotations.html.

When domain objects handle their own validation, they also need to manage their own internationalization. Therefore, the validation keys and text need to be added to the User.properties file.

```
# Validation Messages
validate.email=Please enter a valid email address
validate.notEmpty=Please enter a value
validate.minLength.6=Please enter more than 6 characters
```

■**Note** Once again, different properties files could have been used (i.e., either a package.properties file in a higher level package or a globally configured properties file). My preference for domain objects is to use a property file per domain object as it allows each domain object to specify a different value for common internationalization keys. It also keeps the internationalization information close to the domain object, should you want to use the validation framework outside the scope of the web application (perhaps within the business tier for consistency).

That's it. The error reporting is built into the Struts2 tags, so as long as you are using those tags, the messages will appear (see Figure 5-5).

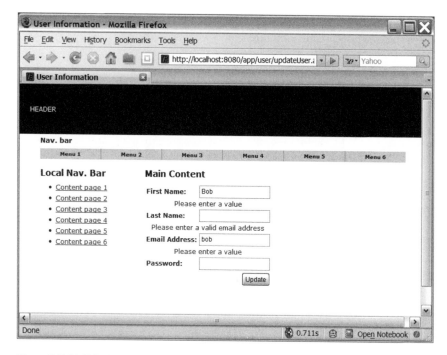

Figure 5-5. *Validation errors displayed next to the field with the problem*

If you don't like the formatting of the message, the CSS classes of errorMessage (for the error's message being displayed) and errorLabel (for the label of the field with the error) can be modified.

OTHER VALIDATION REPORTING OPTIONS

There is an alternative to the built-in error reporting provided by the form field tags. Struts2 provides tags that allow you to place information on the errors anywhere in the JSP template. For the form field errors, the fielderror tag is used. The tag by itself renders a list of all the form field errors:

```
<s:fielderror>
```

General error and user messages can also be communicated to the user. This is achieved using two tags. The error messages are added to the action with the method addActionError("my action error") and viewed in the JSP template using the tag:

```
<s:actionerror />
```

Action messages are added with addActionMessage("my action message") and viewed using the tag:

```
<s:actionmessage />
```

For the action class that is configured via XML and has multiple actions invoking multiple methods, the changes are very similar. The @Validation annotation is added at the class level, and the @Validations(…) annotation (the same as the preceding) is added to the update() method. The rest of the UserAction class stays the same, and the User domain object is the same as for the annotation-based action configuration.

```
@Validation
public class UserAction extends ActionSupport implements ModelDriven, Preparable {

    …

    @Validations( visitorFields = {
            @VisitorFieldValidator(
                    message = "Default message", key = "i18n.key",
                    fieldName= "model", appendPrefix = false) }
    )
    public String update() {
        service.persist(user,emailId);
        return SUCCESS;
    }
}
```

The big difference is in the struts.xml configuration. By default, the @Validations annotation is executed for *any* method providing action logic on the class—it is executed when the findUser.action and updateUser.action are called—resulting in strange behavior. The annotation should instead only be executed when the method it is applied to, update(), is called. The validator interceptor property validateAnnotatedMethodOnly set to a value of true will do the trick.

To apply this property in the interceptor, the stack needs to be referenced in the action configuration, and a param tag must be added. The name attribute value is a concatenation of the interceptor name (that the parameter is to be applied to) and the property name (separated with a period):

```
<interceptor-ref name="paramsPrepareParamsStack">
    <param name="validation.validateAnnotatedMethodOnly">true</param>
</interceptor-ref>
```

Unfortunately, there is no way to configure this globally for the package, so the additional configuration needs to be added to each action configuration (that uses the action class with the validation annotation).

```
<package name="user" extends="struts-default" namespace="/user" >

    …

    <action name="findUser" method="find"
            class="com.fdar.apress.s2.actions.user.UserAction" >
        <result name="input">/WEB-INF/jsp/user/findUser-success.jsp</result>
```

```
        <interceptor-ref name="paramsPrepareParamsStack">
            <param name="validation.validateAnnotatedMethodOnly">true</param>
        </interceptor-ref>
    </action>

    <action name="updateUser" method="update"
            class="com.fdar.apress.s2.actions.user.UserAction" >
        <result name="success" type="redirectAction">index</result>
        <result name="input">/WEB-INF/jsp/user/findUser-success.jsp</result>
        <interceptor-ref name="paramsPrepareParamsStack">
            <param name="validation.validateAnnotatedMethodOnly">true</param>
        </interceptor-ref>
    </action>

</package>
```

Tip You can get more information on interceptor, configuration, and parameter overriding from the Struts2 documentation at `http://struts.apache.org/2.x/docs/interceptors.html`.

Exception Handling

Within an application, exceptions can occur for different reasons and under different circumstances. In most applications, exceptions fall into the following categories:

- An unexpected event occurs or there is a problem accessing a resource, and the user cannot proceed until the issue is fixed (usually by an external entity such as an administrator).

- An exception is used to change the user's workflow.

- An error can be recovered from by interacting with the user.

Of these outcomes, various levels of interactivity and recoverability can be achieved. Some scenarios are completely manageable, whereas others are outright impossible.

Note Like many other features of Struts2, exception mapping is implemented via an interceptor. When using this feature, ensure that the `exception` interceptor is on the interceptor stack for the action. If you are using or extending one of the preconfigured interceptor stacks, the `exception` interceptor will already be there.

Unexpected Errors

As a developer, you are expected to handle all the possible outcomes of the code you are writing. But every now and again, something slips through. It could be a subtle bug in your code, or it might be an undocumented "feature" of an API that is being used. Either way, you need to be prepared to handle this scenario.

Unfortunately, there's not much that can be done. This falls into the outright impossible bucket. All you can do is present an error page to the user. The good news is that this doesn't need to be coded in the action class or even configured for each and every action. It can be defined globally in the `struts.xml` configuration file using the `global-results` and `global-exception-mappings` tags.

```
<package name="base-package" extends="struts-default" >

    <global-results>
        <result name="unknownError">/WEB-INF/jsp/error.jsp</result>
    </global-results>
    <global-exception-mappings>
        <exception-mapping exception="java.lang.Exception" result="unknownError" />
    </global-exception-mappings>

    ...

</package>
```

The `global-results` tag contains one or more `result` tags, which are configured and act just like the `result` tag in the action configuration—a unique value is needed for the name attribute, the `type` (if needed), and the value (default being the JSP location).

More interesting is the `global-exception-mappings` tag, which encloses a list of `exception-mapping` tags that have an attribute for an `exception` (full package and exception class name) and `result` (that is globally configured). If an exception of the configured type is caught, the user is redirected to the specified result. In fact, if the exception caught is a subclass of the configured exception, and the exception is not explicitly configured as a global exception, then it is also redirected to the error page. As an example, take the following configuration:

```
<global-results>
    <result name="unknownError">/WEB-INF/jsp/error1.jsp</result>
    <result name="dbError">/WEB-INF/jsp/error2.jsp</result>
</global-results>
<global-exception-mappings>
    <exception-mapping exception="java.lang.Exception" result="unknownError" />
    <exception-mapping exception="java.sql.SQLException" result="dbError" />
</global-exception-mappings>
```

If a `SQLException` is thrown by the code, the request is redirected to `error2.jsp` (the `dbError` result). However, if an `IOException` is thrown, which is also a subclass of `Exception`, it is forwarded to `error1.jsp` (the `unknownError` result). In this way, you can filter more specific errors and let generic, or unknown errors, be handled in a generic manner.

Changing the Workflow

An extension from the unexpected error scenario is when a part of the application throws an error to indicate that the user should be redirected. This changes the workflow, redirecting the user to somewhere other than where the user is expecting. Typical cases include an authentication module throwing a UserNotAuthenticatedException or a security module throwing an ActionNotAllowedException.

The configuration is also very similar to the unexpected error scenario. The standard exceptions are replaced by the custom application exceptions; the global results names changed to be more descriptive; and the JSPs to be rendered are modified to ones that will either be a dead end (in the case of ActionNotAllowedException) or provide the user with an opportunity to continue (for UserNotAuthenticatedException).

```
<global-results>
    <result name="logon">/WEB-INF/jsp/logon.jsp</result>
    <result name="noAccess">/WEB-INF/jsp/noAccess.jsp</result>
</global-results>
<global-exception-mappings>
    <exception-mapping exception="UserNotAuthenticatedException" result="logon" />
    <exception-mapping exception="ActionNotAllowedException" result="noAccess" />
</global-exception-mappings>
```

Recovery via User Interaction

The last category of exception handling is when the logic can recover from the exception, but it isn't for free. Interaction with the user is required to determine what the next step is. This is a common pattern with database exceptions.

In the code developed so far, entering duplicate primary keys is not explicitly handled. Therefore, when users enter duplicate e-mail addresses, an exception is thrown. This exception is not fatal and can be resolved by asking the users whether they want to change the e-mail address entered or log in to the application.

Before the exception can be configured, the hierarchy needs to be understood. There is a good chance that this exception comes from deep within the layers of the application and will most likely be nested. Creating an object with a primary key that is a duplicate of an existing object, using Hibernate JPA, results in the nested exception hierarchy:

```
javax.persistence.RollbackException
    caused by a org.hibernate.exception.ConstraintViolationException
        caused by a org.hibernate.exception.java.sql.BatchUpdateException
```

To avoid handling a very generic RollbackException, the persist() method on the UserServiceImpl business object is modified using the following pattern:

```
try {
    // start transaction, persist object, commit transaction
} catch (RollbackException e) {
    // rollback transaction
    throw (RuntimeException)e.getCause();
}
```

Now the `ConstraintViolationException` is thrown and can be configured in Struts2, allowing a more precise separation of issues to be made and therefore managed. The exact configuration is a variance on the exception mappings seen previously and differs slightly depending on how the actions were developed.

XML-Configured Actions and Wildcard-Configured Actions

When the actions are configured using XML, there are local equivalents of the global tags. You have already seen one, the `result` tag, which is enclosed within the `action` tag and is reused at a global level within the `global-results` tag. The `exception-mapping` tags, shown in the previous section, can also be used within the `action` tag.

With these configuration elements in place, exceptions can be caught and forwarded to a result locally as well as globally. This allows the exception `ConstraintViolationException` to be intercepted on a per-action basis and be directed to where the user has an opportunity to respond and possibly fix the problem that threw the exception.

```
<action name="updateUser" method="update"
    class="com.fdar.apress.s2.actions.user.UserAction" >
    <result name="success" type="redirectAction">index</result>
    <result name="dupPK">/WEB-INF/jsp/user/findUser-success.jsp</result>
    <exception-mapping result="dupPK"
        exception="org.hibernate.exception.ConstraintViolationException" />
</action>
```

Zero Configuration Actions

There are currently no annotations for exception mapping. So when using zero configuration actions, compromises need to be made. Following are the two available options:

- Use global results and global exception mappings to redirect the user to common pages.

- Use global exception mappings with action result configurations.

The first option has been covered in both of the other sections on exception handling, so you should understand how to configure this option.

The second option is much more useful in this scenario because each action can decide what to do when the exception is encountered. As you know, the exception being thrown is a `ConstraintViolationException`, so a global exception-mapping configuration can be added to the `struts.xml` configuration file. Instead of configuring a matching global result, the exception mapping returns a nebulous `"dupPK"` mapping value.

```
<global-results>
    <result name="unknownError">/WEB-INF/jsp/error.jsp</result>
</global-results>
<global-exception-mappings>
    <exception-mapping result="dupPK"
        exception="org.hibernate.exception.ConstraintViolationException" />
    <exception-mapping result="unknownError" exception="java.lang.Exception" />
</global-exception-mappings>
```

The configured result does not match any global result mappings but is instead intended to match an action result. A new result is added to the UpdateUserAction class with a name attribute value of "dupPK".

```
@ParentPackage("base-package")
@Results({
    @Result(name="success", value="index", type=ServletActionRedirectResult.class),
    @Result(name="dupPK", type=ServletDispatcherResult.class,
            value="/WEB-INF/jsp/user/findUser-success.jsp")
})
public class UpdateUserAction extends BaseUserAction {

    public String execute() throws Exception {
        service.persist(user,emailId);
        return SUCCESS;
    }
}
```

Each individual action can now determine where the user is to be redirected when the ConstraintViolationException exception is thrown.

■**Note** XML-configured actions can also use a local result mapping and a global exception-mapping.

Displaying the Error

Once at the template, the user needs to be provided with feedback to know that something went wrong. Continuing the example of a duplicate primary key, the feedback would be a message asking for a different e-mail address or for the user to log in to the application. The first step is then to determine that an exception has occurred.

When an exception is intercepted by the exception interceptor, two new properties are placed on the Value Stack:

- exception: The description of the message, as provided by the getMessage() method.

- exceptionStack: The full stack trace of the exception.

These can then be used to display feedback to the user (see Figure 5-6). In the findUser-success.jsp template, a test for whether the exception is available or not should suffice to determine whether to show an error message, but if multiple exceptions are being directed to the same template, a more robust filter is needed:

```
<s:if test="exception!=null" >
    <s:text name="info.emailAddressExists" />
</s:if>
```

The key info.emailAddressExists has been entered into the package.properties file as

```
info.emailAddressExists=The email address is already in use, enter another or log in
```

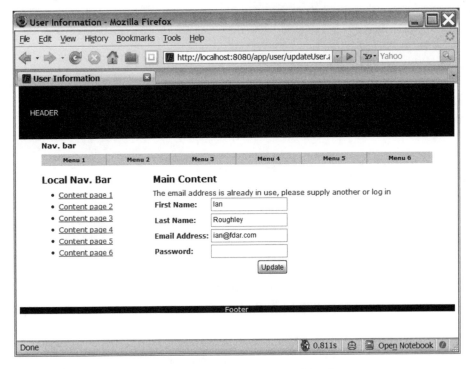

Figure 5-6. *Reporting a thrown exception to the user in a friendly manner*

The additional error information can be retrieved with the property tag:

```
<s:property value="exception" />
<s:property value="exceptionStack" />
```

Caution Showing the exception message or stack trace to the user is never a good idea—always provide friendly messages. An automated process of notifying an administrator or having a process that scans the log files for error messages is also a good solution.

EXCEPTION LOGGING

When an exception class is mapped in the `struts.xml` configuration file, the `exception` interceptor consumes it, pushing it onto the Value Stack. This processing avoids ugly error screens from the application server but can prevent the exception from being logged.

To rectify this behavior and provide logging for all exceptions that are thrown, the `exception` interceptor has additional configuration parameters:

- `logEnable`: Determine if logging is enabled or not.

- `logLevel`: Configures the logging level that the exception will be logged.

- `logCategory`: Configures the logger to use a custom logging category.

The parameters need to be added to the `exception` interceptor configuration. This is usually achieved by creating a new interceptor stack, with the `exception` interceptor (and the new logging parameters) as the first interceptor:

```
<interceptor-stack name="loggingParamsPrepareParamsStack" >
    <interceptor-ref name="exception-logging">
        <param name="logEnabled">true</param>
        <param name="logLevel">ERROR</param>
        <param name="logCategory">com.fdar.apress.s2</param>
    </interceptor-ref>
    <interceptor-ref name="paramsPrepareParamsStack" />
</interceptor-stack>
```

Alternatively, the parameters can be configured on a per-action basis:

```
<action name="updateUser" method="update"
    class="com.fdar.apress.s2.actions.user.UserAction" >
    <result name="success" type="redirectAction">index</result>
    <result name="dupPK">/WEB-INF/jsp/user/findUser-success.jsp</result>
    <exception-mapping result="dupPK"
        exception="org.hibernate.exception.ConstraintViolationException" />
    <interceptor-ref name="paramsPrepareParamsStack">
        <param name="exception.logEnabled">true</param>
        <param name="exception.logLevel">ERROR</param>
        <param name="exception.logCategory">com.fdar.apress.s2</param>
    </interceptor-ref>
</action>
```

However, as described earlier, this option can only be used with XML-based action configuration. Because logging is usually applied to all actions, it's always more convenient and less configuration is required when a custom interceptor stack is created.

File Uploads

The final use case to be implemented is the Upload Portrait to Profile use case, which allows users to upload an image to be associated with their profile. Most of the infrastructure is already in place, and only a few modifications need to be made:

- Update the domain model to support storing the new field.

- Update the JSP template to allow the selection of an image file.

- Update the JSP template to display the current image.

- Modify the action so that it is applied to the domain object to be persisted only when the image is changed.

Starting with the User domain object, the field that stores the image needs to be added. The Hibernate JPA implementation allows a field of type byte[] to map to a database LOB column type:

```
@Entity @Table( name="APP_USER", schema="S2APP" )
public class User implements Serializable {

    ...

    private byte[] portrait;

    @Lob @Column(name="PORTRAIT",nullable=true)
    public byte[] getPortrait() {
        return portrait;
    }

    public void setPortrait(byte[] portrait) {
        this.portrait = portrait;
    }
}
```

After the field and the mapping is added to the domain objects class, Hibernate handles creating the database column in the USER table, as well as managing all the related SQL queries.

Next are the changes to the findUser-success.jsp template (see Figure 5-7). There are three changes in total:

Encoding is added to the form: The attribute enctype="multipart/form-data" defines the encoding for the HTML form. This is the most important step because without it, the image file's contents and the form fields won't be transmitted from the browser.

The form fields to select the image are added: A Struts2 file tag is added to the contents of the form tag. Like the other tags, a key (for an internationalized label) and name (for the property on the action) attribute is supplied.

The existing image is displayed: A regular HTML img tag is used to render an image (if it hasn't been uploaded, a default image is displayed). The Struts2 property tag, using a generated URL, is used within the src attribute. Because there is a default xhtml theme for all tags, which aligns the label and form field using a two-column table, the image tag is spanned across two columns.

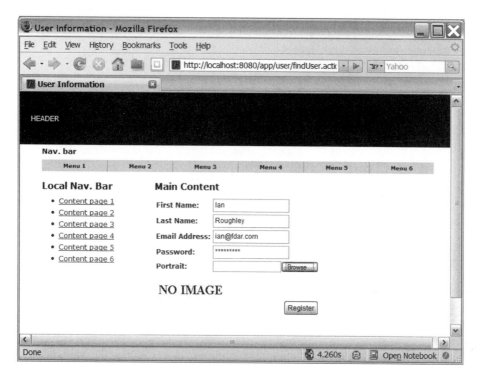

Figure 5-7. *The updated register screen showing the new form elements to upload an image and to view the currently assigned image*

It is interesting to note that the image is not retrieved via a URL ending in `.jpg`, `.gif`, or `.png` but rather an action URL of `/app/user/getPortrait.action`. The result of calling this URL and displaying the returned image for a user is shown in Figure 5-8. More details will be covered as we discuss the action in depth.

Tip If there is no Struts2 equivalent tag for the HTML tag you want to use, or you just prefer the HTML tag, you can use Struts2 `property` tags as values to HTML tag attributes. The resulting code is a little more verbose but just as correct. You can see an example of this style in the `img` tag in the updated `findUser-success.jsp` template.

The `findUser-success.jsp` template now becomes

```
<s:form namespace="/user" action="updateUser" method="post"
    enctype="multipart/form-data">

    // form fields

    <s:file key="user.portrait" name="upload" />
    <tr>
        <td colspan="2">
            <s:url id="image" action="getPortrait" namespace="/user" >
                <s:param name="emailId" value="emailId" />
            </s:url>
            <img src="<s:property value="#image" />" /> <br/>
        </td>
    </tr>

    // submit button code

</s:form>
```

Having a portrait is not necessary, so there are no additional validation requirements.

Figure 5-8. *A retrieved user complete with a portrait image*

Action Modifications

In the action, a new property that corresponds to the value of the file tag's name attribute is added, along with a corresponding setter method. The upload property is of type File and is a temporary file created on the file system of the application server machine. Following are the Struts2 configuration properties that control this process:

- struts.multipart.saveDir: The location to store the temporary file; when not supplied, the system property javax.servlet.context.tempdir is used by default.

- struts.multipart.maxSize: The maximum file size in bytes allowed to be uploaded; the default size is 2097152.

- struts.multipart.parser: The library used to upload the multipart form; valid values are cos, pell, and jakarta (the default).

Values can be assigned to these properties in the struts.xml or struts.properties configuration files. Along with the file itself, two other properties will be set on the action if setter methods are provided: fileName and contentType. Because multiple file tags may be present in a JSP, the setter methods need to be prefixed with the value of the name attribute; hence, for the file tag with a name of "upload", you would need the following:

```
public void setUpload(File upload) { ..}
public void setUploadFileName(String fileName) { ..}
public void setUploadContentType(String contentType) { ..}
```

For all of this to work correctly, once again, an interceptor is needed within the interceptor stack for the action. This is the fileUpload interceptor, and it can be found preconfigured in the fileUploadStack, the paramsPrepareParamsStack, and the defaultStack. We are already using the paramsPrepareParamsStack, so no further changes are needed in configuration.

XML-Configured Actions and Wildcard-Configured Actions

As expected, all the modifications for the XML-configured actions occur in the UserAction class. To gain access to the image and the file name from the user's local machine, the setUpload() and setUploadFileName() methods are implemented.

For the portrait to only be set on the domain object when a file is selected, the update() method is modified to only access the contents of the file (as a byte[] using a helper class method) when the file name is not empty.

```
public String update() {
    if(uploadFileName!=null && !"".equals(uploadFileName)) {
        user.setPortrait(Utils.getBytesFromFile(upload));
    }
    service.persist(user,emailId);
    return SUCCESS;
}
```

One more modification for the action class is not to change behavior but rather to add a new action. The method getInputStream() is introduced, which returns either the image stored in the domain object or a placeholder image (using internationalized text from the package.properties file) as an InputStream.

```
public InputStream getInputStream() {
    if( user==null || user.getPortrait()==null) {
        return Utils.getNoImageInputStream(getText("text.noImage"));
    } else {
        return new ByteArrayInputStream(user.getPortrait());
    }
}
```

To enable the action, a new configuration is added to the struts.xml configuration file.

```
<package name="user" extends="struts-default" namespace="/user" >

    ...
```

```
<action name="getPortrait" class="com.fdar.apress.s2.actions.user.UserAction" >
    <result name="success" type="stream">
        <param name="contentType">image</param>
        <param name="inputName">inputStream</param>
    </result>
</action>

</package>
```

In the configuration, a new result type is used, the `stream` result. This result allows a getter (that returns an `InputStream`) to be configured and the contents streamed back to the requestor. The new method `getInputStream()` added to the action class matches the value configured in the parameter `inputName` and provides the image data.

■**Tip** The `stream` result can be used for any type of binary data you can think of, such as images, PDFs, and Microsoft Office documents.

Along with the `inputName`, the `contentType` has been configured to a value of `"image"`. This could have been more specific had we stored the content type of the uploaded image on the domain object. Because you know it will always be an image, this is specific enough. The complete list of parameters that can be configured for the result are listed here:

- `contentType`: The MIME type of the stream; defaults to `"text/plain"`.

- `contentLength`: The length in bytes; assists the browser in displaying the correct percentage in the progress bar.

- `contentDisposition`: The content disposition header value for specifying the file name; defaults to `"inline"`.

- `inputName`: The name of the property that returns an `InputStream`; defaults to `"inputStream"`.

- `bufferSize`: The size of the copy buffer (from input to output); defaults to `"1024"`.

This configuration returns the image of the current user when the URL `/app/user/get-Portrait.action` is invoked.

Zero Configuration Actions

The same types of modifications need to be made when zero configuration actions are used; they are just in different places. The `setUpload()` and `setUploadFileName()` methods are added to the `BaseUserAction` class, and the `update()` method is modified. These are the same as in the previous section.

Of more interest is the implementation of the new action. Instead of a new method and action configuration in `struts.xml`, a new action class is added:

```
@ParentPackage("base-package")
@Result(name="success", value="inputStream", type=StreamResult.class)
public class GetPortraitAction extends BaseUserAction {

    public InputStream getInputStream() {
        if( user==null || user.getPortrait()==null) {
            return Utils.getNoImageInputStream(getText("text.noImage"));
        } else {
            return new ByteArrayInputStream(user.getPortrait());
        }
    }
}
```

The getInputStream() method is exactly the same as was implemented for the UserAction. Configuration is achieved with the @Result annotation, using a StreamResult.class type and a value of "inputStream". The value, like the XML-configured version, must match a setter or property of the action class.

■**Caution** Make sure that you have the org.apache.struts2.dispatcher.ActionContextCleanUp filter enabled in the web.xml configuration file and applied as the first filter in the chain. This ensures that the environment is clean and ready to accept the upload.

Summary

In this chapter, we covered data manipulation; in particular, creating, updating, and searching for a particular domain object. With the information provided, it should be easy to figure out how to implement a delete feature, which I'll leave for you as an exercise.

The features we discussed in this chapter will be reused and expanded upon throughout the remainder of this book: developing, testing, and configuring actions; working with actions and domain objects; validation; internationalization; and exception handling. Each is an important part of modern web application development and a core element in developing an application with Struts2.

CHAPTER 6

■ ■ ■

Wizards and Workflows

This chapter builds upon the CRUD functionality presented in Chapter 5, showing you how wizards and workflows can be implemented in Struts2. Wizards and workflows collect information from the user in a series of screens. Each screen in the series is small and manageable and allows the application to make intelligent decisions on what information to ask for next. This keeps the user from entering unnecessary information and avoids overwhelming the user by presenting all the information on a single screen.

In many ways, this is analogous to a garden path. The user should be able to go both forward and backward along the path, and there are times that the user will detour from the main path. In a web application, a detour may entail entering additional information that the application needs for the workflow, but the user hasn't yet entered (perhaps the user has registered but not yet completed the profile).

This chapter provides the implementation for a modestly complex workflow, providing an example using several detours. You'll learn about a new interceptor to provide the workflow functionality, complex validation and custom validators, custom tag rendering templates, and flash scope. Each of these features is not limited to wizards and workflows and can be used for any action in a Struts2 application.

The Use Case

The only use case for this chapter, *Create Event*, sounds easy enough by its title. When you review the domain model shown in Figure 6-1, however, you realize the complexity of this use case. Rather than one domain object, as in Chapter 5, there are actually six domain objects: Event, Contestant, Progress, Location, Broadcast, and Address. The good news is that Location is a common base class, and Progress is an enumeration, but this still leaves four classes that need to be dealt with. Adding to the complexity is that an Event can contain many Contestants.

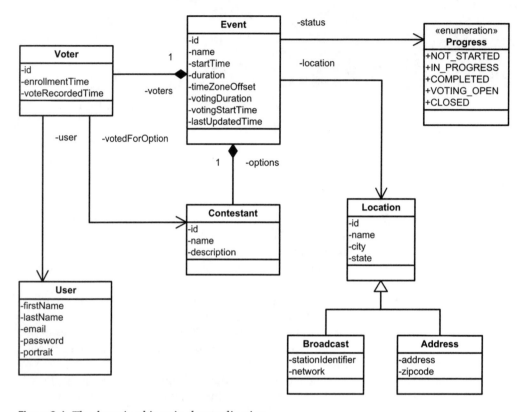

Figure 6-1. *The domain objects in the application*

To collect all the information required to create a new event, you need to make some decisions on the design of the user interface (UI). The options include the following:

1. Collect all the information in one big long form. If new fields need to be added into the form (i.e., when a new contestant is required), the form will be reloaded with the additional fields.

2. The same long form from the preceding option is used. Instead of reloading the entire form when new fields are required, sections are reloaded using AJAX techniques.

3. A series of many small forms is used to collect all the data. The user's progress and the order of the forms presented are strictly controlled to ensure that all the data is collected.

Presenting too much information to users can be overwhelming, so most companies choose the third option. The common name for this type of user interaction is *workflows* or *wizards*.

Within the workflow for the Create Event use case, a number of tasks need to be completed:

- The basic event information needs to be entered.

- The location for the event is selected from a list of known locations.

- If the location isn't known, the user should be able to create a new location.

- The contestants for the event need to be entered.

- There needs to be more than one contestant per event, so the user should be able to add as many as required.

- If a mistake is made, the contestant should be removed and reentered.

■**Note** Within this workflow, information is entered or removed but not updated. This simplistic approach is used to help you learn how to implement workflows instead of focusing on a specific workflow. Updating information is the same as presented in Chapter 5, and those techniques can be applied to workflows from this chapter.

Figure 6-2 is the result of turning the list of requirements into a workflow. Each box represents a screen, page, or view that the user needs to perform a task of entering information or making a choice (selecting from a list or clicking a link). The only screen that might be confusing is the Select Location Type. Because there are two types of locations, Broadcast and Address, the users need to select the type they want to create so the correct fields are presented on the next screen.

In the remainder of this chapter, you will learn different techniques for implementing this workflow. Although all the code for the workflow is not presented (it is available in the Source Code/Download area of the Apress web site at http://www.apress.com), you can combine the techniques presented here with those from Chapter 5 for a complete picture.

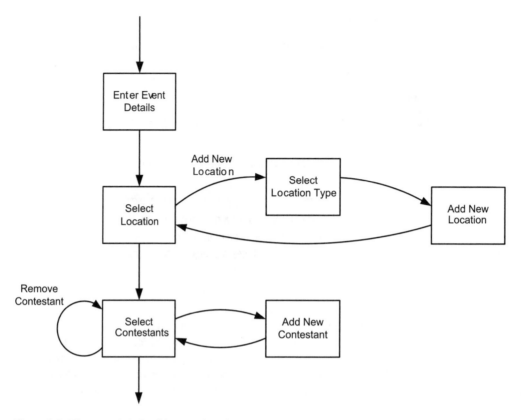

Figure 6-2. *The steps involved in creating a new event*

The Scope Interceptor

The simplest method for creating a workflow in a Struts2 application is to store the data in semipersistent storage for the duration of the workflow (removing it when complete) by using the scope interceptor, which stores and retrieves action properties in the session or application scope.

Reviewing Figure 6-2, you'll notice that even though there are several screens that the user needs to use to enter information, relatively few domain objects are involved. The problem, which is common to workflows, is that the information is built up gradually. All the information to save a correctly populated domain object (including all necessary dependent objects) is not available until the very end.

Following are the domain objects and their dependencies for the Create Event use case:

- Basic event information is entered in the Event domain object. At this stage, there is not enough information to persist the object and have a valid event in the database.

- An existing Location domain object is selected or a new Location domain object is created. The location has no dependency on the event, but the event is required to have a location assigned to it, so it must exist in the database before the event is persisted.

- A Contestant domain object needs to be created for each contestant's information. Contestants are dependent on events and events on contestants, so all these objects need to be persisted together.

The solution is that the Event domain object, associated Location object, and all dependent Contestant objects are stored in the session until the user makes a final confirmation. At this time, the event is saved in the database and is valid for anyone to view.

Caution You may be storing a lot of information, per user, in the session by using this method. This can affect performance and scalability, especially when introducing high-availability clustering. Understanding the nonfunctional requirements of the application you are developing, in particular the user load, will help you determine whether you should proceed with this option or another (which is outside the scope of this book and involves a custom implementation). Pay attention to application server user session limits as well as the total memory being consumed by all user sessions.

Configuration

To isolate the Create Event use case from the other use cases, a new enterEvent package is created for the workflow, which is accessed via the URL namespace /event. To take advantage of the codebehind plug-in, the new package extends the base-package package.

Thus far, the interceptor stack used is the paramsPrepareParamsStack. This stack does not include the scope interceptor, so it must be added. Rather than do this for every action, a new stack is created:

```
<package name="enterEvent" namespace="/event" extends="base-package">

    <interceptors>
        <interceptor-stack name="eventStack">
            <interceptor-ref name="scope">
                <param name="session">model</param>
                <param name="key">partialEvent</param>
            </interceptor-ref>
            <interceptor-ref name="paramsPrepareParamsStack"/>
        </interceptor-stack>
    </interceptors>

    <default-interceptor-ref name="eventStack" />

</package>
```

■**Caution** If the `scope` interceptor is applied to all the actions in a package, then each action in the
package must provide a getter and setter for all of the configured properties. However, every property is
not always needed on every action, which is true for the example when entering a new location. When all
the properties are not needed, you have to decide whether to keep the additional actions in the workflow
with getters and setters that are not used or whether to move the action outside the workflow package or
even outside the workflow altogether.

Two parameters are being used by the `scope` interceptor: the `session` parameter, which
takes a comma-delimited list of properties to store in the session scope, and the `key` parameter, which specifies the name to use when storing the properties. If only one action is used for
the entire flow, the `key` parameter is not required; in this case, you need the `key` parameter to
pass the session-stored properties between actions. The other parameter that can be used is
the `application` parameter, which is similar to the `session` parameter, but the properties are
stored in application scope rather than session scope.

Remember that the order is important. The objects being stored in the session or application scope need to be retrieved and set on the action before any logic is performed, and thus
the `scope` interceptor must be before the `paramsPrepareParamsStack` interceptor in the stack.

Along with the interceptor stack configuration, two actions need special configuration:
one for the action that initiates the workflow, and the other for the action that completes the
workflow. Although all other actions are configured via annotation, these can't be because the
`type` property needs to be overloaded on the `scope` interceptor. The type attribute can have a
value of either `start` or `end`. When the value is `start`, the `scope` interceptor resets the properties in the session (or application scope if the `application` property is used) to their initial
state. A value of `end` does the reverse; it removes the properties from the session (or application) scope, saving the application server memory.

```
<package name="enterEvent" namespace="/event" extends="base-package">

    ...

    <action name="addEventFlow"
        class="com.fdar.apress.s2.actions.event.BaseEventAction">
        <interceptor-ref name="eventStack">
            <param name="scope.type">start</param>
        </interceptor-ref>
        <result>/WEB-INF/jsp/event/enterEventDetails-input.jsp</result>
    </action>

    <action name="completeEvent"
        class="com.fdar.apress.s2.actions.event.BaseEventAction">
        <interceptor-ref name="eventStack">
            <param name="scope.type">end</param>
        </interceptor-ref>
        <result>/WEB-INF/jsp/event/eventReview.jsp</result>
    </action>

</package>
```

In effect, both these actions are pass-through actions. They don't provide any functionality specific to the workflow; instead, they provide an entry and exit point to the workflow. Both these actions extend the `BaseEventAction` class.

■**Caution** It is especially important to have the final action in the workflow configured in XML and different from the action that performs the final saving of data. If they were the same and there was a validation error in final action, the property stored by the `scope` interceptor would no longer be available to the action.

Workflow Elements

All of the workflow elements should be familiar to you; they consist of actions and JSPs. Interlinking them together is the challenge. Figure 6-3 shows how each piece interacts to form the complete workflow.

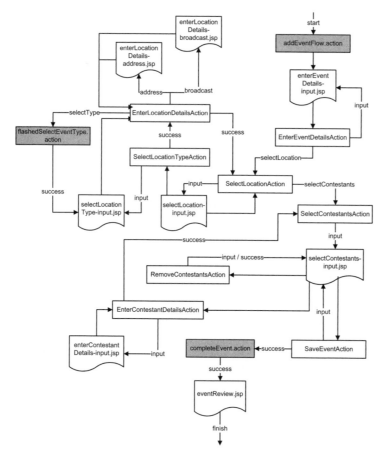

Figure 6-3. *Interactions between actions and JSPs for the Create Event use case using the scope interceptor for the workflow*

Figure 6-3 is a little complex, but it shows all the pieces for the workflow together: the actions (square boxes, grayed ones configured in struts.xml, the others configured via annotations), the JSPs, and the result types (shown on the arrowed lines). Having this complete picture is important and will make explaining the process much easier. If you look through the JSPs and actions, you'll notice that some of the paths in Figure 6-3 are not present. This is because the validation interceptor is used, and when validation fails, it redirects the user back to the "input" view.

The actions and JSPs for the workflow are mostly the same as presented in Chapter 5; each action is model driven with the getter implemented in the BaseEventAction class that is the base class for all the actions in the workflow. Because the scope interceptor stores the "model" property, there also needs to be a setter for the "model" object. This is placed on the BaseEventAction class as well, as the scope interceptor needs both methods to interact correctly with each action.

■**Note** For the implementation, the codebehind plug-in has been used to determine the page name to be rendered when a configuration is not explicitly defined. In the case of a workflow, this does not always make sense. For better clarity, explicitly configure all the results from every action.

CONSOLIDATING THE WORKFLOW ACTIONS

Figure 6-3 describes another important characteristic of the workflow: each step of the workflow is implemented as a separate action class. As discussed in Chapter 5, an action doesn't need to strictly implement an execute() method; instead, any no argument method that returns a String can be used. This opens different implementation possibilities for workflows.

Rather than implement the workflow as individual actions, you can implement the entire workflow as a single action. From a configuration standpoint, the only change is that the key attribute on the scope interceptor configuration is omitted. Because the same action is used for every step, the default name (a unique combination of the property name being stored and the action name) is used.

The difference is conceptual. Is the workflow itself the logic grouping, or is it the individual action? One way to answer this question is to determine if any of the steps in the workflow can be reused, either in other workflows (related or not) or as the logic behind individual pages. If the answer is "yes," then separate actions might be the better choice. Otherwise, it might make sense to consolidate all of the functionality together.

I like to follow the *Single Responsibility Principle* when developing actions. This keeps the action classes small, focused, and easier to test.

With the scope interceptor configured and the base class available, everything needed for the workflow is in place. In the remainder of this section, you'll learn advanced techniques for making the implementation of workflows easier.

■Note These techniques are not limited to workflows and can be used anywhere in a Struts2 application.

Custom Validations

In Chapter 5, you saw how to implement basic validation; the first step in the workflow, the EventEnterDetailsAction action, provides a good example of how to implement custom validators. Before reviewing the action, let's look at the JSP.

```
<head>
    <title><s:text name="createEvent.enterEvent.title" /></title>
</head>
<body>

<s:form action="enterEventDetails" namespace="/event" method="post" >

    <s:textfield key="event.name" name="name" />
    <s:textfield key="event.startDate" name="partialStartDate" />
    <s:textfield key="event.startTime" name="patialStartTime" />
    <s:textfield key="event.timeZoneOffset" name="timeZoneOffset" />
    <s:textfield key="event.votingStartTime" name="partialVotingStartTime" />
    <s:textfield key="event.duration" name="duration" />

    <s:submit key="button.create" />

</s:form>

</body>
</html>
```

Many of the fields in the form correspond directly to the properties on the Event domain object, but there are fields that don't exist. The partialStartDate, partialStartTime, and partialVotingStartTime fields are specified on the action instead of the domain object. Entering a date and time in one form field, in the correct data format, is a challenge for most end users. Having separate fields on the action allows you to accept the data in a user-friendly way and then convert the data so that the domain object can use it.

The UI asks for the date the event is to occur, the time that the event starts, and the time the event creator wants the voting to start. To make data entry for the end user even easier, we want the times to be entered as an hour, an optional colon, and minutes, then "am" or "pm", such as "8:30pm" or "3:30am". As no such validator exists in Struts2, a new one needs to be implemented.

Before looking at the validator, let's look at the action class:

```
@Validation
public class EnterEventDetailsAction extends BaseEventAction implements Preparable {

    …

    public void prepare() throws Exception {
        event = new Event();
        event.setStatus(Progress.NOT_STARTED);
        event.setLastUpdateTime( Calendar.getInstance().getTime() );
    }

    public Date getPartialStartDate() {
        return partialStartDate;
    }

    @RequiredFieldValidator(message="Validation Error", key="validate.notEmpty")
    public void setPartialStartDate(Date partialStartDate) {
        this.partialStartDate = partialStartDate;
    }

    public String getPatialStartTime() {
        return patialStartTime;
    }

    @CustomValidator(type="timeValidator", key="validate.timeOfDay")
    public void setPatialStartTime(String patialStartTime) {
        this.patialStartTime = patialStartTime;
    }

    public String getPartialVotingStartTime() {
        return partialVotingStartTime;
    }

    @CustomValidator(type="timeValidator", key="validate.timeOfDay")
    public void setPartialVotingStartTime(String partialVotingStartTime) {
        this.partialVotingStartTime = partialVotingStartTime;
    }

    @VisitorFieldValidator( message="Default message", fieldName="model",
                            shortCircuit=false, appendPrefix=false)
    public String execute() throws Exception {

        Calendar cal = Calendar.getInstance();
        cal.setTime(partialStartDate);
        TimeUtil timeUtil = new TimeUtil(patialStartTime);
        event.setStartTime(
            timeUtil.resolveDate( partialStartDate, event.getTimeZoneOffset() ) );
```

```
        cal = Calendar.getInstance();
        cal.setTime(partialStartDate);
        timeUtil = new TimeUtil(partialVotingStartTime);
        event.setVotingStartTime(
            timeUtil.resolveDate( partialStartDate, event.getTimeZoneOffset() ) );

        return SUCCESS;
    }
}
```

Following are the highlights of this action class:

- The action implements the `Preparable` interface and provides the `prepare()` method that creates a new event and configures the event with default initialization data.

- There are class properties for `partialStartDate`, `partialStartTime`, and `partialVotingStartTime` (not shown), with matching getters and setters.

- The `execute()` method takes the values from the `partialStartDate`, `partialStartTime`, and `partialVotingStartTime` fields and transforms them into a valid date for the `Event` domain object.

- The validation for the action is a combination of the visitor validation for the `Event` domain object and field validation on the action's setters.

Note The `TimeUtil` class used in the action is a helper class that is also used in the validator code. When instantiated with a `String` value, the utility returns information such as minutes, hours, whether the time is AM or PM, and whether the `String` passed in is valid.

Custom validation annotations are very similar to all the other validation annotations and take the following form:

```
@CustomValidator(type="timeValidator", key="validate.timeOfDay")
```

The similarities include the `message` (message to display), `key` (key for the message to display), `fieldName` (used when the annotation is not placed directly on the field), and `shortCircuit` attributes (determines whether other validations should be executed when the current validation fails). The main difference is the `type` attribute. This attribute defines which custom validator to use from the `validation.xml` configuration file.

If you only use the provided validations, you never need to provide a `validation.xml` configuration file because the default file from Struts2 is used. When using custom validations, you need to copy the `default.xml` configuration file (from the `com\opensymphony\xwork2\validator\validators` directory of the XWork JAR) to the root directory of your classpath (changing the name to `validators.xml`) and then add the new validator's configuration.

The updated `validators.xml` configuration file is

```xml
<?xml version="1.0" encoding="UTF-8"?>
<!DOCTYPE validators PUBLIC
        "-//OpenSymphony Group//XWork Validator Config 1.0//EN"
        "http://www.opensymphony.com/xwork/xwork-validator-config-1.0.dtd">
<validators>
  <validator name="required"
    class="com.opensymphony.xwork2.validator.validators.RequiredFieldValidator"/>
  <validator name="requiredstring"
    class="com.opensymphony.xwork2.validator.validators.RequiredStringValidator"/>
  <validator name="int"
    class="com.opensymphony.xwork2.validator.validators.IntRangeFieldValidator"/>
  <validator name="double"
    class="com.opensymphony.xwork2.validator.validators.DoubleRangeFieldValidator"/>
  <validator name="date"
    class="com.opensymphony.xwork2.validator.validators.DateRangeFieldValidator"/>
  <validator name="expression"
    class="com.opensymphony.xwork2.validator.validators.ExpressionValidator"/>
  <validator name="fieldexpression"
    class="com.opensymphony.xwork2.validator.validators.FieldExpressionValidator"/>
  <validator name="email"
    class="com.opensymphony.xwork2.validator.validators.EmailValidator"/>
  <validator name="url"
    class="com.opensymphony.xwork2.validator.validators.URLValidator"/>

    …

  <!-- Our custom validators -->
  <validator name="timeValidator" class="com.fdar.apress.s2.util.TimeValidator"/>

</validators>
```

The configuration provides a `name` attribute that is unique across all the validators and a `class` attribute that provides the functionality.

Next is the validator itself. When implementing a validator, the Struts2 `Validator` interface is implemented. To make creating validators even easier, two supporting classes can be extended: `ValidatorSupport` and `FieldValidatorSupport`. The only difference is that the `FieldValidatorSupport` is used when validating a specific field (as opposed to the action) and provides the getters and setters to obtain the field name.

In both cases, the method `validate(Object obj)` needs to be implemented. To report problems, and hence fail the validation, the `addFieldError(…)` and `addActionError(…)` methods are used. These methods are provided by a `ValidatorContext` instance, passed in before the validation is performed. As a field validator is being implemented, the field that the validator is currently validating against is obtained with a call to `getFieldName()`.

With all these pieces in place, the only step left is the logic. The complete custom time validator is shown here:

```
public class TimeValidator extends FieldValidatorSupport {

    public void validate( Object obj ) throws ValidationException {

        String fieldName = getFieldName();
        Object value = this.getFieldValue(fieldName, obj);

        if( value == null || !(value instanceof String)
                || !( new TimeUtil( (String)value ).isValid() ) ) {
            addFieldError( fieldName, obj );
        }

    }

}
```

When implementing validation, you should be aware of the following notes specific to the workflow:

- Each domain object that you place the validation annotations on may require its own internationalization file (depending on the strategy you have selected) when the annotation attribute key is used.

- When using `@VisitorFieldValidator` on a field as opposed to the preceding `execute()` method (with the `appendPrefix` attribute set to `true`), the default message needs to be empty; otherwise, both the action message and the domain model message are displayed. An example can be found in the `EnterContestantDetailsAction` action.

With the validator complete, so too is the first page of the workflow. Figure 6-4 shows the fields, along with the results of one successfully validated field and one that has failed.

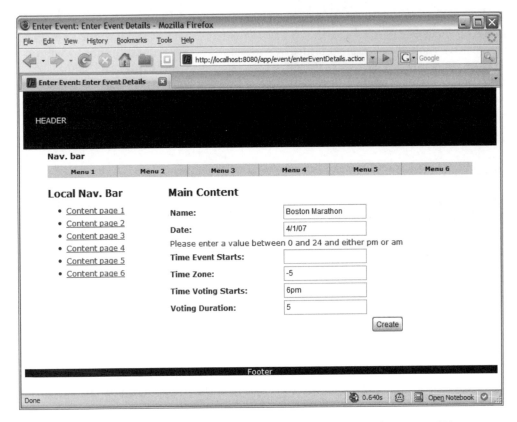

Figure 6-4. *The Enter Event Details page showing the results of the failed custom validator*

Customizing the Rendering of Struts2 Tags

In Chapter 3, we discussed how the architecture of Struts2 provided a much more flexible design than tag libraries, allowing a tag to be constructed of logic in Java and rendering using templates (that could be bundled together into a theme). The workflow created takes advantage of this flexibility in two specific places:

- In the selectLocationType-input.jsp template, to render a list of radio buttons vertically underneath each other, rather than horizontally next to each other

- In the selectContestants-input.jsp template, to render a list of check boxes vertically underneath each other, rather than horizontally next to each other

Instead of creating individual templates, we'll create a theme that allows you to expand upon these two cases as the project evolves. The theme we'll create will be called "apress" and is nothing more complex than a directory name that Struts2 can find tag templates in. To implement the theme, a directory /template/apress is created in the root web application directory.

In the theme directory, make a copy of the template to be modified (the original template file can be found in the Struts2 JAR file under the /template directory). Whenever possible, start off using the simple theme, which provides the simplest implementation. Now that there is a base implementation, you can make changes to the template to provide the required change in rendering.

The files that need to be modified for the special workflow rendering are the `radiomap.ftl` and `checkboxlist.ftl` templates. To each of these templates, an HTML `<br/>` tag is inserted so that each of the elements is rendered on a new line. The resulting view for the `selectLocationType-input.jsp` page can be seen in Figure 6-5.

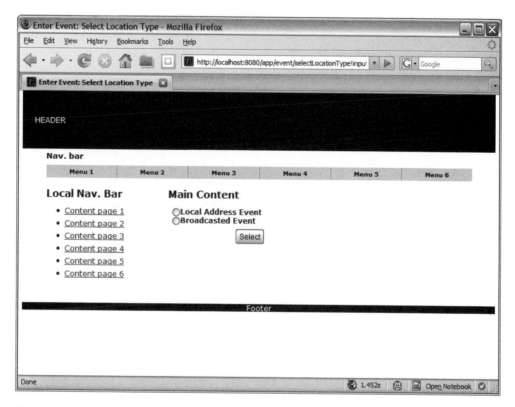

Figure 6-5. *Rendering radio buttons vertically rather than horizontally (the default)*

■**Tip** When writing templates, don't forget to include header or footer templates. These are common templates that provide features such as layout and error rendering code. Usually, the templates from the `simple` theme can be reused from any new theme that you create. This saves time and ensures consistency across all the tags in the application.

To use the new theme, a `theme` attribute with the value `"apress"` needs to be added to all tags that want to use the new theme for rendering. In `selectLocationType-input.jsp`, this is a change to the `radio` tag only:

```
<s:radio theme="apress" list="types" name="typeClass"
        listKey="class.name" listValue="getText(class.name)" />
```

CHANGING THE TEMPLATE RENDERING LANGUAGE

Templates do not need to be written in Freemarker. They can be rendered in Freemarker, Velocity, or JSP templates. To change the template rendering language, use the property `struts.ui.templateSuffix`, which can be modified in the `struts.properties` or the `struts.xml` configuration files.

The one caveat to be aware of is that all templates need to be the same language. You cannot have some templates rendered in Freemarker and others in JSP. So, if you change the templating language away from Freemarker, the first task will be to rewrite all the existing templates in the new language.

Using this technique, many libraries of themes can be built up. It is not uncommon to have multiple themes per project—perhaps one for a double column layout, and another for a triple column layout. The themes can be reused between projects, and, if you are using Freemarker or Velocity templates, they can be packaged separately in JAR files to make sharing easier.

Working with Subclassed Domain Objects

When creating a location, the user has the option to create an address location (for a physical address where the event is to be held) or a broadcast location (for a radio or television network that the event is being broadcast on). Because both of these location types share properties, the domain model (refer to Figure 6-1) is composed of a `Location` class that is subclassed by an `Address` class and a `Broadcast` class.

As well as reusing properties in the super class, we'll try to make the workflow dynamic by reducing duplicate code and configuration as much as possible and allowing the addition of new subclasses with minimal work.

The starting point is the `SelectLocationTypeAction` class, which is used to generate the list of types that are presented to the user (the results of which were shown in Figure 6-5). In the `prepare()` method, a list is created with an instance of each of the subclasses of the `Location` class. There is no additional functionality provided by the `input()` method.

```
@Result(type=ServletActionRedirectResult.class,value="enterLocationDetails")
public class SelectLocationTypeAction extends BaseEventAction
        implements Preparable
{

    private Integer typeId;
    private List<Location> types;

    ...

    public List<Location> getTypes() {
        return types;
    }
}
```

```
    public void prepare() throws Exception {
        types = new ArrayList<Location>();
        types.add(new Address());
        types.add(new Broadcast());
    }

    public String input() throws Exception {
        return INPUT;
    }

}
```

Once complete, the user is redirected to the selectLocationType-input.jsp JSP, and the list that has been created in the action is rendered in the `<s:radio ... />` tag. An OGNL expression in the listKey attribute allows the name of the class to be used as the value to be submitted when selected in the form. And, by creating an entry in the package.properties for the full package and class name of the Address and Broadcast classes, the display value rendered in the listValue attribute for the user can be modified to a user friendly (and internationalized) value.

```
<head>
    <title><s:text name="createEvent.selectLocationType.title" /></title>
</head>
<body>

<s:form action="enterLocationDetails" namespace="/event" method="post" >

    <s:radio theme="apress" list="types" name="typeClass"
            listKey="class.name" listValue="getText(class.name)" />
    <s:hidden name="setup" value="true" />

    <s:submit key="button.select" />

</s:form>

</body>
</html>
```

The other important field in the JSP is the hidden setup field, which allows the next action to identify whether it should forward back to the current JSP with a validation error, forward to a location input view, or save the entered location.

In the execute() method of the EnterLocationDetailsAction class, you can review the details of the logic. When the typeClass property (set by the radio list) is null, meaning that the user clicked "submit" without selecting a type, a field validation error is added and the user redirected back to the previous page with the "selectType" result.

■Note The getText(…) method comes from the ActionSupport class (in the class hierarchy) and allows internationalized text to be retrieved using a supplied key. There are many forms of the getText(…) method, but because we are using the version that takes an internationalization key as the first parameter, the second parameter is a list of substitution values for the text. In this scenario, there are no such parameters, which is why an empty String array is provided.

```
public class EnterLocationDetailsAction
        extends BaseEventAction implements Preparable {

    private String setup;
    private String typeClass;

    ...

    public String execute() throws Exception {

        if( typeClass==null ) {
            addFieldError("typeClass",
                        getText("validate.selectType",new String[]{}));
            return "selectType";

        } else {

            String objType =
                typeClass.substring(typeClass.lastIndexOf(".")+1).toLowerCase();
            if( setup!=null ) {
                return objType;
            } else {
                ...
            }
            ...

        }
    }
}
```

If a location type was selected, the next test is to determine if the setup property is not null (the value is valid only when the user is coming from the selectLocationType-input.jsp template). In this case, we want to direct the user to the correct input screen enterLocationDetails-address.jsp for entering address information, or enterLocationDetails-broadast.jsp for entering broadcast information. Because the codebehind plug-in is being used, the suffix of the JSP is the same as the result being returned: the name of the domain object. The full class name of the selected domain object is being passed into the action, so the result value can be easily determined.

In the case of each result, the JSPs will be similar, but there are some points to note:

- Each JSP must provide all the form fields for data the user needs to enter (both the Location class properties and the subclass properties).

- Because the domain model is not the object managed by the action being model driven, each of the form fields must include the domain object name and property (i.e., broadcast.state).

- A hidden form field is required to reconvey the selected class of the domain object back to the action using the name "typeClass".

All of these conditions have been satisfied in the enterLocationDetails-broadast.jsp template shown here:

```
<head>
    <title>
        <s:text name="createEvent.enterLocationDetails.broadcast.title" />
    </title>
</head>
<body>

<s:form action="enterLocationDetails" namespace="/event" method="post" >

    <s:textfield key="broadcast.name" name="broadcast.name" />
    <s:textfield key="broadcast.city" name="broadcast.city" />
    <s:textfield key="broadcast.state" name="broadcast.state" />
    <s:textfield key="broadcast.network" name="broadcast.network" />
    <s:textfield key="broadcast.stationIdentifier"
        name="broadcast.stationIdentifier" />

    <s:hidden name="typeClass"/>

    <s:submit key="button.create" />

</s:form>

</body>
</html>
```

Returning to the EnterLocationDetailsAction class, the prepare() method is invoked. This method creates an instance of the correct domain object, using the class name that was originally passed from the selectLocationType-input.jsp JSP. To collect user-entered data (and return data if there was a validation error), the action also requires both getters and setters for each of the domain object types.

Tip The main object managed by the `scope` interceptor is not always the `model` property. By using another property name, each action in the workflow that implements the `ModelDriven` interface can supply a different type. To determine which style to use, first determine if the property being stored is used in the majority of the actions in the workflow. If so, this property is also the best choice to use as the model.

Finally, validation needs to be performed for the domain object. Validation annotations are placed on the `Location`, `Address`, and `Broadcast` domain objects but not on the action class itself. If annotations were placed on the action, on the `setAddress(…)` and `setBroadcast(…)` methods, both would need to pass every time. This is incorrect because only one domain object is entered (and only one requires validation, not both), so validation needs to be invoked manually.

Note Another validation option for the action is to implement the `Validateable` interface (provided in `ActionSupport`), which has a `validate()` method. In this scenario, it would not have been possible because the interceptors that work with the `Validateable` interface forward the user to the same action with the result type "`input`". The complexity of this action requires the failed validation result to be the name of the domain object's class.

Invoking the validation framework manually is not difficult and can be used outside Struts2 completely, that is, to validate the domain objects when the data comes from another source (XML files, web service calls, etc.). Following are the steps for using the validators:

1. Create the validator class; in this case, the `VisitorFieldValidator`.

2. Configure any properties. For the action, you set the field name to use and configure the validator to append the property prefix to the field name.

3. Create a validator context, and apply it to the validator. The `DelegatingValidatorContext` provides a default implementation and can be created using a subclass of `ActionSupport` (or any class implementing the `ValidationAware`, `TextProvider`, and `LocaleProvider` interfaces).

4. Invoke the `validate(…)` method of the validator passing in the object to validate; in this case, it is the current action.

To determine whether validation errors were found, use the `hasErrors()`, `hasFieldErrors()`, and `hasActionErrors()` methods on the action. If an error is found, you return the name of the domain object as the result.

```java
@Results( value={
    @Result(type=ServletActionRedirectResult.class,
        value="selectLocation",params={"method","input"}),
    …
})
public class EnterLocationDetailsAction
        extends BaseEventAction implements Preparable {

    …

    public void prepare() throws Exception {
        if( typeClass!=null ) {
            Class clazz = Class.forName(typeClass);
            location = clazz.newInstance();
        }
    }

    …

    public Broadcast getBroadcast() {
        return (Broadcast)location;
    }

    public void setBroadcast( Broadcast location ) {
        this.location = location;
    }

    public Address getAddress() {
        return (Address)location;
    }

    public void setAddress( Address location ) {
        this.location = location;
    }

    public String execute() throws Exception {

        if( typeClass==null ) {
            …
        } else {
            String objType =
                typeClass.substring(typeClass.lastIndexOf(".")+1).toLowerCase();
            if( setup!=null ) {
                return objType;
            } else {
```

```
                    VisitorFieldValidator validator = new VisitorFieldValidator();
                    validator.setAppendPrefix(true);
                    validator.setValidatorContext(new DelegatingValidatorContext(this));
                    validator.setFieldName(objType);
                    validator.validate(this);

                    if( hasFieldErrors() ) {
                        return objType;
                    }
                }

            service.create((Location)location);
            return SUCCESS;
            }
        }
}
```

With the successful completion of the action, the selectLocation action is invoked. This action is configured via an @Result annotation and provides an additional parameter params={"method","input"} that has not been seen before. Every result can include additional parameters, in this case, providing the method of the action class to invoke the action's logic.

Implementing flash Scope

In the previous section, we skipped over one piece of the configuration, that is, when the EnterLocationDetailsAction action returns a selectType result indicating that the user didn't select a location type and needs to be redirected back to make a selection. Because of the decision to split the SelectLocationTypeAction action from the EnterLocationDetailsAction action, the dispatcher or redirect result types cause problems. For the dispatcher result type, the list of location types isn't available, and for the redirect result type, the error messages aren't available. This is the same problem that comes up in the post-redirect pattern and is solved using flash scope.

Flash scope provides access to the context of the previously invoked action, as well as the current action, when the result type is a redirect. This is important because when the user refreshes the browser rather than clicking a link or button on the page, the context of the previous action is lost and the current page refreshed. In the case of a post-redirect, it is exactly what is required. The post is not submitted twice, and any messages from saving data are removed.

Struts2 does not have an implementation of flash scope, but WebWork (the predecessor of Struts2) does. Porting the FlashInterceptor and FlashResult from WebWork to Struts2 is trivial, and the results are included in this chapter's source code in the Source Code/Download area of the Apress web site (http://www.apress.com). The interceptor can be used alone (to store and retrieve the action to flash scope), or the interceptor can be used in combination with the result type. For implementing the workflow requirements, the interceptor and result type are used in combination.

In either configuration—the action returning the `flash` result type or configured with the `flash` interceptor—the action executed is placed in the Value Stack ahead of the action invoked during the redirect. Because of this, you should only use the `flash` scope when needed.

Before using the interceptor, it must be configured. This can be done in the packages that require it, or in a default project package. Either way, the configuration requires only a unique interceptor name and the class name of the interceptor.

```
<interceptors>
    <interceptor name="flash"
        class="com.opensymphony.webwork.interceptor.FlashInterceptor" />
    <interceptor-stack name="eventStack">
        ...
    </interceptor-stack>
</interceptors>
```

> **Caution** When using the result type in an annotation, no further configuration is required. However, if you were to use XML configuration, the additional step of configuring the result type would be needed.

Using the flash result is the same as using any other result. Provide the class name as the `type` attribute value, and the URL to redirect to as the `value` attributes value. There is only one flash result type, so a URL needs to be provided and not an action name. In the following `EnterLocationDetailsAction` action, the "selectType" returns a flash result type.

```
@Results( value={
    @Result(type=ServletActionRedirectResult.class, value="selectLocation",
            params={"method","input"}),
    @Result(type=FlashResult.class, name="selectType",
            value="/event/flashedSelectEventType.action")
})
public class EnterLocationDetailsAction
        extends BaseEventAction implements Preparable {
    ...
}
```

The next step is the configuration of the action being invoked. This action is configured in the `struts.xml` configuration file so that the `flash` interceptor can be applied. By providing a different action name, the `flash` interceptor is only applied when needed and not to all the `selectEventType.action` requests.

> **Caution** The name of an action configured in XML cannot be the same as an action that is configured via convention (that is, guessed from class name). This would be convenient in this case, but unfortunately, the configuration via convention always wins, and hence the XML configured version is never invoked.

The interceptor uses the parameter `operation`, which takes the value `Retrieve`. If the interceptor (rather than the result type) was being used to store the current action into `flash` scope after execution, the value `Store` would be used instead. There is also a key parameter, which is used to change the name under which the `flash` scope action is stored in the session. This parameter is not used unless a conflict is noticed. The configuration, which is similar to the annotation version for the `flashedSelectEventType.action`, then becomes the following:

```
<action name="flashedSelectEventType"
        class="com.fdar.apress.s2.actions.event.SelectLocationTypeAction">
    <interceptor-ref name="flash">
        <param name="operation">Retrieve</param>
    </interceptor-ref>
    <interceptor-ref name="eventStack" />
    <result>/WEB-INF/jsp/event/selectLocationType-input.jsp</result>
</action>
```

This style of operation is not restricted to use in workflow situations and can be useful in many different scenarios.

■**Note** Like many open source project features, the reason for WebWork providing the `flash` scope functionality and not Struts2 is simple. The `flash` scope result type and interceptor were part of a branch to WebWork called *Able*, which Patrick Lightbody created. At some point, a committer on WebWork thought that it was useful enough to commit into the main code base, but as of yet, no one has committed it into the Struts2 code base.

Action Validation Using OGNL

A useful validator that has not been mentioned is the `ExpressionValidator`, which allows you to provide an OGNL expression to determine if validation should succeed. The expression can take advantage of the current action's properties, as well as any objects or properties available via the Value Stack.

Within the workflow, this validator has been taken advantage of in two places: the `RemoveContestantsAction` (where the user must select at least one contestant to remove) and the `SaveEventAction` (where there must be more than one contestant added to complete the event).

The validator is similar to all other validators, with the OGNL expression being provided via the `expression` attribute. Although the `ExpressionValidator` can be applied at the field level, it is more commonly found at the action level. Here is the configuration for the `RemoveContestantsAction` class:

```
@Validation
public class RemoveContestantsAction extends BaseEventAction {

    private List<String> selectedContestants;

    …

    @Validations( expressions = {
        @ExpressionValidator(message="Default message",
            key="validate.mustSelectOne",
            expression="selectedContestants!=null && selectedContestants.size>0" )
    })
    public String execute() throws Exception {
        …
    }
}
```

The validation for the SaveEventAction class is very similar; the difference is that two or more contestants must have been added to the event. Because the Event object is placed in the Value Stack ahead of the action, the OGNL expression needs to be options.size rather than model.options.size (options is the property containing the list of contestants on the event).

```
@Validations( expressions={
    @ExpressionValidator(message="Default message",
        key="validate.moreThanTwoOptions",
        expression="options!=null && options.size>1" )
})
public String execute() throws Exception {
    …
}
```

An Alternative Approach to Entering Contestants

In the design of the Create Event workflow (refer to Figure 6-2), working with contestants happens with three distinct actions: listing the current contestants, adding a new contestant, and removing existing contestants.

The first screen the user sees, shown in Figure 6-6, is the one listing the current contestants for the event (an empty list if none have been entered). This screen also provides a link to add a new contestant and a check box and submit button to remove existing contestants.

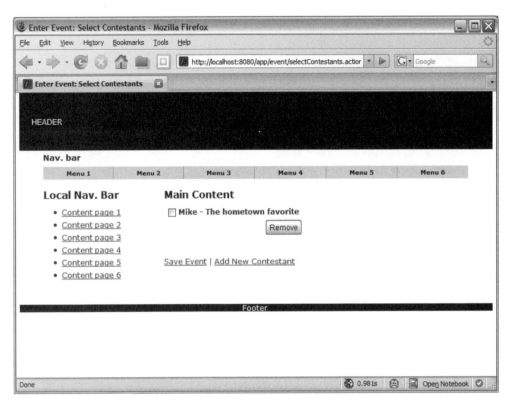

Figure 6-6. *The central page in the workflow for listing contestants, adding new contestants, and removing existing contestants*

When adding a new contestant, a different screen is used as shown in Figure 6-7.

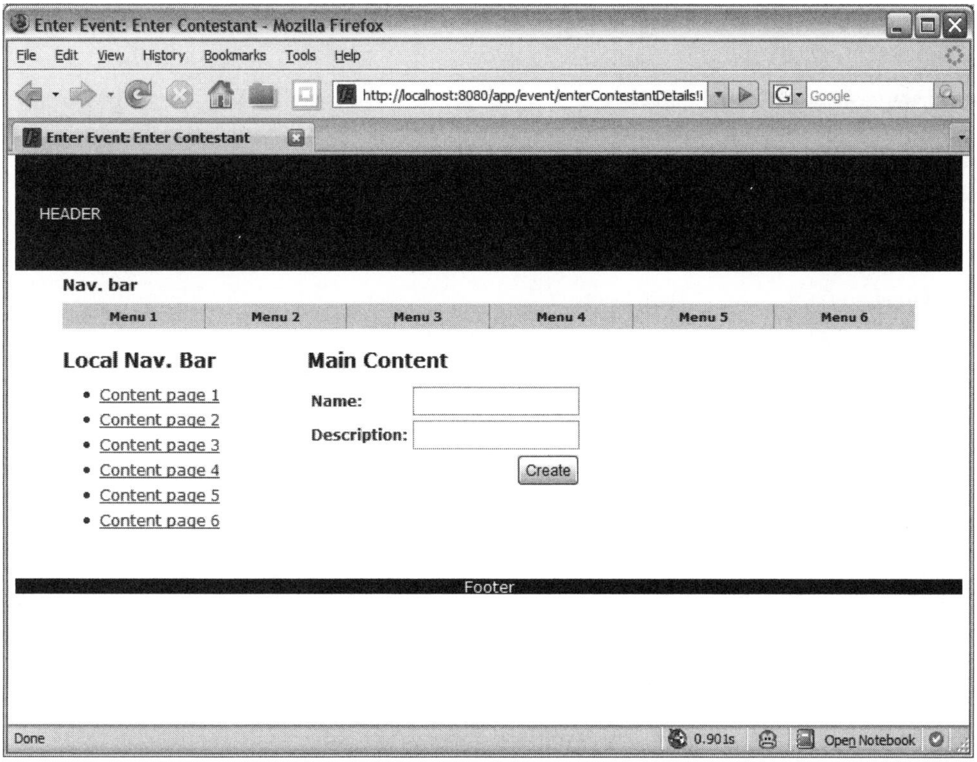

Figure 6-7. *Entering a new contestant for an event*

To remove an existing contestant, the user selects the check box associated with the contestant (from the contestant list screen) and then clicks the Remove button. There is no screen for this action; instead, the list contestants screen is redisplayed (with the removed contestant no longer present).

This is a common workflow pattern for working with a list of dependent objects; however, when only a few data elements are being added (the name and description as opposed to 20 fields of data), this pattern can be frustrating to the user.

A much better approach is to allow the user to enter all the data from the same screen (see Figure 6-8). This allows the data to be entered much faster by eliminating the wait for browser-server communication and page rendering, and there is no longer a need for the remove functionality. The changes to implement this style of data entry are very easy and involve only the selectContestants-input.jsp template and the SaveEventAction class.

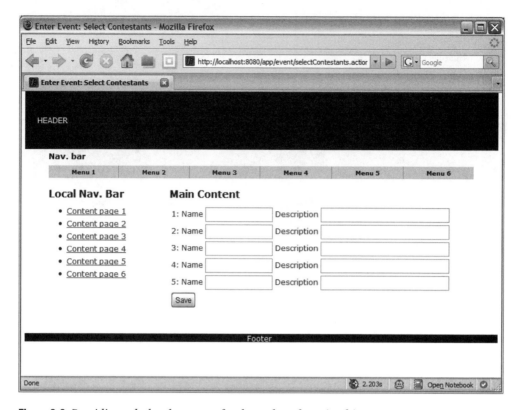

Figure 6-8. *Providing tabular data entry for dependent domain objects*

We will review both these files, starting with the `selectContestants-input.jsp` template:

```
<html xmlns="http://www.w3.org/1999/xhtml" xml:lang="en" lang="en">

<head>
    <title><s:text name="createEvent.selectContestants.title" /></title>
</head>
<body>

<s:actionerror />

<s:form action="saveEvent" namespace="/event" method="post" theme="simple">

    <table>
        <s:iterator value="{0,1,2,3,4}" status="stat">

            <tr>
                <td>

                    <s:property value="#stat.index+1" />:
```

```
                <s:text name="contestant.name" />
                <s:textfield key="contestant.name"
                    name="options[%{#stat.index}].name" size="15"/>

                <s:text name="contestant.description" />
                <s:textfield key="contestant.description"
                    name="options[%{#stat.index}].description" size="35"/>
            </td>
        </tr>
    </s:iterator>

    <tr><td><s:submit key="button.save" /></td></tr>
    </table>

</s:form>

</body>
</html>
```

The first change is that the list of elements in the template is generated using an `iterator` tag with a value of `"{0,1,2,3,4}"`. Because the contestants do not initially exist on the `Event` object, this OGNL value provides a list with five elements (each being an integer value from 0 to 4) so that form elements are created for five contestants.

To distinguish each contestant's form elements, each is placed in a new row of a table. At the start of the row, the ordinal of the contestant is rendered:

```
<s:property value="#stat.index+1" />
```

The ordinal is different from the index, as it starts at one rather than zero. Using the special status `iterator` object (assigned to the `stat` property in the `iterator` tag), the current index in the iterator can be accessed and its value incremented by one.

■**Note** The `iterator` status object has many more useful properties, and the full list can be found in the JavaDocs at `http://struts.apache.org/2.x/struts2-core/apidocs/org/apache/struts2/views/jsp/IteratorStatus.html`.

Next are the `textfield` tags for the contestant's name and description. By using a special format for the `name` attribute, the data entered by the user for the contestant automatically triggers the following events in the Struts2 framework:

- A new `Contestant` object is created if one does not already exist for the current index.

- The user-entered form field data values are set on the `Contestant` object.

- The `Contestant` object is added to the list managed by the action or, in this case, the model object.

The format is the path to the list, followed by the index of the object in square brackets, followed by the property of the dependent object. For regular HTML tags, the following code allows the user to enter two contestants' data, which is saved in the options property of the domain object—exactly what is required.

```
<input type="text" name="options[0].name" />
<input type="text" name="options[0].description" />

<input type="text" name="options[1].name" />
<input type="text" name="options[1].description" />
```

Because a Struts2 iterator tag is being used, the name attribute is adjusted slightly to be generated from the current index. Here is the form field for the contestant's name:

```
<s:textfield key="contestant.name" name="options[%{#stat.index}].name" />
```

The index value (inside the square brackets) needs to be %{#stat.index} rather than just #stat.index so that the index value is calculated, instead of the string literal being used. This is the trickiest part of the expression and is easy to forget.

■**Note** All this magic is, in fact, simple type conversion. Because generics are used to specify the type of object contained in the list, Struts2 can automatically perform all the steps to populate the new elements within the list. Similar functionality is available for Maps, as well as property file configuration for when generics are not used. For more information on the use and configuration of type converters, check out the Struts2 documentation at http://struts.apache.org/2.x/docs/type-conversion.html.

EDITING DEPENDENT OBJECTS

Retrieving values from a list and presenting them for editing is just as simple and requires only two modifications. The first is that the OGNL path to the list of objects is used (in this case, the value options as the property for the contestants on the Event object) instead of an OGNL-generated list as the value of the iterator. The other change is the id property of the contestant is added as a hidden form field, so that the contestant is updated and not created. Following are the changes to the selectContestants-input.jsp template:

```
<s:iterator value="options" status="stat">

    <tr>
        <td>
            <s:hidden name="options[%{#stat.index}].id" />

            <s:property value="#stat.index+1" />:
```

```
                <s:text name="contestant.name" />
                <s:textfield key="contestant.name"
                    name="options[%{#stat.index}].name" size="15"/>

                <s:text name="contestant.description" />
                <s:textfield key="contestant.description"
                    name="options[%{#stat.index}].description" size="35"/>
            </td>
        </tr>
    </s:iterator>
```

To complete the example, the SaveEventAction class needs to be modified for two reasons. The first is to remove contestants that have no information entered for them (this could have been avoiding using JavaScript to insert new rows to the table as required); the second is that the contestant is not associated to the event that it belongs to, and the association needs to be made so the contestant is persisted to the database correctly. The resulting code is

```
public class SaveEventAction extends BaseEventAction {

    …

    public String execute() throws Exception {

        List<Contestant> results = new ArrayList<Contestant>();
        for(Contestant c: event.getOptions() ) {
            if( !"".equals(c.getName()) && !"".equals(c.getDescription()) ) {
                c.setEvent(event);
                results.add(c);
            }
        }

        event.setOptions(results);
        service.create(event);

        return SUCCESS;
    }
}
```

Summary

In this chapter, the scope interceptor was used to store and retrieve action properties in the HTTP session scope; a flash scope implementation was introduced by using an interceptor and result type to allow access to the previously executed action properties after a post-redirect (to keep the user from being able to accidentally double submit a request); expression validators were used for complex intra-property validations; custom validators were created and configured to handle a special time input; and a new UI theme was created and configured with different tag rendering templates to change how the tag looks.

By now you should feel comfortable implementing most user-facing business logic. In the next chapter, the focus turns to the application logic, and you'll learn how to provide security for your web application.

CHAPTER 7

■■■

Security

Security is one of those features that is considered from the very beginning of an application but usually implemented as late as possible in the development cycle. More often than not, a custom security implementation is used without considering the alternatives.

In this chapter, we will discuss the security attributes of authorization and authentication. These are not the only attributes that should be considered in an application, but they are the attributes needed when integrating security into the application. For example, this doesn't mean that a channel security (using HTTPS) requirement isn't important; it just means that the channel security attribute isn't as closely integrated into the application logic as authorization and authentication.

Lastly, note that Struts2 doesn't provide any special security features. Everything that we will cover in this chapter is a specific implementation of the general concepts of the framework. This means that if you have a different option, there's no reason that it can't be implemented by modifying the approaches being explored.

The Use Cases

The requirements for authorization and authentication in the application are condensed into the following use cases:

Logon User: Users need to authenticate before they are allowed to access restricted features of the application. The precondition of this use case is that users have completed the Register use case. For authentication, users enter their username (the e-mail address entered during registration) and password; if the values match those stored during the registration process, the users are given access to the restricted functionality.

Logoff User: Along with logging on to the application, users should be able to log off. This signifies that the users no longer want to access the restricted section of the web application.

By today's web application standards, this is a very simple security requirement, which allows the exploration of three different options for authorization and authentication:

- *Container-based authentication*: The application server or the servlet container provides the authentication services. This option frees the developers from concerning themselves with a lot of the security infrastructure and isolates the web application from requiring functionality to administer the users.

- *Using existing libraries (Acegi)*: Existing security libraries can be integrated. This frees the developers from developing the entire infrastructure but allows integration points for more complex configuration and integration.

- *Custom authentication/authorization*: The last option is to develop the entire infrastructure. Although developing everything "in house" is usually frowned upon, this option does allow a level of detail that the other options cannot provide.

Each of these alternatives has its own pros and cons, so you must determine which fits best into your application. In this chapter, you will learn the differences through practical examples.

Container-Based Authentication

In container-based authentication, the J2EE or servlet container that the web application is deployed to handles the authentication for the web application. The main benefit, and drawback, to container-based authentication is that it is specific to the J2EE or servlet container being used to deploy the web application. If the container is advanced and supports many integration options, your job is easy. On the other hand, if you are using a bare-bones container, a lot of work may be involved to provide the expected security. The other concern is *when* the container is going to change, either from the developer's environment to the production environment, or to a new container after the web application has been deployed to production.

Because Jetty is being used as the servlet container in our application, this section covers the specifics of configuring Jetty's authentication. For the most part, the configuration is similar across all containers.

Configuring the Container

This is the container-specific part of the configuration. In the example, we are using the Maven2 plug-in for Jetty, and so we need to add some additional configuration to the pom.xml configuration file:

```
<plugin>
    <groupId>org.mortbay.jetty</groupId>
    <artifactId>maven-jetty-plugin</artifactId>
    <version>6.0.1</version>
    <configuration>
        <scanIntervalSeconds>10</scanIntervalSeconds>
        <webAppSourceDirectory>${basedir}/src/main/webapp</webAppSourceDirectory>
        <webXml>${basedir}/src/main/webapp/WEB-INF/web.xml</webXml>
        <classesDirectory>${basedir}/target/classes</classesDirectory>
```

```
    <userRealms>
        <userRealm implementation="org.mortbay.jetty.security.HashUserRealm">
            <name>ApressRealm</name>
            <config>etc/realm.properties</config>
        </userRealm>
    </userRealms>
    </configuration>
</plugin>
```

The new section is the userRealms tag, and is described in the following list:

- userRealm: The implementation attribute specifies the class that provides the authentication mechanism; in this case, it is a simple in-memory hash (using the HashUserRealm class), but Jetty also provides a JAAS (Java Authentication and Authorization Service) implementation (using the JAASUserRealm class) and a JDBC (using the JDBCUserRealm class) implementation.

- name: The unique name of the security realm that is being configured; the name selected must exactly match the name configured in the web.xml configuration file (shown in the next section).

- config: The name and location of the property file that contains authentication information for the users; this is specific to the HashUserRealm class, and other implementations require different information.

■**Note** The configuration shown is used with Maven2. When another build system is used, XML configuration files provide the same information. More information about configuring security realms in Jetty can be found at http://docs.codehaus.org/display/JETTY/Realms.

As the simple hash implementation for user management was selected, the next step is to create the property file that contains the list of users for the application. From the config tag, you know that the file is called etc/realm.properties. The structure of the file is also simple, although different from the expected Java properties file format; it consists of a single line for each user, consisting of the username, colon, and password followed by a comma-delimited list of role names (that are completely optional).

```
Username: password [,rolename]
```

The test file for container-managed authentication contains two users, one with a role of user and the other with a role of registered:

```
user1:welcome,user
user2:welcome,registered
```

Configuring the Web Application

After the container is configured, the next step is to configure the web application. This involves the web.xml configuration file and is not specific to Struts2 web applications. In fact, the configuration in this section is defined as part of the servlet security specification and is the same when configuring any web application.

There are two parts to configuring the web.xml file. First is the security-constraint tag, which defines the URL resources to be protected. The requirements state that a user must be logged in to enter an event, and because the event workflow uses the enterEvent package, the configuration needs to protect all actions in the /event namespace. Because this namespace maps to the /event URL path (or http://localhost:8080/app/event), we can use the value /event/*. This value is assigned via the url-pattern tag within the web-resource-collection tag. The web-resource-name tag provides a user-friendly way to identify the collection of URLs.

■**Caution** Configuring URLs with the wildcard * character includes not only those resources in the current URL path but also all subpaths and resources contained within the subpaths. So if there was an /event/admin path, all those actions would also be protected.

Along with the URLs being protected are the roles that are allowed to access them. The roles are configured via the role-name tag in the auth-constraint tag. Multiple values are allowed, but as our requirements are simple, there is only one role configured in the example. Role names configured here must match those provided in the etc/realm.properties file.

```
<security-constraint>
    <web-resource-collection>
        <web-resource-name>Secure Pages</web-resource-name>
        <url-pattern>/event/*</url-pattern>
    </web-resource-collection>
    <auth-constraint>
        <role-name>registered</role-name>
    </auth-constraint>
</security-constraint>
```

After the resources are configured, the authentication mechanism is configured using the login-config tag. Many authentication options are available, including BASIC, FORM, DIGEST, and CLIENT-CERT. For the user to enter login information in a JSP and to provide feedback on any problems, the FORM option has been selected and is specified in the auth-method tag. Different authentication mechanisms can be used for different realms, so next we need to configure the realm as the value for the realm-name tag. The value ApressRealm is taken directly from the Jetty configuration in the previous section.

■**Caution** The realm names must match; otherwise, resources you expect to be protected won't be, and other resources will be protected that shouldn't be.

Along with FORM authentication, URLs for the login page (using the form-login-page tag) and the error page (using the form-error-page tag) are configured. Both these values are set to /logon.action. In the case of a login failure, the auth request parameter is added to the URL, which allows an error message to be presented to the user.

```
<login-config>
    <auth-method>FORM</auth-method>
    <realm-name>ApressRealm</realm-name>
    <form-login-config>
        <form-login-page>/logon.action</form-login-page>
        <form-error-page>/logon.action?auth=false</form-error-page>
    </form-login-config>
</login-config>
```

■**Tip** If you are not using internationalization, a JSP could be specified instead of an action. For internationalization to work correctly in Struts2, the resources need to be loaded, which occurs during an actions request/response processing.

The logon action is a pass-through action leading directly to a JSP, so the struts.xml configuration is straightforward and uses the BaseAction action class already developed:

```
<package name="home-package" extends="struts-default" namespace="/">

    ...

    <action name="logon" class="com.fdar.apress.s2.actions.BaseAction" >
        <result name="success">/logon.jsp?auth=${auth}</result>
    </action>

</package>
```

■**Tip** Using an action configured in this manner provides the same functionality as an ActionForward in Struts1. In fact, if internationalization (or a different option for the properties file) was being used instead of the com.fdar.apress.s2.actions.BaseAction class, the com.opensymphony.xwork2.ActionSupport class (which comes with Struts2) could have been used.

The use of auth=${auth} in the result is new. Similarly to actions and JSPs, the result configuration has access to the Value Stack. By including OGNL expressions, dynamic values can be used in the result configuration. The difference is that instead of using %{ and }, the delimiting characters are ${ and }. So by providing the expression auth=${auth} in the result configuration, the request parameter value for auth passed to the logon.action is forwarded onto the logon.jsp template. From the previously configured form-error-page tag's URL, a value of false is passed when the authentication fails; otherwise, it is an empty value.

This brings us to the logon.jsp page, which is not exactly configuration but is used to integrate authentication into the web application. The JSP is broken into two logical parts: the top part providing a message if authentication has failed; and the bottom part allowing the user to enter authentication information and to submit the request.

Because the error feedback from the container-managed authentication is sparse, that is, *it failed*, the message displayed to the user also needs to be generic. In both the web.xml and struts.xml configuration files, an auth request parameter is being passed along. Using a Struts2 if tag, the value for the auth request parameter can be evaluated to see whether a value is present. This is achieved using the expression !''.equals(#parameters.auth). If the expression returns a true result (there is a value for the auth request parameter), a message is displayed to the user.

```
<head>
    <title><s:text name="home.logon" /></title>
</head>
<body>

<s:if test="!''.equals(#parameters.auth)">
    <s:text name="auth.failed" /><br/><br/>
</s:if>

<form action="<%=request.getContextPath()%>/j_security_check" method="POST" >
  <s:text name="logon.username"/> <input type="text" name="j_username" /> <br/>
  <s:text name="logon.password"/> <input type="password" name="j_password" /> <br/>
  <input type="submit" value="<s:text name="button.logon" />" />
</form>

</body>
</html>
```

The form that allows the user to enter authentication information is always present. For FORM-based, container-managed authentication to work, the following requirements must be satisfied:

- The form must be submitted to the URL /j_security_check in the current web application context.

- The name of the username form field must be j_username.

- The name of the password form field must be j_password.

For these requirements, using Struts2 form tags doesn't make much sense because the Struts2 tags, especially the form tags, provide help to construct URLs and manage interactions and data between the user interface and the action. In this case, the interaction is between the user interface and the servlet/J2EE container with no data being passed or retrieved from actions. So it's simpler not to use the Struts2 form and form field tags; instead, the JSP uses pure HTML syntax for the form and form fields, along with Struts2 tags to provide internationalized text for the form field labels and the label for the submit button.

To provide the web application's context in the form's `action` attribute, the scriptlet `<%=request.getContextPath()%>` is used. For simple properties like the context path or constant values, this is an acceptable method that can avoid introducing the `ServletRequestAware` interface; however, in general, scriptlets promote poor programming habits such as reducing modularization and increasing the cost of making changes.

This completes the configuration necessary to protect a web application using container-based authentication. If a user is unknown or logs on with incorrect information, the container returns the user to the logon page, with a friendly message asking the user to "try again." If the user authenticates correctly, the user is granted access to the requested resource.

Accessing Role Information

Protecting URL resources is a good start, and for a simple application like the one we are building, a simple protected or unprotected switch is enough. When the application becomes more complex with multiple roles, then both the actions and the JSPs need to access the current user's role to determine whether logic should be executed and to determine which sections of the JSP should be rendered.

Because container-based authentication uses the servlet specification, all the methods that expose authenticated user and role information are available via the `HttpServletRequest` class, and this object is available to actions when they implement the `ServletRequestAware` interface. From the Struts2 framework standpoint, the `HttpServletRequest` object now has multiple responsibilities: request and response responsibilities and user authentication responsibilities. For this reason, Struts2 has separated the user authentication responsibilities into the `PrincipalProxy` class, which is preferred when working with the authenticated user and contains only authenticated user information.

The `PrincipalProxy` interface provides the following information:

```
public interface PrincipalProxy {

    boolean isUserInRole(java.lang.String string);

    java.security.Principal getUserPrincipal();

    java.lang.String getRemoteUser();

    boolean isRequestSecure();

}
```

Just as the `HttpServletRequest` class has the `ServletRequestAware` interface, the `PrincipalProxy` class has the `PrincipalAware` interface:

```
public interface PrincipalAware {

    void setPrincipalProxy( PrincipalProxy principalProxy );
}
```

When an action implements the `PrincipalAware` interface, and the `servletConfig` interceptor is applied to the action, the user authentication information is retrieved from the

HttpServletRequest (where the container has placed it) and assigned to the action using the PrincipalAware interface. By implementing the interface in a base class, the user information becomes available to all actions that extend the base class.

```
public class BaseAction extends ActionSupport implements PrincipalAware {

    protected PrincipalProxy principal;

    public void setPrincipalProxy(PrincipalProxy principalProxy) {
        this.principal = principalProxy;
    }

    public PrincipalProxy getPrincipal() {
        return principal;
    }
}
```

Along with the setter, a matching getter is implemented, which allows JSP code to access the user information. An example is displaying the current user and testing whether a user is in a specific role:

```
<s:property value="principal.remoteUser" /> <br/>
<s:if test="principal.isUserInRole('registered')" />
    …
</s:if>
```

In fact, on the home page, there are links that should be displayed only to users that have been authenticated (Update Profile) and links that are displayed to users that are not authenticated (Logon and Register). The index.jsp template now becomes more complicated:

```
<s:if test="principal.remoteUser==null">

    <s:url id="register" action="findUser" namespace="/user" />
    <s:a href="%{register}"><s:text name="link.register" /></s:a>

    <s:url id="logon" action="logon" namespace="/" />
    | <s:a href="%{logon}"><s:text name="link.logon" /></s:a>

</s:if>
<s:else>
    <s:text name="text.remoteUser" />
        <s:property value="principal.remoteUser" /> <br/><br/>

    <s:url id="update" action="findUser" namespace="/user" >
        <s:param name="emailId" value="principal.remoteUser" />
    </s:url>
    <s:a href="%{update}"><s:text name="link.updateProfile" /></s:a>
</s:else>
```

```
<s:if test="principal.isUserInRole('registered')">
    <s:url id="newEvent" action="addEventFlow" namespace="/event" />
    | <s:a href="%{newEvent}"><s:text name="link.addEvent" /></s:a>
</s:if>
```

The Roles Interceptor

At the beginning of this section, the configuration to restrict a URL to be accessed by a particular role was configured with the security-constraint tag in the web.xml configuration file.
Another option that provides the same functionality is the roles interceptor.

The functionality between web.xml-based configuration and role interceptor-based configuration is exactly the same: to provide role-based access to a URL. The difference is how the
configuration is achieved. Using web.xml configuration, any URL can be constrained to be
accessed only by the specified roles. When using the roles interceptor, the URL can be configured to be accessed only by the specified roles (as in the web.xml configuration case) or to
allow all roles except those specified to access the URL. Depending on the number of roles in
the application, this may require much less configuration.

Another benefit of using the roles interceptor is that the configuration information is
closer to the application, in the struts.xml configuration file. Being closer to the action configuration allows developers to easily determine which role a user requires to access the
package or action.

The interceptor has two parameters: allowedRoles for those roles that are allowed access
to the resource; and disallowedRoles for those roles that are not allowed access. Each parameter value can provide a single value or a comma-delimited list of values.

```
<interceptors>
    <interceptor-stack name="secure">
        <interceptor-ref name="roles">
            <param name="allowedRoles">registered</param>
        </interceptor-ref>
        <interceptor-ref name="paramsPrepareParamsStack"/>
    </interceptor-stack>
</interceptors>
```

■Tip It's best to use this configuration when packages have the same role requirement, so you can configure the interceptor and assign it as the default for the package.

Implementing Acegi

The next authentication option is applicable when an existing security library is used. The
library that has been chosen is Acegi. *Acegi* is a fully featured and popular security framework
that was originally created for the Spring community. Although it does rely heavily on the
Spring Framework, it can be used in other contexts. This section discusses how to integrate
Acegi with Struts2.

Similarly to the previous section on container authentication, the scope of security being discussed will be limited to authentication and authorization at the URL and web application (action and JSP) level only. Acegi does have many advanced features that you can research and include in your web applications, including channel security and domain object access control.

■**Note** To find out more about the Acegi project, including the advanced features and configurations that are different from those used here, visit the Acegi documentation at `http://www.acegisecurity.org`.

Configuring Acegi

Before we can configure Acegi, we need to integrate it into the project by adding a new dependency to the Maven `pom.xml` configuration file:

```
<dependency>
    <groupId>org.acegisecurity</groupId>
    <artifactId>acegi-security</artifactId>
    <version>1.0.4</version>
</dependency>
```

When the project is next built, Maven will download the Acegi libraries, along with all the libraries that Acegi is dependent upon. Because Acegi relies heavily on the Spring Framework, many of these files will be Spring Framework libraries.

■**Note** Acegi uses a lot of the Spring Framework libraries in its implementation. If your application does not also use the Spring Framework, and you want to limit the dependencies being introduced into your project, you may want to reconsider using Acegi. In this case, your options are to seek out an alternative library or to implement your own authentication as shown in the next section.

Next we need to configure the Acegi servlet filter. Using a filter allows Acegi to intercept URL requests to a web application and provide custom security processing. In fact, as seen in the following filter configuration, the filter implementation class `FilterToBeanProxy` is actually a proxy to a second class (the `FilterChainProxy` class) that is defined in the Spring Framework configuration.

```
<filter>
    <filter-name>Acegi Filter Chain Proxy</filter-name>
    <filter-class>org.acegisecurity.util.FilterToBeanProxy</filter-class>
    <init-param>
        <param-name>targetClass</param-name>
        <param-value>org.acegisecurity.util.FilterChainProxy</param-value>
    </init-param>
</filter>
```

Along with the filter configuration is the filter mapping. Note that the `filter-name` tag value matches the filter configuration's `filter-name` tag exactly, and the `url-pattern` tag's value of /* ensures that all requests to the web application are processed by the Acegi filter. Providing the most general mapping possible here allows more specific filtering to be performed at a later stage in the configuration (in the `applicationContext-acegi-security.xml` configuration file).

```
<filter-mapping>
    <filter-name>Acegi Filter Chain Proxy</filter-name>
    <url-pattern>/*</url-pattern>
</filter-mapping>
```

■**Caution** Remember, the order that the filter mappings are defined in the `web.xml` configuration file is the order in which they are processed. Because security is one of the more important concerns, it should be one of the first and should definitely be before the Struts2 dispatch filter. If the security filter is not before the Struts2 filter, any user with any role can invoke the Struts2 actions.

The Acegi Application Context Configuration File

In the web application, there is already a Spring Framework `applicationContext.xml` configuration file. When integrating Acegi, you have the option of adding the security configuration to the existing `applicationContext.xml` configuration file or creating a new configuration file specific to security. To keep the security configuration separate from the domain object configuration, we chose the second option, with the configuration file name being `applicationContext-acegi-security.xml`.

The addition of a second configuration file has already been taken into account in the `web.xml` configuration. Rather than specifying the complete file name for each and every configuration file, we used the wildcard `classpath*:applicationContext*.xml`. Therefore, any configuration file name starting with `applicationContext` on the classpath is automatically loaded.

```
<context-param>
    <param-name>contextConfigLocation</param-name>
    <param-value>classpath*:applicationContext*.xml</param-value>
</context-param>
```

Because we are interested in the integration of Acegi and Struts2 and not a detailed discussion of Acegi, the `applicationContext-acegi-security.xml` configuration file from the Acegi example WAR has been used as a starting point.

■**Note** If you are already familiar with Acegi, you may have noticed that several elements have been removed, including functionality for switching users, channel security, and user caching. All of these features are compatible with Struts2 and were only removed to simplify the configuration and make clearer the elements of interest for the integration configuration.

The first bean of interest is the FilterChainProxy configuration because it is called from the Acegi filter defined in the web.xml configuration file. Being a filter, the value of the value tag is a list of processing instructions. Some of these instructions, such as PATTERN_TYPE_APACHE_ANT, are built-in processing macros or instructions on how to process the remainder of the list's instructions. Others are specific rules on how to process specific URLs.

```
<bean id="filterChainProxy" class="org.acegisecurity.util.FilterChainProxy">
    <property name="filterInvocationDefinitionSource">
        <value>
            CONVERT_URL_TO_LOWERCASE_BEFORE_COMPARISON
            PATTERN_TYPE_APACHE_ANT
            /event/**=httpSessionContextIntegrationFilter,logoutFilter,
                authenticationProcessingFilter,basicProcessingFilter,
                securityContextHolderAwareRequestFilter,anonymousProcessingFilter,
                exceptionTranslationFilter,filterInvocationInterceptor
        </value>
    </property>
</bean>
```

The last instruction is the most important. This instructs Acegi on how to handle the URL /event/**. As ANT patterns are matched, this processing instruction matches all resources under the /event URL. At this stage, it is not important to understand everything that is happening for the URL processing but rather the following:

- Many steps are involved in processing a configured URL.

- The order that the steps are configured is important.

- Each of the steps refers to another bean configured in the Spring Framework configuration files.

- Each step can be configured further in its own configuration.

The step that warrants further investigation is the very last one: the filterInvocationInterceptor configuration. Where the filterChainProxy bean configured the steps in processing a URL, the filterInvocationInterceptor configuration defines the roles that are allowed access to a particular URL.

```
<bean id="filterInvocationInterceptor"
        class="org.acegisecurity.intercept.web.FilterSecurityInterceptor">
    <property name="authenticationManager">
        <ref bean="authenticationManager"/>
    </property>
    <property name="accessDecisionManager">
        <ref local="httpRequestAccessDecisionManager"/>
    </property>
```

```
<property name="objectDefinitionSource">
    <value>
        CONVERT_URL_TO_LOWERCASE_BEFORE_COMPARISON
        PATTERN_TYPE_APACHE_ANT
        /event/**=ROLE_USER
        /**=ROLE_ANONYMOUS,ROLE_USER
    </value>
</property>
</bean>
```

The application has the simple requirement that a user is either authenticated or not authenticated, which maps nicely to the Acegi default roles of ROLE_ANONYMOUS and ROLE_USER. Each URL pattern, as well as a specific action, is configured here with the roles that are allowed access. As expected, the /event URL can only be accessed by users that have been authenticated.

■**Caution** Always remember to place the more specific URL patterns before the generic URL patterns.

Remember to always leave the pattern /** accessible to everyone. Just like in container-managed authentication, Acegi has special URLs that are used for logging in, logging off, and switching user roles. They are accessed from this reference location.

■**Tip** We are only touching the surface of role configuration in Acegi; many more configuration options are available, and more information on this type of configuration can be found in the Acegi documentation.

Implementing a Custom Authentication Provider

The other important bean configuration is the daoAuthenticationProvider bean. This configuration is referenced by the authenticationManager bean, which in turn is accessed by the basicProcessingFilter bean in the URL processing configuration.

To provide an application-specific service to return user objects that Acegi will use, modify the daoAuthenticationProvider configuration to reference a different userDetailsService bean. By default, InMemoryDaoImpl and JdbcDaoImpl (which enforces a default database structure) are available; each provides restrictions that may or may not be acceptable in your application.

Because there is already a UserService service in the application that provides access to User objects, the daoAuthenticationProvider bean can be configured to take advantage of this service. The existing userService configuration is

```
<bean id="userService" class="com.fdar.apress.s2.services.UserServiceImpl" />
```

Updating the configuration is simple. Create a bean reference to the userService bean that is already defined:

```
<bean id="daoAuthenticationProvider"
      class="org.acegisecurity.providers.dao.DaoAuthenticationProvider">
    <property name="userDetailsService"><ref bean="userService"/></property>
</bean>
```

■**Note** If needed, a password-encoding mechanism is available that uses an MD5 hash. For simplicity, this step has been omitted from the example.

This completes the configuration. The next step is to make changes to the service, which involves implementing the UserDetailsService interface provided by Acegi:

```
public class UserServiceImpl implements UserService, UserDetailsService {

    …

    public UserDetails loadUserByUsername(String s)
            throws UsernameNotFoundException, DataAccessException {
        User u = findByEmail(s);
        if( s==null || "".equals(s.trim()) || u==null ) {
            throw new UsernameNotFoundException(s);
        }
        return new PermissionedUser(u);
    }
}
```

The interface adds one method, loadUserByUsername(). Because the e-mail address is being used as the username, the findByEmail() method in the same service is used to find the correct User object. When no username is passed to the method, or a user matching the supplied username is not found, the method must throw a UsernameNotFoundException. The exception signifies that there is a problem and that the user should not be allowed to progress any further.

If a User object is found, the method returns a PermissionedUser. The PermissionedUser object is a wrapper around the User object that provides authentication and authorization information and must implement the UserDetails Acegi interface.

```
public class PermissionedUser implements UserDetails {

    private User user;

    public PermissionedUser( User user ) {
        this.user = user;
    }
```

```java
public User getUser() {
    return user;
}

public String getPassword() {
    return user==null ? "" : user.getPassword();
}

public GrantedAuthority[] getAuthorities() {
    return new GrantedAuthority[] { new GrantedAuthorityImpl("ROLE_USER") };
}

public String getUsername() {
    return user==null ? "" : user.getEmail();
}

public boolean isAccountNonExpired() {
    return true;
}

public boolean isAccountNonLocked() {
    return true;
}

public boolean isCredentialsNonExpired() {
    return true;
}

public boolean isEnabled() {
    return true;
}

}
```

The only tricky method in this class is getAuthorities(). This method returns the authorities, which in this case are roles, that the user has been granted. Because we are only using the ROLE_ANONYMOUS and ROLE_USER roles, any user that has registered is automatically assigned the ROLE_USER role.

Authenticating the User

With Acegi configured, the last step is to allow users to authenticate themselves. This is performed using a logon JSP called acegilogon.jsp, which users are directed to for the initial logon as well as when an incorrect username or password is entered. The configuration of this URL is specified in the authenticationProcessingFilterEntryPoint and the authenticationProcessingFilter bean configurations.

Just like in the container-managed authentication, when an error occurs, a request parameter is added to the URL (in this case, login_error=1) so that a message can be displayed. The struts.xml configuration file also needs to have a mapping from the action to the JSP that is rendered:

```
<action name="acegilogin" class="com.fdar.apress.s2.actions.BaseAction" >
    <result name="success">/acegilogin.jsp?login_error=${login_error}</result>
</action>
```

The resulting JSP also looks very similar to the container-managed version:

```
<html>

<head>
    <title><s:text name="home.logon" /></title>
</head>
<body>

<s:if test="#parameters.size()>0">
    <s:text name="text.error.reason" />:
    <s:property value="#session['ACEGI_SECURITY_LAST_EXCEPTION'].message" /><br/>
    <s:text name="text.register"/><br/><br/>
</s:if>

<form action="<%=request.getContextPath()%>/j_acegi_security_check" method="POST" >
    <s:text name="logon.username"/>
        <input type="text" name="j_username" /> <br/>
    <s:text name="logon.password"/>
        <input type="password" name="j_password" /> <br/>
    <input type="submit" value="<s:text name="button.logon" />" />
</form>

</body>
</html>
```

The differences are that the URL for authentication is /j_acegi_security_check rather than /j_security_check and accessing the error message is different. Instead of checking for a particular request parameter, the test checks for the number of request parameters. When there are more than zero request parameters, the authentication message is displayed.

Acegi also provides a message regarding what the specific authentication problems are. This message is retrieved from the HTTP session scope using the key ACEGI_SECURITY_LAST_EXCEPTION. So the Strut2 tag and OGNL expression:

```
<s:property value="#session['ACEGI_SECURITY_LAST_EXCEPTION'].message" />
```

is exactly the same as the JSP scriptlet:

```
<%= ((AuthenticationException) session
    .getAttribute(AbstractProcessingFilter.ACEGI_SECURITY_LAST_EXCEPTION_KEY))
    .getMessage() %>
```

Accessing Role Information

The biggest difference between container-managed authentication and integrating an authentication library is accessing the user's role information. Instead of having the roles available via the HttpServletRequest (and thus the PrincipalProxy object), additional work needs to be done.

■**Tip** The Acegi libraries could be integrated into an interceptor that created a PrincipalProxy and assigned it to actions that implemented the PrincipalAware interface, but this would be additional work and require the exact placement of the new interceptor in existing stacks. A better solution is to work with the library being integrated to find the path of least resistance with the simplest and most feature-full implementation, while still taking advantage of the Struts2 framework features, which is what we've tried to do here.

To access the user's role in an action, an annotation-based approach is used. A marker annotation, @AcegiPrincipal, is placed on setter methods that have one parameter, the PermissionedUser. The annotation class is

```
@Target(ElementType.METHOD)
@Retention(RetentionPolicy.RUNTIME)
public @interface AcegiPrincipal {
}
```

A matching interceptor looks for methods with the marker annotation (using reflection) and, if found, calls the setter using the user from the Acegi security context. Because we are only interested in the user (we only care whether a user is registered, not about any particular role), the principal is retrieved from the Authentication object and assigned to the action without any role information. The object type returned from the getPrincipal() method will be the same object type returned from the loadUserByUsername() method on the UserServiceImpl service shown earlier, in this case, the PermissionedUser class.

```
public class AcegiInterceptor extends AbstractInterceptor {

    public String intercept(ActionInvocation invocation) throws Exception {

        Object action = invocation.getAction();
        Authentication currentUser =
            SecurityContextHolder.getContext().getAuthentication();

        if( currentUser!=null ) {
            for( Method m: action.getClass().getDeclaredMethods() ) {
                if( m.getAnnotation(AcegiPrincipal.class)!=null
                        && currentUser.getPrincipal() instanceof PermissionedUser ) {
```

```
                    m.invoke(action,currentUser.getPrincipal());
                }
            }
        }
        return invocation.invoke();
    }
}
```

Because this is the first interceptor developed, there are a few things to point out:

- Most interceptors extend the `AbstractInterceptor` class and provide an `intercept()` method. If an initialize or destroy method is needed, the `Interceptor` interface can be implemented (be wary though, interceptors are initialized and destroyed once per web application life cycle, not per request like actions).

- The `invocation.invoke()` call invokes the remaining interceptors on the current execution stack until the action is finally invoked. Unless you are short-circuiting the result, this method should always be called.

- The `ActionInvocation` object contains everything the interceptor needs: the action being invoked, the `ActionProxy` (configuration information for the action), and the `ActionContext` (request, session, the Value Stack, and other environmental and context information).

- It's really easy to develop interceptors.

Because the interceptor was easy to develop, with the `ActionInvocation` object containing everything the interceptor needs to access, testing should also be easy. The test case is broken into two parts: the first is the test itself; and the second is a test action that contains the annotation. Here is the complete test case:

```
public class AcegiInterceptorTestCase extends TestCase {

    public void testIntercept() throws Exception {

        AcegiInterceptor interceptor = new AcegiInterceptor();

        TestAction action = new TestAction();
        MockActionInvocation ai = new MockActionInvocation();
        ai.setAction(action);

        SecurityContextImpl sc = new SecurityContextImpl();
        Authentication auth =
            new TestingAuthenticationToken(
                new PermissionedUser(
                    new User()),"password",new GrantedAuthority[] {} );
        sc.setAuthentication( auth );
        SecurityContextHolder.setContext(sc);
```

```
            assertNull(action.getUser());
            interceptor.intercept(ai);
            assertNotNull(action.getUser());
            assertEquals(auth.getPrincipal(),action.getUser());
        }

    class TestAction {

        private PermissionedUser user;

        public PermissionedUser getUser() {
            return user;
        }

        @AcegiPrincipal
        public void setUser(PermissionedUser user) {
            this.user = user;
        }

        public String execute() {
            return Action.SUCCESS;
        }
    }
}
```

■**Note** The test classes being developed use the same libraries as Chapter 5; they are JUnit
(http://www.junit.org) and JMock (http://www.jmock.org).

The basic steps of unit testing are the following:

1. Create the object under test. This is the interceptor.

2. Create the supporting objects. This includes the test action, mock objects, and real
   objects.

3. Execute the method being tested, and assert the results are correct. In this instance, we
   are asserting that no user is on the action before the interceptor is invoked and that a
   user exists for the action after the interceptor is invoked.

From the Struts2 framework side, the MockActionInvocation class is very helpful. It
allows us to set and get objects from an ActionInvocation instance that would normally be
prepopulated and unmodifiable. The same features are available on the Acegi side by using
the TestingAuthenticationToken class.

Configuring a custom interceptor is the same as any other interceptor. A unique name is provided along with the class name, and then the interceptor is available to be referenced by its unique name from within interceptor stacks.

To ensure that all actions that want access to the authenticated user information have access to it, an authenticated stack is created in the home-package (that all other packages extend). Because the interceptor is assigning a user to an action (remember that a servlet filter is doing the authentication checking), order doesn't matter. For simplicity, it has been placed first. Each inheriting package should extend the authenticated stack to have access to the new functionality without needing to duplicate the interceptor stack configuration.

```
<package name="home-package" extends="struts-default" namespace="/">

    <interceptors>
        <interceptor name="acegi"
            class="com.fdar.apress.s2.util.AcegiInterceptor" />
        <interceptor-stack name="authenticated">
            <interceptor-ref name="acegi"/>
            <interceptor-ref name="paramsPrepareParamsStack"/>
        </interceptor-stack>
    </interceptors>

    <default-interceptor-ref name="acegi" />

    ...

</package>
```

Following the lead from our testing action, we see that any action that wants access to the authenticated user needs to have an annotated setter. This modification is made to the BaseAction class, so that all actions that extend it will have access to the authenticated user information.

```
public class BaseAction extends ActionSupport {

    private PermissionedUser user;

    @AcegiPrincipal
    public void setAuthenticatedUser(PermissionedUser user) {
        this.user = user;
    }

    public PermissionedUser getAuthenticatedUser() {
        return user;
    }
}
```

Along with the setter, a getter has been added to the BaseAction class. The getter allows JSPs to access authenticated user information from the action. In the index.jsp template, the user object provides the username to create the correct URL for editing the authenticated user's profile.

```
<s:url id="update" action="findUser" namespace="/user" >
    <s:param name="emailId" value="authenticatedUser.username" />
</s:url>
<s:a href="%{update}"><s:text name="link.updateProfile" /></s:a>
```

Acegi has an additional benefit. It provides JSP tag libraries for accessing current user authority information. Just like the container-managed authentication version, the Acegi index.jsp template needs to show some links to users that are authenticated and show different links to those that are not. The Acegi tag libraries make this easy with the authorize tag, using the ifNotGranted and ifAllGranted attributes to list the role name.

```
<%@ page contentType="text/html; charset=UTF-8" %>
<%@ taglib uri="/struts-tags" prefix="s" %>
<%@ taglib prefix="authz" uri="http://acegisecurity.org/authz" %>

<html>
<head>
    <title><s:text name="home.title" /></title>
</head>
<body>

<authz:authorize ifNotGranted="ROLE_USER">

    <s:url id="register" action="findUser" namespace="/user" />
    <s:a href="%{register}"><s:text name="link.register" /></s:a>

    <s:url id="login" action="acegilogin" namespace="/" />
    |   <s:a href="%{login}"><s:text name="home.logon" /></s:a>
</authz:authorize>
<authz:authorize ifAllGranted="ROLE_USER">
    <s:url id="update" action="findUser" namespace="/user" >
        <s:param name="emailId" value="authenticatedUser.username" />
    </s:url>
    <s:a href="%{update}"><s:text name="link.updateProfile" /></s:a>

    |   <a href="<%=request.getContextPath()%>/j_acegi_logout">
            <s:text name="link.logoff" /></a>
</authz:authorize>

<s:url id="newEvent" action="addEventFlow" namespace="/event" />
|   <s:a href="%{newEvent}"><s:text name="link.addEvent" /></s:a>

</body>
</html>
```

Integrating Acegi provides a higher-level control over the configuration and credentials of the users using the web application. Users can be created by your application logic and those same business services used to look up users for authentication, which avoids any application external servlet or J2EE interaction.

Using Acegi, the roles for a user can be dynamically assigned and new roles created by the application on the fly. When using container-managed security, the roles are usually static. For this reason, container-managed security is usually preferred when the roles (and security requirements) are simple and not changed often. More complex security requires integrating a security library (such as Acegi) or implementing a custom solution.

Custom Authentication and Authorization

Custom authentication is the most complex of all the options because you cannot rely upon existing infrastructure or libraries to help, and every step for authentication needs to be implemented.

Before you can implement a custom solution, a few design decisions need to be made. The first is that the solution will be Struts2 based, which means the elements of Struts2 will be used to enforce authorization and authentication before looking to outside options (such as a servlet filter).

The other decision is how to determine who the currently logged in user is. For this, you can use an HTTP session object. If there is an object (matching a known key) in the HTTP session, then the user is authenticated and logged in; otherwise, the user is unknown and still requires authentication.

Preventing Unauthorized Access

The fist step in developing a custom solution is to ensure that only the users that are authorized are allowed to access a resource. In the container-based solution, this problem was handled outside the scope of the web application (by the container), and in the Acegi solution, a servlet filter was configured. In the custom solution, we will use a combination of an annotation and an interceptor.

The annotation will be a class-level annotation, marking the action as one that can only be executed when the user is authenticated.

```
@RequiresAuthentication
public class LogoffAction extends BaseAction {

    …

    public String execute() {
        …
    }
}
```

Like the Acegi annotation, the @RequiresAuthentication is very simple. The only difference is that the target of the annotation is a TYPE, instead of a METHOD:

```
@Target(ElementType.TYPE)
@Retention(RetentionPolicy.RUNTIME)
public @interface RequiresAuthentication {
}
```

■**Note** A simple class-level annotation can be used because the security requirements are simple: a user is authenticated and can use the application, or they cannot. If more complex role-based security is required, the annotation could be enhanced to specify the roles that are allowed to invoke the action. This is left as an exercise for you.

The annotation is not much good alone and requires an interceptor to restrict access to the user if the annotation is present, but the user has not yet authenticated. This is one of the features of the interceptor that is to be developed. There are other features that the interceptor also requires:

- *Securing packages*: As well as securing individual actions, the interceptor can be configured with Struts2 packages that always require user authentication.

- *Error message*: If the action implements the ValidationAware interface (which all actions extending ActionSupport do), the interceptor should add a message into the action error messages that can be displayed to the user.

- *Internationalization*: If the action implements the TextProvider interface, the interceptor should provide an internationalized error message to the action (otherwise, a default English message is added).

- *Redirect to a logon page*: If the user is not authenticated, the user is redirected to the logon page.

The following SecurityInterceptor fulfills all these requirements:

```
public class SecurityInterceptor extends AbstractInterceptor {

    public static final String USER_OBJECT = "user";
    public static final String LOGIN_RESULT = "authenticate";

    public static final String ERROR_MSG_KEY = "msg.pageRequiresRegistration";
    public static final String DEFAULT_MSG =
        "This page requires registration, please logon or register";

    private List<String> requiresAuthentication;

    public void setRequiresAuthentication( String authenticate ) {
        this.requiresAuthentication = stringToList(authenticate);
    }
```

```
    public String intercept(ActionInvocation invocation) throws Exception {

        User user =
            (User)invocation.getInvocationContext()
                .getSession().get(USER_OBJECT);
        Object action = invocation.getAction();
        boolean annotated =
            action.getClass().isAnnotationPresent(RequiresAuthentication.class);

        if( user==null && ( annotated ||
                requiresAuthentication(invocation.getProxy().getNamespace()) ) ) {
            if( action instanceof ValidationAware) {
                String msg = action instanceof TextProvider ?
                        ((TextProvider)action).getText(ERROR_MSG_KEY) : DEFAULT_MSG;
                ((ValidationAware)action).addActionError(msg);
            }
            return LOGIN_RESULT;
        }

        return invocation.invoke();
    }

    private List<String> stringToList(String val) {
        // changes a comma-delimited String list into a List of Strings
    }

    private boolean requiresAuthentication( String namespace ) {
        // returns true when the parameter matches
        //    an element of requiresAuthentication
    }
}
```

There are a couple of interesting points in this class. The first is that setting the package names on the interceptor is achieved using a setter, the same as if the interceptor was a simple POJO. The setter is called during the configuration of the interceptor, and a comma-delimited string of package names is passed in.

```
private List<String> requiresAuthentication;

public void setRequiresAuthentication( String authenticate ) {
    this.requiresAuthentication = stringToList(authenticate);
}
```

The other code of interest is the main logic loop. After initializing the necessary objects, the user is checked for existence, and if null (not authenticated), the action is checked to determine if an annotation is present, and finally the Struts2 package is checked to determine if it is in the list of protected packages. If any of these conditions are true, the remaining action processing is aborted, and the result LOGIN_RESULT is returned. Otherwise, the action processing continues as normal.

```
if( user==null && ( annotated ||
        requiresAuthentication(invocation.getProxy().getNamespace()) ) ) {
    …
    return LOGIN_RESULT;
}


return invocation.invoke();
```

Configuring Authorization

You have already seen the first way to configure authorization by annotating an action class. The other way is to configure the packages to protect via the interceptor. With this alternative, additional configuration information is added to the interceptor's configuration. A param tag, with the name attribute matching the setter of the interceptor (shown in the preceding interceptor code) and the value being the package list, is used to convey the required values.

```
<interceptor name="security"
        class="com.fdar.apress.s2.util.SecurityInterceptor" >
    <param name="requiresAuthentication">/event,/admin</param>
</interceptor>
```

To ensure that all actions include the new security interceptor, the security interceptor configuration as well as a new securedBasicStack interceptor stack is created in the home-package. The new stack is then configured as the default interceptor:

```
<package name="home-package" extends="struts-default" namespace="/">

    <interceptors>
        <interceptor name="security"
                class="com.fdar.apress.s2.util.SecurityInterceptor" >
            <param name="requiresAuthentication">/event,/admin</param>
        </interceptor>
        <interceptor-stack name="securedBasicStack">
            <interceptor-ref name="security" />
            <interceptor-ref name="defaultStack" />
        </interceptor-stack>
    </interceptors>

    <default-interceptor-ref name="securedBasicStack" />

    …

</package>
```

Tip Whenever possible, it's always a good idea to configure interceptors and interceptor stacks in your application's base package. This way, any package that inherits from the base package (either directly or indirectly) has access to the interceptor or interceptor stack without needing to reconfigure it. But be careful—sometimes interceptor stacks can be redefined in subpackages by accident. Also, having an interceptor stack included twice in a request could lead to hard-to-find issues, not to mention the double processing that will occur.

As well as the `home-package`, the `base-package` needs to be configured. This package has a different stack requirement than the `home-package`, and you need to ensure that security is applied. Just like in the `home-package`, a new `securedStack` interceptor stack is defined and configured as the default interceptor:

```
<package name="base-package" extends="home-package" >

    <interceptors>
        <interceptor-stack name="securedStack">
            <interceptor-ref name="security" />
            <interceptor-ref name="paramsPrepareParamsStack" />
        </interceptor-stack>
    </interceptors>
    <default-interceptor-ref name="securedStack" />

    …

</package>
```

Caution The annotated actions use this package for configuration, which may not have been obvious. If unexpected behavior occurs (in this case, no authorization), check that the interceptor stacks are configured correctly in the necessary packages.

The final configuration is the global authentication result. When the security interceptor returns the `authenticate` value (a constant in the `SecurityInterceptor` class), Struts2 needs to determine what to render to the user. This is configured in the `struts.xml` configuration file for the `home-package`:

```
<package name="home-package" extends="struts-default" namespace="/">

    <global-results>
        <result name="authenticate">/WEB-INF/jsp/logon.jsp</result>
    </global-results>

    …

</package>
```

■**Caution** Just like the filter in the Acegi implementation, if the interceptor is not applied to the package or action, the request is not secure, and any user may access it. For secure applications, this is a good endorsement for including the security interceptor in a base package, as it will always be included. Even if it isn't used, it's always better to have a security interceptor available for future enhancements.

Implementing Authentication

In each of the other authentication options, there was a JSP dedicated to obtaining the user's authentication credentials: the logon JSP. The same JSP is present for custom authentication; however, there are some differences:

- The form is created using the Struts2 tag libraries.

- Instead of calling a nebulous URL, a Struts2 action is being invoked when the form is submitted.

- The authentication messages are rendered using the Struts2 tags.

The only item that has not been introduced is the `actionerror` tag. This tag renders any error messages that have been set on the action as a list. With this last piece of knowledge, the `logon.jsp` is

```
<html>

<head>
    <title><s:text name="home.logon" /></title>
</head>
<body>

<s:actionerror />

<s:form action="logon" namespace="/" method="POST" >
    <s:textfield key="logon.username" name="username"/>
    <s:password key="logon.password" name="password"/>
    <s:submit type="submit" key="button.logon" />
</s:form>

</body>
</html>
```

The business logic to log on or authenticate a user and to log out a user has not been needed before. This logic is contained in the `LogonAction` class and the `LogoutAction` class.

The `LogonAction` class combines the functionality of an action, the getters and setters for the username and password fields, with the business logic to determine if the user is valid from the `UserDetailsService` class in the Acegi implementation. It uses the `UserService` business service to find a user, and, if valid, places the `User` object in the HTTP session.

If unsuccessful, an action error is added to the action (the same as the interceptor), and the user is returned to the logon JSP.

```java
public class LogonAction extends BaseAction implements ServletRequestAware {

    private String username;
    private String password;

    protected UserService service;
    private HttpServletRequest request;

    public static final String FAILURE = "failed";

    public void setUserService(UserService service) {
        this.service = service;
    }

    public void setServletRequest(HttpServletRequest httpServletRequest) {
        this.request=httpServletRequest;
    }

    public String getUsername() {
        return username;
    }

    public void setUsername(String username) {
        this.username = username;
    }

    public void setPassword(String password) {
        this.password = password;
    }

    public String execute() throws Exception {
        User user = service.findByEmail(username);
        if( user!=null && null!=username && !"".equals(username)
                && password.equals(user.getPassword()) ) {
            request.getSession(true)
                .setAttribute(SecurityInterceptor.USER_OBJECT,user);
            return SUCCESS;
        } else {
            addActionError(getText("auth.failed"));
            return FAILURE;
        }
    }
}
```

Where the logon action added the User object to the HTTP session, the logoff action removes it. In fact, rather than searching for and removing the object explicitly, the entire HTTP session can be invalidated. This removes all objects at once, providing a clean slate.

For demonstration purposes, the logoff action has the @RequiresAuthentication annotation, which means it can only be called after the user has logged on. If called before logging on, the user is directed to the logon page.

```
@RequiresAuthentication
public class LogoffAction extends BaseAction implements ServletRequestAware {

    private HttpServletRequest request;

    public void setServletRequest(HttpServletRequest httpServletRequest) {
        this.request=httpServletRequest;
    }

    public String execute() throws Exception {
        request.getSession().invalidate();
        return SUCCESS;
    }
}
```

To complete the actions, their configuration is added to the struts.xml configuration file:

```
<package name="home-package" extends="struts-default" namespace="/">

    ...

    <action name="logon" class="com.fdar.apress.s2.actions.LogonAction" >
        <result name="success" type="redirectAction">index</result>
        <result name="failed" >/WEB-INF/jsp/logon.jsp</result>
    </action>

    <action name="logoff" class="com.fdar.apress.s2.actions.LogoffAction" >
        <result name="success" type="redirectAction">index</result>
    </action>

</package>
```

Accessing Role Information

The earlier design decision of placing the authenticated user object into the HTTP session makes determining the role of the user easy. For the action, it means implementing the ServletRequestAware interface and then using the request to gain access to the object:

```
User user = request.getSession(true).getAttribute(SecurityInterceptor.USER_OBJECT);
```

This could be done for each and every action that requires access to the user, or it could be placed on the BaseAction for all implementing actions to have access to automatically.

Accessing the user object in a JSP is equally simple. The OGNL expression `#session['user']` (where user is the value of the key from the `SecurityInterceptor` class) is used to obtain the user. For this simple example of using no roles, checking for existence is enough. However, if roles were available and required, the `User` object could provide access methods to that information.

The `index.jsp` template that restricts access to various links becomes

```
<html>

<head>
    <title><s:text name="home.title" /></title>
</head>
<body>

<s:if test="#session['user']==null">
    <s:url id="register" action="findUser" namespace="/user" />
    <s:a href="%{register}"><s:text name="link.register" /></s:a>
</s:if>
<s:else>
    <s:url id="update" action="findUser" namespace="/user" >
        <s:param name="emailId" value="#session['user'].email" />
    </s:url>
    <s:a href="%{update}"><s:text name="link.updateProfile" /></s:a>

    <s:url id="logoff" action="logoff" namespace="/" />
|   <s:a href="%{logoff}"><s:text name="link.logoff" /></s:a>
</s:else>

<s:url id="newEvent" action="addEventFlow" namespace="/event" />
|   <s:a href="%{newEvent}"><s:text name="link.addEvent" /></s:a>
</body>
</html>
```

Another option is to create a custom tag library to access the `User` object and its methods, similar to the Acegi tag libraries.

When facing the decision of integrating an external library (such as Acegi) or providing a custom implementation, the deciding factors are the features and level of integration that are required.

Summary

In this chapter, we have covered three different variations of securing a Struts2 application from the perspective of authorization and authentication. The concepts and ideas are the same, but the implementations differ. Depending on the level of integration, more or less development work is required to implement the solution. The level of control also changes depending on the solution selected.

Although the examples were simple, the concepts and infrastructure of the examples remain the same when implementing more complex role-based authorization systems.

CHAPTER 8

■ ■ ■

Searching and Listings

In this chapter, you will learn how to add searching to the web application, as well as how to render the subsequent result lists. The functionality will be introduced using two different options: a quick search feature that appears on every page, and a search form that the user requests via HTML link.

The Use Cases

The use cases being developed in this chapter all revolve around searching for events, and listing event information. However, the use cases will not be implemented individually; instead, they will manifest themselves under two new features of the application:

- *A quick search form*: This feature will be present on all screens at the top right. It will allow users to search by the name or partial name of an event.

- *A search form*: The search form will allow the user to perform an exhaustive search using many different criteria. This will be a separate screen that the user can select using the left navigation.

Each of the use cases from Chapter 4 will be developed as part of the quick search form, the search form, or both. To recap, the use cases that are being developed are the following:

Search for Events by Name: By entering an event name or a partial event name, the user will be able to search for matching events. This use case will be available through the quick search form and the search form.

Search for Events by Location: The user will be able to search for events by providing a city and state for the location. This use case will be available only through the search form.

Search for Events by Contestant: The user will be able to search for events by providing the names of the contestants that are competing in the event. This use case will also only be available through the search form.

Before delving into each use case, changes to support the new functionality need to be made to the application. This is the topic of the following section.

Setting the Stage

Before starting development on the new use cases, a few changes need to be made to the current screen layout. Along with updating the screen layout, several other changes will be introduced to facilitate developing the use cases for this chapter.

Updating the Screen Layout

Until now, the screen layout from the starter archetype has been used unmodified. The structure should be familiar to anyone who has viewed a web application, with a panel for the header, footer, navigation, and the primary content, as shown in Figure 8-1. In previous development, this structure was not taken advantage of, and all hyperlinks, data entry, and information to be viewed was placed in the main content panel. It's now time to break this habit, splitting out the navigational elements and moving them into the correct navigational panels.

Figure 8-1. *The current screen layout showing the header, footer, navigation, and content panels*

The first step is to move all the navigation elements from the index.jsp template, which was rendered in the main content panel, to the navigation panel (the final results of the updates are shown in Figure 8-2). This functionality is provided by SiteMesh and was introduced in Chapter 2.

SiteMesh is a little different from other templating technologies in that it uses the decorator design pattern to embellish HTML with additional HTML provided in a secondary file. The second HTML file, known as the *decorator*, uses special tags to denote when the title (between the ⟨title⟩ tags), the header (between the ⟨head⟩ tags), and the body (between the ⟨body⟩ tags) from the original HTML should be inserted. The decoration of the HTML with the decorator occurs in real time, and SiteMesh can decorate all HTML sources, whether produced by JSP, PHP, Perl, or Ruby (although if you are using other languages, you would most likely avoid deploying it to a servlet container, which SiteMesh needs to operate within).

The decorator that SiteMesh selects is determined by the decorators.xml configuration file. In this file, you can associate URL patterns, request parameters, or event browser agent information with different decorator files. This mechanism makes SiteMesh extremely powerful.

Tip There are also SiteMesh tags to obtain additional properties from the original HTML, as well as for the page to specify which template it wants to use and to decorate inline or external content from within the page itself. Information on all the available tags can be found in the SiteMesh documentation at http://www.opensymphony.com/sitemesh/tags.html.

Most other templating technologies, such as Apache Tiles, take the opposite approach and use a template that specifies the subparts that need to be included. SiteMesh can also work in this mode, although it's usually the last configuration option used.

The decorator template used in the web application is called main.jsp, and it can be found in the /src/main/webapp/WEB-INF/decorators directory. When this file is stripped down to the basic elements, it becomes the following:

```
<html xmlns="http://www.w3.org/1999/xhtml" xml:lang="en" lang="en">
<head>
  <title><decorator:title default="Struts Starter"/></title>
  <decorator:head/>
</head>
<body id="page-home">
  <div id="page">
    <div id="header" class="clearfix">
      <!-- header code -->
    </div>

    <div id="content" class="clearfix">
      <div id="main">
        <decorator:body/>
      </div>

      <div id="local">
        <!-- navigation code -->
      </div>

    </div>
```

```
      <div id="footer" class="clearfix">
        <!-- footer code -->
      </div>

  </div>

</body>
</html>
```

For the navigation panel, the HTML element of interest is the `<div id="local">` tag. The JSP code from the `index.jsp` template is placed between the opening and closing tags. While modifying the decorator, internationalized text is added for the header and footer (with the matching key/value pairs placed into the `package.properties` file). The final decorator template is as follows:

```
<%@ page contentType="text/html; charset=UTF-8" pageEncoding="UTF-8" %>
<%@taglib prefix="decorator" uri="http://www.opensymphony.com/sitemesh/decorator" %>
<%@taglib prefix="page" uri="http://www.opensymphony.com/sitemesh/page" %>
<%@taglib prefix="s" uri="/struts-tags" %>

<html xmlns="http://www.w3.org/1999/xhtml" xml:lang="en" lang="en">
<head>
  <title><decorator:title default="Struts Starter"/></title>
  <link href="<s:url value='/styles/main.css'/>" rel="stylesheet"
      type="text/css" media="all"/>
  <decorator:head/>
</head>
<body id="page-home">
  <div id="page">
    <div id="header" class="clearfix">
      <s:text name="header.text" />
    </div>

    <div id="content" class="clearfix">
      <div id="main">
        <decorator:body/>
      </div>
```

```
    <div id="local">
      <h3><s:text name="leftnav.title"/></h3>
      <ul>
        <s:if test="#session['user']==null">
          <s:url id="register" action="findUser" namespace="/user" />
          <li><s:a href="%{register}"><s:text name="link.register" /></s:a></li>
        </s:if>
        <s:else>
          <s:url id="update" action="findUser" namespace="/user" >
            <s:param name="emailId" value="#session['user'].email" />
          </s:url>
          <li>
            <s:a href="%{update}"><s:text name="link.updateProfile" /></s:a></li>
          <s:url id="logoff" action="logoff" namespace="/" />
          <li><s:a href="%{logoff}"><s:text name="link.logoff" /></s:a></li>
        </s:else>

        <s:url id="newEvent" action="addEventFlow" namespace="/event" />
        <li><s:a href="%{newEvent}"><s:text name="link.addEvent" /></s:a></li>
      </ul>
    </div>

  </div>

  <div id="footer" class="clearfix">
    <s:text name="footer.text" />
  </div>

  </div>

</body>
</html>
```

Note All the Struts2 tags available to the web application's JSPs are also available in the SiteMesh decorator.

Figure 8-2. *The screen layout showing with the navigation moved from the main content panel to the navigation panel*

Creating a Friendly Home Page

Although the navigation is now separate from the main content, the initial screen that is presented to the user (as shown in Figure 8-2) is a little confusing. Apart from two links, no information is displayed, and the user is not given any direction on how to proceed. To make the home page more inviting, we'll modify it to provide direction to the user as well as list the most recently added events.

The first part is easy. A Struts2 text tag is added to the index.jsp template. In the package.properties properties file, the home.welcomeText key is associated with an internationalized value that will be rendered.

Rendering the list of events is a little different from what you have seen before. The option you currently have available is to create an action that obtains a list of events and has the following result configuration:

```
@Result(name="success",value="/WEB-INF/jsp/index.jsp")
```

Although this works, to use the same list of events in different pages involves significant effort. Following are the options that are currently available:

- Subclass (not copy!) the original action class and provide a different configuration.

- Use XML configuration rather than annotation configuration.

Using either of the preceding options also leads to problems when constructing pages with many unrelated parts (for example, diverse data in a portal application). Because Java does not allow multiple inheritance, the easiest way to provide reuse while avoiding duplication by cut and paste is to use helper classes that are referenced from the action (as well as other actions providing similar functionality). The resulting action would be an aggregator of the functions of many other actions. This is too much responsibility for one action, and it doesn't allow for the maximum reuse in action logic or rendering.

A better option is to invoke an action in a JSP template via the Struts2 `action` tag. When the `action` tag is used in a JSP, the developer has the option of including the result produced by the invoked action in the current JSP. Even if the result is not included, the invoked action will be available on the Value Stack (and hence have its methods available to the current JSP). The tag has three attributes:

- `name`: The name of the action to invoke.

- `namespace`: The namespace that the action is configured under.

- `executeResult`: Whether the result that is configured for the action should be invoked (inserting the HTML generated into the calling JSP template) or just the `execute()` method of the action (providing access to the action's data via the Value Stack) should be invoked.

In addition to the attributes, `param` tags can be nested to pass in parameter information. The following is the final `index.jsp` template to call a new `showRecentEvents` action and display the most recent ten entries:

```
<html xmlns="http://www.w3.org/1999/xhtml" xml:lang="en" lang="en">
<head>
    <title><s:text name="home.title" /></title>
</head>
<body>

<p><s:text name="home.welcomeText"/></p>

<div>
    <p><s:text name="home.mostRecentTen"/></p>
    <s:action name="showRecentEvents" namespace="/search" executeResult="true" >
        <s:param name="number">10</s:param>
    </s:action>
</div>

</body>
</html>
```

■**Tip** Use the `action` tag to create focused actions that can be easily reused. Actions developed in this style follow the *Single Responsibility Principle* and follow proven good programming styles.

The action showRecentEvents corresponds to an action class ShowRecentEventsAction. You also know that a parameter number is used, and so the setNumber(int number) setter must exist on the action class.

```java
@ParentPackage("base-package")
@Result(name="success",value="/WEB-INF/jsp/search/listEvents-partial.jsp")
public class ShowRecentEventsAction extends BaseAction {

    private int number;
    private List<Event> results;
    private EventService service;

    public void setEventService(EventService service) {
        this.service = service;
    }

    public void setNumber(int number) {
        this.number = number;
    }

    public List<Event> getResults() {
        return results;
    }

    public String execute() throws Exception {
        results = service.findAllEvents(number);
        return SUCCESS;
    }
}
```

To obtain the events to display, the execute() method uses a new findAllEvents() method on the EventService API. To access the result of the action in the JSP being rendered, a getResults() method is supplied on the action.

As expected from setting executeResult="true", a SUCCESS result from the action renders the listEvents-partial.jsp template and not the index.jsp template. One possible option for the listEvents-partial.jsp is to iterate over the results (provided by the getResults() method on the action), displaying each in turn. The resulting JSP code for this option is

```jsp
<%@ page contentType="text/html; charset=UTF-8" %>
<%@ taglib uri="/struts-tags" prefix="s" %>

<s:iterator value="results">
    <h3><s:property value="name" /></h3>
    <div>
        <!-- render fields from the Event class -->
    </div>
</s:iterator>
```

The iterator tag does pretty much what you would expect: it iterates over a collection (any class that implements the `java.util.Collection` or `java.util.Iterator` interface). The collection is specified using the `value` attribute, which in this case is the `result` property that corresponds to the `getResults()` method on the action class. For each value in the collection, the code inside the `iterator` tag is executed, and the current value of the collection is placed on the top of the Value Stack. Hence, the code

```
<s:property value="name" />
```

could be thought of as (where i is the current location in the loop)

```
<s:property value="results[i].name" />
```

There are two other attributes for the `iterator` tag. An `id` attribute can be used to provide the current object in the loop with an identifier that can be referenced via OGNL (the value being equivalent to `results[i]`). This allows you to specify the name of the property rather than using the object on the top of the Value Stack (great for when you have an `iterator` tag within another `iterator` tag, and you need to reference properties from both). The previous example becomes the following:

```
<s:iterator id="next" value="results">
    <h3><s:property value="#next.name" /></h3>
    …
</s:iterator>
```

The final attribute, `status`, when used in the `iterator` tag, provides access to an instance of the `IteratorStatus` class. This class provides information about the current iteration, such as the current index, whether this is the first element or the last element, and whether this row is an odd row or an even row.

```
<s:iterator status="rowstatus" value="results">
    <s:if test="#rowstatus.odd" >…
        <!-- highlight row in a different color -->
    </s:if>
    …
</s:iterator>
```

Note The properties available via the `IteratorStatus` class can be found in the Struts2 JavaDoc at http://struts.apache.org/2.x/struts2-core/apidocs/org/apache/struts2/views/jsp/IteratorStatus.html.

Modularizing the List Rendering

Another option is available for rendering the event list. Instead of placing the code for rendering the event inside the logic that iterates over the list, it can be split out. This allows the same code to be used whether the event is rendered in a list or whether it is rendered at the main element in a page.

Note This is similar to the JSP 2.0 tag file feature, where the tag libraries are built from JSP or XML code fragments rather than Java code, making it easier for non-Java developers to write tags and reuse code.

The first step is to modify the partial JSP template `listEvents-partial.jsp` from the version in the previous section. There is still an `iterator` tag; however, the differences are that a `component` tag has been introduced and some additional logic is used to handle the case when no events have been found (see Figure 8-3).

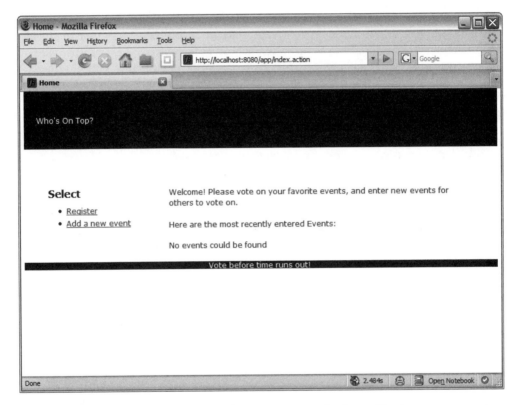

Figure 8-3. *The home screen layout when there are no events in the application*

You can think of the `component` tag as an *extract method* refactoring. It takes common presentation code that is spread across many JSP templates and moves it to a common tag that anyone can use to provide consistent rendering/behavior. An additional benefit is that maintaining the code is simpler because changes only need to be applied to one place.

```
<%@ page contentType="text/html; charset=UTF-8" %>
<%@ taglib uri="/struts-tags" prefix="s" %>
```

```
<s:if test="results.size()==0">
    <s:text name="text.noEvents" />
</s:if>
<s:else>
    <s:iterator id="next" value="results">
        <s:component template="eventListing.jsp" theme="apress">
            <s:param name="event" value="#next" />
        </s:component>
    </s:iterator>
</s:else>
```

Using the component tag is similar to using an include tag of either the Struts2 or JSP variety. The difference is conceptual, in that the component tag is meant to be a user interface widget rather than already preformatted text. As such, it includes the Struts2-specific theme attribute, as well as all the JavaScript event attributes, CSS attributes, and HTML attributes found on the other Struts2 tags.

Two attributes are being used to specify the location of the template: the template attribute that provides the name of the template, in this case eventListing.jsp; and the theme attribute that provides additional directory information. The base directory that Struts2 uses is /templates (in the web root), so by aggregating the attribute information, the file being used by the component tag is /template/apress/eventListing.jsp.

Another feature is that the template using the component tag can pass parameters to the component template being used during rendering (the Struts2 include tag has the same feature). These are specified using the param tag and can be of any object type. By using the id attribute of the iterator tag, the listEvents-partial.jsp template can pass the current object in the iteration with the specific name event. On the receiving end (the eventListing.jsp template), the parameter is accessed by prepending parameters. to the property name. So the name of the event passed to the component template is accessed as

```
<s:property value="parameters.event.name" />
```

Armed with all of this information, you should have a good idea of what the eventListing.jsp template will look like. Here is the complete eventList.jsp listing to complete the picture (Figure 8-4 shows what the user sees):

```
<%@ page contentType="text/html; charset=UTF-8" %>
<%@ taglib uri="/struts-tags" prefix="s" %>

<p>
<h3><s:property value="parameters.event.name" /></h3>
<s:text name="display.event.date"/>
    <s:date name="parameters.event.startTime" format="MMM d, yyyy"/> <br/>
<s:text name="display.event.start"/
    <s:date name="parameters.event.startTime" format="hh:mm a" /> <br/>
<s:text name="display.event.voting"/>
    <s:date name="parameters.event.votingStartTime" format="hh:mm a"/> <br/>
</p>
```

Note Information on the specifics of the `date` tag can be found in the Apache documentation at `http://struts.apache.org/2.x/docs/date.html`.

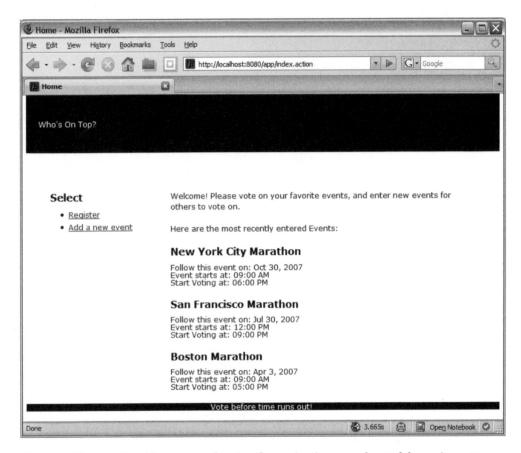

Figure 8-4. *The completed home page showing the navigation moved out of the main content panel and the most recent event listing in the main content panel*

Search for Events by Name

Searching for the name (or title) of the event is the first use case that we'll implement. As you would expect, when the number of events in the web application becomes larger, this will be a very commonly used feature.

To make it quick and easy for the user to perform a search, a quick search form has been placed on each and every page in the user interface. This means modifying the `main.jsp` SiteMesh decorator again. The quick search form will be in the common upper-right corner position for web applications. For this placement, a new HTML `div` tag for the quick search form must be added immediately preceding the `div` tag used for the main content.

A style attribute has been added to position the quick search form, halfway between the header and the content for the page. The new layout can be seen in Figure 8-5 and is achieved using the following main.jsp decorator:

```
<html xmlns="http://www.w3.org/1999/xhtml" xml:lang="en" lang="en">
<head>…</head>
<body id="page-home">
  <div id="page">
    <div id="header" class="clearfix">
      <s:text name="header.text" />
    </div>

    <div align="right" style="position:relative;top:-40px;">
      <s:form namespace="/search" action="searchByTitle"
          method="POST" theme="simple">
        <s:text name="text.search" />
        <s:textfield name="titlePartial" size="15"/>
        <s:submit key="button.search"/>
      </s:form>
    </div>

    <div id="content" class="clearfix">
      <div id="main">
        <decorator:body/>
      </div>

      <div id="local">
        <!-- nav links -->
      </div>

    </div>

    <div id="footer" class="clearfix">
      <s:text name="footer.text" />
    </div>

  </div>

</body>
</html>
```

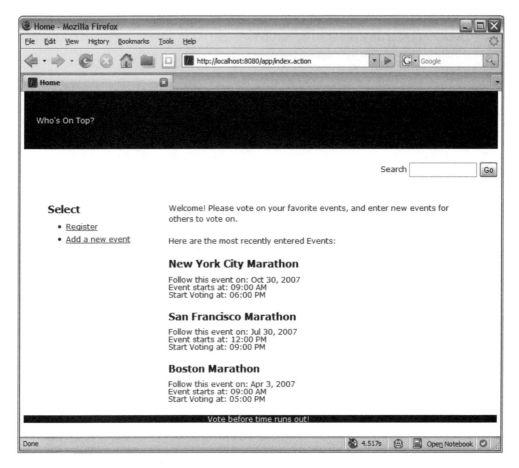

Figure 8-5. *The home page showing the quick search form*

The form is a little different from what you have seen before in that it uses the `simple` theme, specified by `theme="simple"`. This theme provides rendering that is the same as if pure HTML was used without tables and other special formatting, which allows the quick search form to have a small inline footprint on the screen.

■**Caution** Be careful when specifying the action value. If the extension is specified in the `action` attribute value (i.e., `action="searchByTitle.action"`), Struts2 thinks you are providing a complete URL and will ignore the `namespace` attribute value.

When the user enters a value and submits the form, the `searchByTitle.action` URL is called, which in turn invokes the `SearchByTitleAction` action class:

```
@ParentPackage("base-package")
@Result(name="success",value= "/WEB-INF/jsp/search/listEventResults.jsp")
public class SearchByTitleAction extends BaseAction {

    private String titlePartial;
    private String userInfo;

    private List<Event> results;
    private EventService service;

    public void setEventService(EventService service) {
        this.service = service;
    }

    public void setTitlePartial(String titlePartial) {
        this.titlePartial = titlePartial;
    }

    public List<Event> getResults() {
        return results;
    }

    public String getUserInfo() {
        return userInfo;
    }

    public String getEventTemplate() {
        return "apress";
    }

    public String execute() throws Exception {
        results = service.findByTitle(titlePartial);
        userInfo = "".equals(titlePartial) ?
                getText("searchBy.all") :
                getText("searchBy.title", new String[]{titlePartial});
        return SUCCESS;
    }
}
```

This action class uses a new findByTitle() method on the EventService business service that takes the partial title value entered by the user and searches all the event names. If the partial title value is contained within an event name, the event is returned and stored in the results list property of the action.

There are two other special features of the action class. The first is that the action has a getEventTemplate() method that provides template information that is used to decide which template renders the event information (this feature will be discussed more later). Second, the action needs to provide information about which query has been executed. This is achieved by setting the `userInfo` property. A key is used to look up the final value, which could be a simple `String`, or it can also pass in values from the action to include in the final value.

When the action is complete, it forwards the user to the `listEventResults.jsp` template. This JSP has been made as generic as possible, as explained in the following list:

- The HTML `title` tag value is set to `Search Results`, so it can be used for any search.

- The information about the query that will be presented to the user is obtained from the action that was previously executed.

- The JSP assumes that the list of results could be an empty list.

- The rendering of the event uses the previously developed `eventListing.jsp` template (called via the `component` tag); however, the JSP obtains the template directory to apply to the `eventListing.jsp` template from the previously executed action.

The last feature is interesting because it allows the action to determine how the event is rendered. Having advance knowledge of the upcoming features in the application in this case is a good thing because it allows this feature to be added ahead of time. The other use cases to be implemented are search on location and contestant; these use cases will also render the location and contestant information in the results. This means that either a new JSP needs to be created for each different search, or the template `/apress/eventListing.jsp` needs to be changed. By allowing the action to specify the template's location, the template can be specified in part by the controller, which avoids multiple search result JSPs.

Note Always be careful when allowing the action to provide rendering information to the JSP. In this case, a template or file system directory is provided by the action, rather than the template name. This is a higher level of information than the template name (which could have also been specified by the action). Remember that the action is a controller, and you want to avoid creating dependencies in the action layer from JSPs. However, when a compromise such as this provides some control (but not too much) and allows the JSP template to be made more generic (to handle the view for multiple use cases), it's a better option than duplicating the JSP code.

Figure 8-6 shows the user's view of the search results, rendered by the JSP:

```
<html xmlns="http://www.w3.org/1999/xhtml" xml:lang="en" lang="en">

<head>
    <title><s:text name="searchResults.title" /></title>
</head>
<body>

<h4><s:text name="searchResults.query"/> <s:property value="userInfo" /></h4>
```

```
<div>
    <s:if test="results.size()==0">
        <s:text name="text.noEvents" />
    </s:if>
    <s:else>
        <s:iterator id="next" value="results">
            <s:component template="eventListing.jsp" theme="%{eventTemplate}">
                <s:param name="event" value="#next" />
            </s:component>
        </s:iterator>
    </s:else>
</div>

</body>
</html>
```

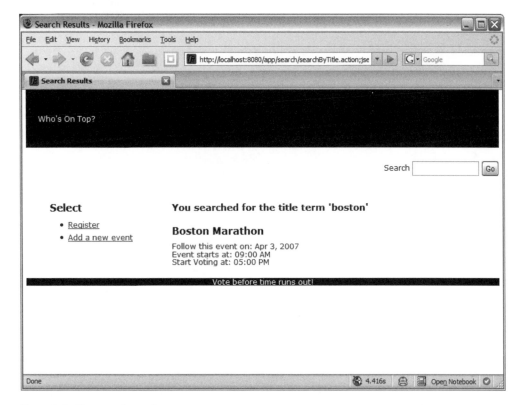

Figure 8-6. *The search results screen*

PAGINATION

Pagination is a topic that is usually discussed along with search results and lists; however, pagination is not introduced and not implemented in the example application in this chapter.

The reason for this is that pagination is not purely an action layer concern in a web application, and therefore needs to be designed with the entire application as well as the nonfunctional requirements (especially performance and memory consumption characteristics) in mind. Table 8-1 highlights the options available, complexity of the solution, and concerns.

Table 8-1. *Pagination Implementation Options and Concerns*

Option	Implementation Complexity	Description/Concerns
Pagination in the JSP	Easy	The list of all the result objects is returned from the action, and the JSP decides which elements should be displayed. The web application needs to keep track of the current page by using a request parameter, hidden form parameter, or even a session object. The server is worked hard because all the results are searched for and returned on each pagination request. Caching at the business service or database layer can help.
Storing the result list in the HTTP session	Medium	The list of result objects is obtained from the business or database layer and placed into the HTTP session. The JSP can then access the result list and decide which elements should be displayed. The business services or database layer is accessed less (once per search versus once per search result page change), but now the results are taking up memory resources on the application server. Large result sets and clustering/high-availability concerns need to be taken into account.
Business service or database returning a partial result set	Hard	When the action calls the business service or database, only a partial result list is returned. The list contains all the results for the current page being rendered to the user but nothing else. Memory and performance concerns at the web application side are diminished, but the overall complexity of the solution increases. Rather than the business service or database layer returning a list, an object needs to be returned that contains a partial list as well as telemetry information (how many pages, which page the user is viewing, etc.). The complexity of the business service or database object increases because now the starting and ending records need to be taken into account, the management of the data increases (were any new records entered while a user is halfway through viewing a result list, and how is this event handled), and rendering the data using the telemetry object is more complex than before.

The good news is that the `iterator` tag and the `status` attribute (which is an `IteratorStatus` class instance) are the fundamental tags used to implement all of these options.

The other option is to use a preexisting library to provide the required functionality. Displaytag (`http://displaytag.sourceforge.net`) is a great choice for a standard HTML user interface, and Yahoo! (`http://developer.yahoo.com/yui/datatable/`) provides an AJAX-enabled option. These are not the only options available but provide a good place to start.

Developing a Search Form

One option for developing the remaining search use cases is to create a new search form for each individually, with different input options and different search action classes. Although this is a valid option, a business decision was made that users would more likely want all the options together. They could then decide to enter either the location information or the contestant information to search on, or they might use both together.

Developing this scenario is very similar to the previous use case. The search form is not added to the SiteMesh decorator, but a link to the search form needs to be added to the navigation links. The link uses the Struts2 `url` and `a` tag and calls the `/app/search/searchEvents.action` URL.

```
<div id="local">
  <h3><s:text name="leftnav.title"/></h3>
  <ul>
    <s:if test="#session['user']==null">
      <s:url id="register" action="findUser" namespace="/user" />
      <li><s:a href="%{register}"><s:text name="link.register" /></s:a></li>
    </s:if>
    <s:else>
      <s:url id="update" action="findUser" namespace="/user" >
        <s:param name="emailId" value="#session['user'].email" />
      </s:url>
      <li><s:a href="%{update}"><s:text name="link.updateProfile" /></s:a></li>

      <s:url id="logoff" action="logoff" namespace="/" />
      <li><s:a href="%{logoff}"><s:text name="link.logoff" /></s:a></li>
    </s:else>

    <s:url id="newEvent" action="addEventFlow" namespace="/event" />
    <li><s:a href="%{newEvent}"><s:text name="link.addEvent" /></s:a></li>

    <s:url id="search" action="searchEvents" namespace="/search" />
    <li><s:a href="%{search}"><s:text name="link.search" /></s:a></li>
  </ul>
</div>
```

The search form doesn't need access to a specialized action for data but, at the same time, the decorator cannot call the JSP directly because internationalization information won't be available. To solve both these issues, a new search package is added to the struts.xml configuration file, and a configuration is added for the searchEvents.action that uses the common BaseEventAction to redirect to the search.jsp template:

```
<struts>

    ...

    <package name="searching" namespace="/search" extends="base-package">
        <action name="searchEvents"
                class="com.fdar.apress.s2.actions.event.BaseEventAction">
            <result>/WEB-INF/jsp/search/search.jsp</result>
        </action>
    </package>

</struts>
```

Clicking on the Advanced Search link on the home screen now brings the user to the search form (see Figure 8-7) rendered by the following JSP template:

```
<html xmlns="http://www.w3.org/1999/xhtml" xml:lang="en" lang="en">

<head>
    <title><s:text name="search.title" /></title>
</head>
<body>

<s:form namespace="/search" action="searchForEvent" method="POST" >

    <tr>
        <td colspan="2">
            <h4><s:text name="search.location.criteria" /></h4>
        </td>
    </tr>
    <s:textfield key="search.location.name" name="locationName"/>
    <s:textfield key="search.location.city" name="locationCity" />
    <s:textfield key="search.location.state" name="locationState" />

    <tr>
        <td colspan="2">
            <h4><s:text name="search.contestant.criteria" /></h4>
        </td>
    </tr>
    <s:textarea key="search.contestant" name="contestants" />
```

```
    <s:submit key="button.advSearch" />

</s:form>

</body>
</html>
```

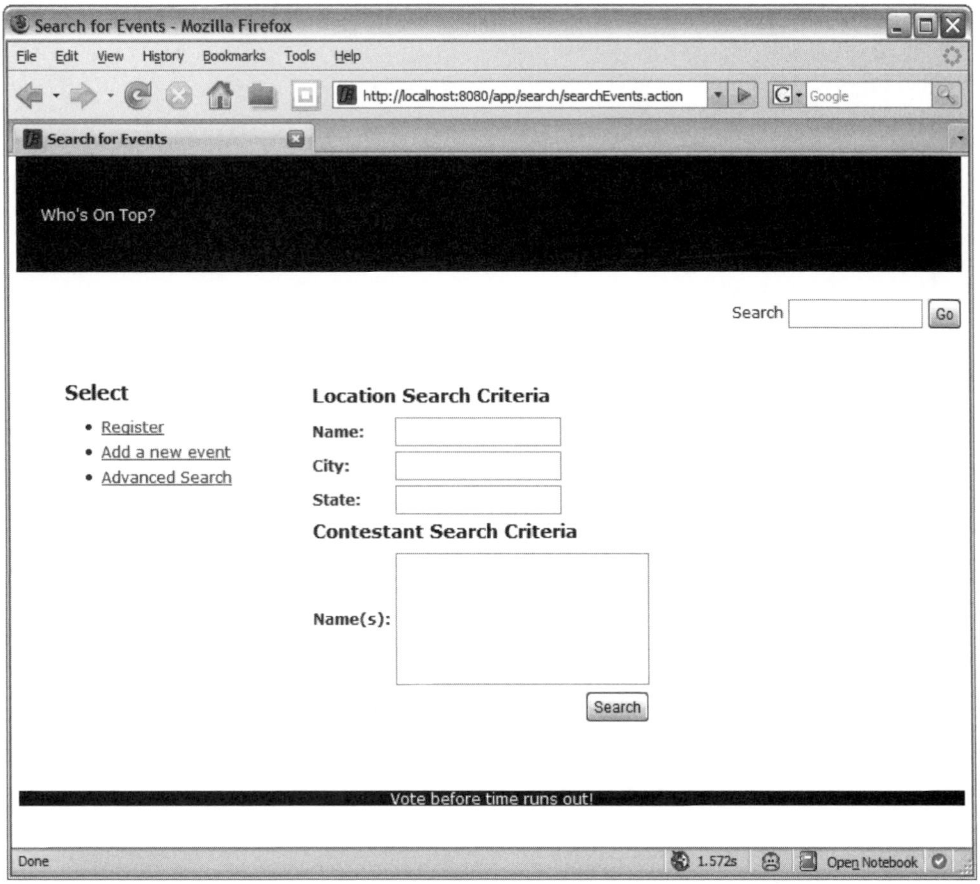

Figure 8-7. *The advanced search form screen*

The action that the search form submits to is very similar to the SearchByTitleAction action class. In fact, the only differences are the number of setter methods (for the fields being submitted from the search form), the result is returned from the getEventTemplate() method, and the logic is in the execute() method.

```
@ParentPackage("base-package")
@Result(name="success",value= "/WEB-INF/jsp/search/listEventResults.jsp")
public class SearchForEventsAction extends BaseAction {
```

```java
    private String locationName;
    private String locationCity;
    private String locationState;
    private String contestants;

    private String userInfo;
    private List<Event> results;
    private EventService service;

    public void setEventService(EventService service) {
        this.service = service;
    }

    public void setLocationName(String locationName) {
        this.locationName = locationName;
    }

    public void setLocationCity(String locationCity) {
        this.locationCity = locationCity;
    }

    public void setLocationState(String locationState) {
        this.locationState = locationState;
    }

    public void setContestants(String contestants) {
        this.contestants = contestants;
    }

    public List<Event> getResults() {
        return results;
    }

    public String getUserInfo() {
        return userInfo;
    }

    public String getEventTemplate() {
        return "apress/extended";
    }

    public String execute() throws Exception {
        results = service.findEventsByExample(
            createQueryLocation(), createContestantsList() );
        userInfo = getText("searchBy.advanced");
        return SUCCESS;
    }
```

```
    private Location createQueryLocation() {
        // create a Location instance for the individual fields
    }

    private List<String> createContestantsList() {
        // create a list of strings
    }
}
```

Note The method `findEventsByExample()` is not implemented in the example code, and so the resulting JSP will always contain all the events entered into the application. Having the logic implemented would not change the Struts2 code being discussed, it would only reduce the number of results being returned and hence displayed.

Even better than only having a few changes in the action class is that the `listEventResults.jsp` template has not changed at all. The very same JSP that was used to display the results for the quick search results is used for the advanced search results. When you think about it, this makes sense. All the same things are being rendered, so why should the template that iterates over the list change? What did change is the rendering of the individual event.

The `SearchByTitleAction` action class returned the value apress from the `getEventTemplate()` method, so the event was rendered using the `/template/apress/eventListing.jsp` template. This same method in the `SearchForEventsAction` returns a value of apress/extended, so the template changed to `/template/apress/extended/eventListing.jsp`. The new template's formatting is shown in Figure 8-8 and in the following listing:

```
<%@ page contentType="text/html; charset=UTF-8" %>
<%@ taglib uri="/struts-tags" prefix="s" %>

<p>
<h3><s:property value="parameters.event.name" /></h3>
<ul>
    <li>
        <s:text name="display.event.date"/>
        <s:date name="parameters.event.startTime" format="MMM d, yyyy"/>
    </li>
    <li><s:text name="display.location" />
        <s:property value="parameters.event.location.name" /> :
        <s:property value="parameters.event.location.city" />,
        <s:property value="parameters.event.location.state" />
    </li>
    <li><s:text name="display.contestants" />
```

```
            <s:iterator status="rowstatus" value="parameters.event.options">
                <s:property value="name"/>
                <s:if test="#rowstatus.last==false" >,</s:if>
            </s:iterator>
        </li>
    </ul>
</p>
```

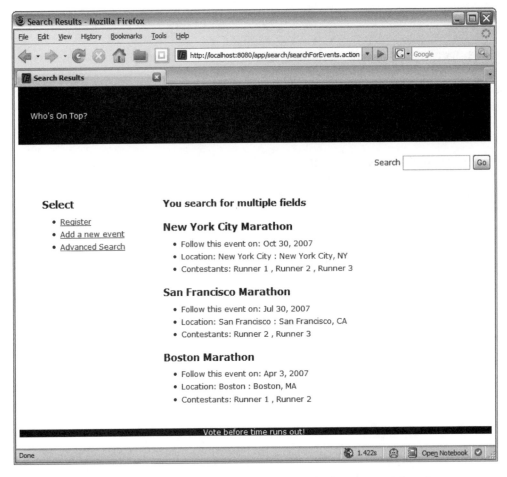

Figure 8-8. *The advanced search results, using a new* eventListing.jsp *template theme*

Consolidating List Actions

The final consideration for the search use cases is whether the code can be optimized or consolidated.

From the very beginning, the listEventResults.jsp template was developed with reusability in mind. Because there were several search uses cases, and each needed to display results, a common results page was developed. To provide the generic canvas that any action could use, the template used properties from the calling action to provide context information to the user. The downside of this approach is that each and every calling action is now required to provide these properties. When the search actions were being developed, the commonality required to render the result was missed, and it's now time to return and extract the common elements.

The first step is to create a base class and extract the common elements. Each of these elements has been covered in detail previously:

- The property and setter that allows the EventService business service to be used by the action

- The property and getter for the list of resulting events

- The property and getter for the description of the search that was just performed

- A getter that allows the JSP to select the correct template to render the event details

The base class BaseSearchAction (listing is shown next) is the result of extracting the common elements. To ensure that developers subclass the action class correctly, and all the elements necessary to render the results are provided, the class is made abstract along with the getEventTemplate() method.

```
public abstract class BaseSearchAction extends BaseAction {

    protected String userInfo;

    protected List<Event> results;
    protected EventService service;

    public void setEventService(EventService service) {
        this.service = service;
    }

    public List<Event> getResults() {
        return results;
    }

    public String getUserInfo() {
        return userInfo;
    }

    public abstract String getEventTemplate();

}
```

After a search base class is created, each of the search use case action implementations can be refactored to extend it. The resulting action classes are much smaller, and more importantly, focused on a single responsibility: providing the functionality of the use case with the clutter of the search result infrastructure removed.

The SearchByTitleAction action becomes

```
@ParentPackage("base-package")
@Result(name="success",value= "/WEB-INF/jsp/search/listEventResults.jsp")
public class SearchByTitleAction extends BaseSearchAction {

    private String titlePartial;

    public void setTitlePartial(String titlePartial) {
        this.titlePartial = titlePartial;
    }

    public String getEventTemplate() {
        return "apress";
    }

    public String execute() throws Exception {
        results = service.findByTitle(titlePartial);
        userInfo = "".equals(titlePartial) ?
                getText("searchBy.all")
                : getText("searchBy.title", new String[]{titlePartial});
        return SUCCESS;
    }
}
```

The SearchForEventsAction action class (listing is shown next) is longer than the SearchByTitleAction action class; however, it provides the same focus on a single responsibility.

```
@ParentPackage("base-package")
@Result(name="success",value= "/WEB-INF/jsp/search/listEventResults.jsp")
public class SearchForEventsAction extends BaseSearchAction {

    private String locationName;
    private String locationCity;
    private String locationState;
    private String contestants;

    // setters for the form field properties

    public String getEventTemplate() {
        return "apress/extended";
    }
```

```
public String execute() throws Exception {
    results = service.findEventsByExample(
        createQueryLocation(), createContestantsList () );
    userInfo = getText("searchBy.advanced");
    return SUCCESS;
}

private Location createQueryLocation() {
    // create a Location instance for the individual fields
}

private List<String> createContestantsList() {
    // create a list of strings
}
}
```

There is yet another option for combining the search actions. Instead of developing a base class and individual subclasses, you can place all the logic for all of the search use cases in a single action class.

This approach is useful when the parameters being passed to the different search use cases are similar; that is, there is approximately the same number of terms, and they are of the same type. Under this circumstance, the only difference is the action logic method (the renamed execute() method).

When the use cases are like the search use cases developed in this chapter, separate action classes should be used. If all the use cases are lumped together, the action class is too overrun with properties that are conditional on the use case being invoked. This leads to confusion about when properties are being used and when they aren't and is a bad example if used in other areas of the web application.

As an example of how it can be achieved, the code for an all-encompassing SearchAction is provided here:

```
public class SearchAction extends BaseAction {

    private String userInfo;
    private String eventTemplate;

    private List<Event> results;
    private EventService service;

    // all the search use cases' properties (quick search and advanced search)

    public void setEventService(EventService service) {
        this.service = service;
    }
```

```
        public List<Event> getResults() {
            return results;
        }

        public String getUserInfo() {
            return userInfo;
        }

        public String getEventTemplate() {
            return eventTemplate;
        }

        public String searchByTitle() {
            // the quick search logic
        }

        public String searchByLocationAndContestants() {
            // the advanced search logic
        }

    }
```

Summary

By now, you should have a good understanding of how to implement search functionality and how to display the results. Along with the search functionality, you saw techniques for creating focused actions, dividing up the view rendering into multiple JSPs, and creating generic JSP templates. You should also be comfortable modifying SiteMesh templates to provide additional user interface elements, as well as adding new links to the navigation panel.

During the development of the web application, the underlying business service implementation of the search functionality was intentionally not discussed because it's not relevant to accessing and rendering the results using Struts2. If you look into the provided code, you'll see that the underlying implementation is a simple Hibernate query. This is one of the many different ways to perform searching and, as indicated in the sidebar on pagination, there are many technology considerations, as well as nonfunctional considerations, that need to be taken into account when selecting an implementation.

From a purely technological standpoint, Hibernate or direct JDBC using SQL or stored procedures can be used, or a library such as Lucene can be integrated. Each of these methods has pros and cons. The important thing to remember, and the reason why this was not discussed earlier, is that the implementation details do not (and should not) have an impact on how the results are obtained and how they are rendered. Everything discussed in this chapter is applicable to any of these implementations.

CHAPTER 9

▪ ▪ ▪

Syndication and Integration

In the new era of Web 2.0 development, developing an island of functionality that users access from a web browser is no longer enough. Web sites are a main focus and a starting point but no longer the only means of accessing the information. Mashups are one example of an alternative way to access and use data from a web site; a mashup takes information from many different sources and combines it in ways that were not considered by the original developer. Google Maps is a great example of this technology. It is remarkably easy to take an API or RSS feed and combine it with a Google Map to provide a geographical representation of what was originally purely textual information. Further still, web sites have sprung up that are themselves mashups. The bulk of their functionality is simply aggregated content from other sites, with an overlay of social networking functionality to bring it all together.

In this chapter, you will learn about the different options to provide syndication and integration in web applications. First we'll discuss a RSS (Really Simple Syndication) feed, then consuming the RSS feed to create a mashup, and finally providing a REST (Representational State Transfer) style web service to access data.

Caution Before the code in this chapter can be run, several artifacts need to be installed into the local Maven2 repository. The instructions on how to install the required artifacts can be found in the section "Configuration for the GeoRSS Module."

The Use Case

This chapter has only one use case: *Publish Event Information*. The event information that has been entered by users should be available externally, as well as through the web application. By exposing event details to a wider audience and beyond the boundaries of our original site, more people will be exposed to our service. In turn, this has the possibility to bring more people to our web application.

To implement this use case, you will first implement an RSS feed. Additionally, a RESTful web service will be developed to provide another integration option for the web application.

Implementing RSS

The first style of syndication being implemented is RSS (Really Simple Syndication), more specifically RSS version 2.0.

RSS was first available in 1999 in the "My Netscape" portal and was the first syndication technology to gain widespread acceptance and use. Since then, the acronym RSS has several different interpretations depending on the version:

- *RSS 2.0*: Really Simple Syndication.

- *RSS 1.0 & 0.90*: RDF (Resource Description Framework) Site Summary.

- *RSS 0.91*: Rich Site Summary.

At its core, RSS is XML, where each different version of RSS has a slightly different DTD or XML Schema. Here is an example of RSS 2.0 source that comes from a feed on the Apache Software Foundation's site:

```
<?xml version="1.0" encoding="UTF-8"?>
<rss version="2.0">

  <channel>

    <title>Apache Software Foundation Struts2 RSS Feed</title>
    <link>http://cwiki.apache.org/confluence</link>
    <description>
      The 5 most recent creations of or modifications to pages,
      blogposts, mails, comments, attachments less than 200.0 days
      old in space Apache Struts 2 Wiki.
    </description>

    <item>
      <title>Articles and press (updated)</title>
      <link>
        http://cwiki.apache.org/confluence/display/S2WIKI/Articles+and+press
      </link>
      <description>&lt;div id="PageContent"&gt; …</description>
      <pubDate>Thu, 14 Jun 2007 15:04:43 GMT</pubDate>
      <guid>
          http://cwiki.apache.org/confluence/display/S2WIKI/
            Projects+Using+WebWork+or+Struts2</guid>
    </item>

    <item>
      <title>Companies that provide Struts 2 support (updated)</title>
      <link>
        http://cwiki.apache.org/confluence/display/S2WIKI/Companies+that
          +provide+Struts+2+support
```

```
    </link>
    <description>&lt;div id="PageContent"&gt; …</description>
    <pubDate>Sun, 27 May 2007 01:27:04 GMT</pubDate>
    <guid>
      http://cwiki.apache.org/confluence/display/S2WIKI/
        Companies+that+provide+Struts+2+support</guid>
  </item>

  …

  </channel>
</rss>
```

Basically an RSS feed has a `channel`. A `channel` has basic information that includes `title`, `link`, and `description`, as well as a list of `item` elements. The `item` elements provide the detailed information, which includes the same elements as the `channel` (`title`, `link`, and `description`) and additional fields for `pubDate` and `guid`. These are not the only elements available, but they are the required elements. More information can be obtained from the RSS specification.

■**Note** The RSS 2.0 specification can be obtained at `http://www.rssboard.org/rss-specification`; here you will find an extensive list of the optional elements not included in this example.

In Chapter 8, functionality was developed to retrieve a list of events and render the results in HTML. The same functionality can be reused here; however, to render RSS rather than HTML, the result format needs to be changed. The chosen option for rendering RSS is a new result type. Using a new result type allows any action that contains a list of `Event` objects to be turned into a RSS feed quickly and easily.

To generate the correct XML for the RSS feed, the Rome library will be used. Rome is an open source library that supports all of the RSS version formats, as well as Atom.

■**Note** Atom is a concurring standard with RSS and provides a complete publishing protocol that is HTTP-based. It is also an IETF (Internet Engineering Task Force) standard, RFC 4287 (`http://www.ietf.org/rfc/rfc4287.txt`). A good reference for the differences between the RSS and Atom protocols can be found in the Wikipedia at `http://en.wikipedia.org/wiki/Atom_%28standard%29`.

As well as creating feeds, Rome provides functionality to read feeds, aggregate feeds, and convert between different feed formats. Most importantly, Rome allows you to interact with the feed using Java objects rather than the raw XML. Figure 9-1 shows an example of the completed RSS result type displaying event information in a browser.

■**Tip** More information on the Rome library can be obtained from `https://rome.dev.java.net`.

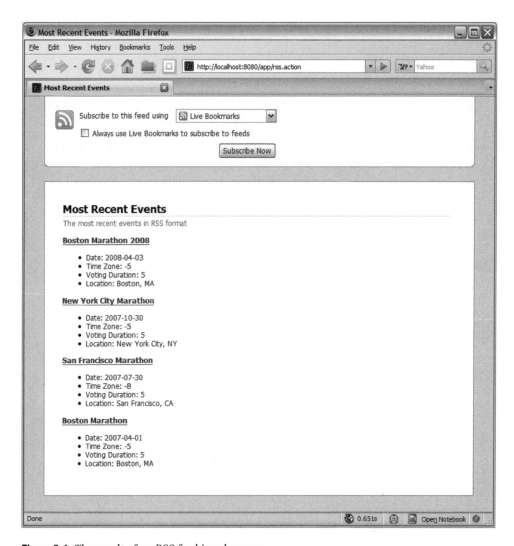

Figure 9-1. *The result of an RSS feed in a browser*

The Rome JAR files are included in the application by adding the following dependency to the Maven `pom.xml` configuration file:

```
<dependency>
    <groupId>rome</groupId>
    <artifactId>rome</artifactId>
    <version>0.9</version>
</dependency>
```

Results and Result Types

In previous chapters, you have learned how to use existing Struts2 result types. Now you'll learn how to implement a new result type. The basic implementation is easy; simply implement the Result interface.

```
public interface Result extends Serializable {

    public void execute(ActionInvocation invocation) throws Exception;
}
```

When the result is configured for an action, the execute() method is invoked to generate the final outcome that is returned to the user.

As you can see, result types are very similar to actions in that a result is executed (by a provided execute() method). In the dispatcher, velocity, and freemarker results, the outcome is returning HTML to the user, but there are other options. The redirect and redirectAction results forward the user to a different URL or action, the stream result streams data directly to the browser using a specific MIME type, and the httpheader result can modify the HTTP headers in the response.

Result types are also similar to interceptors in that all the information that is needed to execute must be obtained from the ActionInvocation object. This makes results slightly different from actions, which can gain access to additional objects from the executing environment via dependency injection. (Although objects cannot be injected, parameters that are specified in the result configuration are injected into setter on the result type.)

Configuring Result Types

Most of the actions previously developed have been configured via annotations. The same approach could be taken for configuring the action using the new RSS result type: create a new action (a copy, because an action already exists with the same functionality) and configure it with the RSS result type annotation. However, this means that exactly the same code is required with the only difference being a different result annotation.

Because the action class has already been developed, all that is needed is a different configuration. By providing a new action configuration in the struts.xml configuration file, a new URL can be used to invoke the same action class, and a different result type can be used in rendering the result.

There are two elements in configuring a new result type. The first is declaring the implementation class of the new result type, along with the unique name that will be used to specify the result type in the action's configuration. This is done at the package level, before the actions are configured. The name attribute specifies the unique name to use in further configuration, and the class attribute specifies the class name of the new result type:

```
<struts>

  <package name="home-package" extends="struts-default" namespace="/">

    <result-types>
      <result-type name="eventRSS" class="com.fdar.apress.s2.util.RssEventResult" />
    </result-types>

    ...

  </package>

  ...

</struts>
```

Next, the action needs to be configured. The action name feed (corresponding to the
http://localhost:8080/app/feed.action URL) is used and, as discussed, reuses the
ShowRecentEventsAction class. This class expects a "number" value to be specified, which is
achieved using the param tag.

Lastly, the result configuration is added to the action configuration. As usual, the name
attribute specifies which result from the invoked action method this configuration applies to.
The type attribute matches the unique name configured in the name attribute of the
result-type tag. Enclosed in the result tag is another param tag, specifying a parameter name
of inputName with a value of results. Just as the first param tag set a value on the action class,
this param tag sets a value on the result type. The action class has a method called
getResults(), which returns a list of the found events, so this parameter tells the result type
which property contains the list of events.

■Note In Chapter 5, the StreamResult class was configured using annotations and also used a parameter inputName to specify where to obtain the data to use in rendering the result. This configuration is exactly
the same; the only difference is that XML is used for configuration rather than annotations.

```
<struts>

    <package name="home-package" extends="struts-default" namespace="/">

        ...

        <action name="feed"
                class="com.fdar.apress.s2.actions.search.ShowRecentEventsAction" >
            <param name="number">10</param>
            <result name="success" type="eventRSS" >
                <param name="inputName">results</param>
```

```
            </result>
        </action>
    </package>

    …


</struts>
```

In the XML format for RSS, recall that channel information was applied to all the item elements. Because the action previously developed only provides the items, there needs to be a way to specify the channel's title, link, and description fields. These values are added as parameters to the result configuration.

Finally, because the Rome library can handle different versions of RSS, a feedType parameter is added. The final configuration for the action becomes the following:

```
<action name="rss"
        class="com.fdar.apress.s2.actions.search.ShowRecentEventsAction" >
    <param name="number">10</param>
    <result name="success" type="eventRSS" >
        <param name="inputName">results</param>
        <param name="feedType">rss_2.0</param>
        <param name="title">Most Recent Events</param>
        <param name="link">http://localhost:8080/app/rss.action</param>
        <param name="description">The most recent events in RSS format</param>
    </result>
</action>
```

Implementing the RSS Result Type

With the configuration known, you should already have a good idea of what the result type code should be. For each of the param tag properties (inputName, feedType, title, link, and description), there needs to be a setter method, some of which provide default values. So the RSS result type class, which has been named RssEventResult, starts off as the following:

```
public class RssEventResult implements Result {

    private String inputName = "inputList";
    private String feedType = "rss_2.0";

    private String title;
    private String link;
    private String description;

    public void setInputName(String inputName) {
        this.inputName = inputName;
    }
}
```

```
        public void setFeedType(String feedType) {
            this.feedType = feedType;
        }

        public void setTitle(String title) {
            this.title = title;
        }

        public void setLink(String link) {
            this.link = link;
        }

        public void setDescription(String description) {
            this.description = description;
        }

        public void execute(ActionInvocation invocation) throws Exception {

            // execution logic here
        }
}
```

Next, the execute() method needs to be implemented. The implementation follows the same steps needed for any result type that is writing data to the response stream:

1. Obtain the HttpServletResponse object from the actions execution context.

2. Set the content type on the response.

3. Obtain the data to process, most likely from the Value Stack (which in turn accesses the property from the previously executed action).

4. Write the content to the response.

5. Flush and close the response output stream.

To write content to the response output stream, a SyndFeedOutput object is created, and the RSS result is generated by calling the output() method. The parameters for the output() method are a SyndFeed object and the stream to write the result to (the response output stream). To create a SyndFeed object, a new createFeed() method is used. Here is the code for the execute() method of the result type:

```
public class RssEventResult implements Result {

    private static final String MIME_TYPE = "application/xml";

    ...

    public void execute(ActionInvocation invocation) throws Exception {
```

```
    HttpServletResponse response =
        (HttpServletResponse) invocation.getInvocationContext()
            .get(StrutsStatics.HTTP_RESPONSE);
    response.setContentType(MIME_TYPE);

    List<Event> events =
        (List<Event>) invocation.getStack().findValue(inputName);

    try {

        SyndFeedOutput feedOutput = new SyndFeedOutput();
        feedOutput.output(
            createFeed(events,feedType,(TextProvider)invocation.getAction()),
            response.getWriter());
        response.getWriter().flush();

    } finally {
        if( response.getWriter() != null ) {
            response.getWriter().close();
        }
    }

  }

  ...

}
```

The last step is to create the actual feed content, which is performed in the createFeed() method. Rome allows you to create the feed items using these objects: SyndFeedImpl, SyndEntryImpl, and SyndContentImpl. In total, three new methods are created for setting the correct data on the feed objects:

- createFeed(): Sets the channel information.

- createEntry(): Sets the item information.

- createDescription(): Creates the description or the content of the feed entry.

Each of the implementations should be straightforward, either directly setting known data on the objects or creating HTML content (in the case of the description). The only exception is the link field. A link should provide a URL to view more information about the entry, and so the code creates a URL (using the base URL provided by the channel's link attribute in the result configuration) with the form http://localhost:8080/app/api/event/ 123 (where 123 is the ID of the item's event, event is the action name, and the package name is api).

Note The format of the URL may look a little strange if you haven't encountered RESTful URLs before. For the moment, only the format of the URL is important—that it refers to an event with an id of "123". A non-RESTful URL for the same event (if the action existed and was mapped) would be http://localhost:8080/app/api/viewEvent.action?id=123. RESTful URLs are covered later in this chapter.

```
protected SyndFeed createFeed(
        List<Event> events,String feedType, TextProvider textProvider)
        throws IOException,FeedException {

    SyndFeed feed = new SyndFeedImpl();
    feed.setFeedType(feedType);

    feed.setTitle(title);
    feed.setLink(link);
    feed.setDescription(description);

    List entries = new ArrayList();
    for( Event next: events ) {
        entries.add( createEntry(next,textProvider) );
    }

    feed.setEntries(entries);
    return feed;
}

private SyndEntry createEntry(Event event, TextProvider textProvider) {

    SyndEntry entry = new SyndEntryImpl();
    entry.setTitle(event.getName());
    entry.setLink(
        link.substring(0,link.lastIndexOf("/")+1)+"api/event/"+event.getId());
    entry.setPublishedDate(event.getStartTime());

    SyndContent description = new SyndContentImpl();
    description.setType("text/html");
    description.setValue(createDescription(event,textProvider));
    entry.setDescription(description);
```

```java
        return entry;
    }

    private String createDescription(Event event, TextProvider textProvider) {

        DateFormat df = new SimpleDateFormat("yyyy-MM-dd");
        StringBuilder sb = new StringBuilder();

        sb.append("<ul>");
        sb.append("<li>")
                .append(textProvider.getText("event.startDate"))
                .append(": ")
                .append(df.format(event.getStartTime()))
                .append("</li>");
        sb.append("<li>")
                .append(textProvider.getText("event.timeZoneOffset"))
                .append(": ")
                .append(event.getTimeZoneOffset())
                .append("</li>");
        sb.append("<li>")
                .append(textProvider.getText("event.duration"))
                .append(": ")
                .append(event.getDuration())
                .append("</li>");
        sb.append("<li>")
                .append(textProvider.getText("event.location"))
                .append(": ")
                .append(event.getLocation().getCity())
                .append(", ")
                .append(event.getLocation().getState())
                .append("</li>");
        sb.append("</ul>");

        return sb.toString();
    }
```

CHANGING THE FEED FORMAT

To change the format of the RSS feed, the `RssEventResult` class could be subclassed, and any of the `createFeed()`, `createEntry()`, or `createDescription()` methods overloaded. This method is not as easily reusable as the method described for lists in Chapter 8; however, it is also much more likely that you will be changing, updating, or displaying the event information in different HTML formats before the RSS description format changes.

If you do have a case for changing the format often, or perhaps even specifying user-specific formats, the same technique can be used as in Chapter 8. There are several ways to achieve the results:

- Remove the formatting methods from the result type, and instead use a specialized formatter object (called via a factory) to separate the result type code from the formatting code.

- Use a regular dispatcher result type (that calls a JSP template) that generates the RSS format in the JSP template. The JSP templates can then use all the Struts2 tags, including the `component` tag.

- Use a Freemarker or Velocity result type, which generates the RSS format. For this scenario, a templating language is a better choice than JSPs because they provide built-in control structures (without needing additional external libraries, that is, tags), which are more efficient. Additionally, maps can be used to pass information from the action to the template to make the template more generic. Although the same can be achieved in JSPs with tags, the resulting code is more cryptic to read.

From the second and third options, you should have guessed that instead of implementing a result type, the XML format of the RSS feed could have been manually coded. This is great for the easy XML formatting cases, but as soon as the XML becomes complex (especially when combining several different namespaces), using a specialized library and creating a custom result type is by far the easiest solution.

Implementing an Atom Feed

Now that the RSS feed functionality has been developed, extending it to create an Atom feed is trivial. In fact, the only change required is to modify the value of the `feedType` parameter from `rss_2.0` to `atom_0.3` in the action's configuration. This value can be any feed type supported by the Rome library. When new feed types are added to Rome, all that is required for the application to support the new type is to update the Rome JAR file and to change the value to the new type.

To provide both an RSS and Atom feed, using the same action, the following configuration can be added to the `struts.xml` configuration file. The feeds can then be accessed with the URLs `http://localhost:8080/app/rss.action` and `http://localhost:8080/app/atom.action`, respectively.

```
<struts>

    <package name="home-package" extends="struts-default" namespace="/">

        ...

        <action name="rss"
                class="com.fdar.apress.s2.actions.search.ShowRecentEventsAction" >
            <param name="number">10</param>
            <result name="success" type="eventRSS" >
                <param name="feedType">rss_2.0</param>
                <param name="inputName">results</param>
            </result>
        </action>

        <action name="atom"
                class="com.fdar.apress.s2.actions.search.ShowRecentEventsAction" >
            <param name="number">10</param>
            <result name="success" type="eventRSS" >
                <param name="feedType">atom_0.3</param>
                <param name="inputName">results</param>
            </result>
        </action>


    ...

</struts>
```

If you implemented a JSP template, Freemarker template, or Velocity template with hand-coded RSS, making the change to support the Atom protocol would not have been as easy.

Consuming the RSS Feed with a Mashup

Having the RSS feed is one thing, but it isn't useful until someone consumes it. To test that the event location RSS feed provides enough data, as well as the correct data, the next step is to consume the feed. To make the code more interesting, instead of using a test case, a mashup will be implemented using the RSS feeds and Google Maps to visualize the location of the events provided.

To visually display the location of the events on a map, two things need to occur:

1. The physical address for the event entered by the user needs to be geo-coded (a fancy way of saying that the latitude and longitude needs to be found for a street address).

2. The geo-coded location information needs to be added to the RSS feed, along with the event information.

An advantage of using Rome is that it provides a plug-in system that allows developers to create modules for encoding and decoding data that is not part of the core RSS standard. This allows new content types to be added into existing feeds, for the new data to be consistently and properly formatted, and for the data to be placed into the correct XML namespaces.

■**Tip** The full list of plug-in modules for Rome can be found at `http://wiki.java.net/bin/view/Javawsxml/RomeModules`.

For describing geographic information, there is a GeoRSS standard. If you were to add the necessary changes to the previous RSS feeds source, the outcome would be the following:

```
<rss xmlns:content="http://purl.org/rss/1.0/modules/content/"
     xmlns:georss="http://www.georss.org/georss"
     xmlns:taxo="http://purl.org/rss/1.0/modules/taxonomy/"
     xmlns:rdf="http://www.w3.org/1999/02/22-rdf-syntax-ns#"
     xmlns:geo="http://www.w3.org/2003/01/geo/wgs84_pos#"
     xmlns:dc="http://purl.org/dc/elements/1.1/"
     xmlns:gml="http://www.opengis.net/gml" version="2.0">
  <channel>
    <title>Most Recent Events</title>
    <link>http://localhost:8080/app/rss.action</link>
    <description>The most recent events in RSS format</description>
    <item>
      <title>Boston Marathon 2008</title>
      <link>http://localhost:8080/app/api/event/3</link>
      <description>…</description>
      <pubDate>Thu, 03 Apr 2008 13:00:00 GMT</pubDate>
      <guid>http://localhost:8080/app/api/event/3</guid>
      <dc:date>2008-04-03T13:00:00Z</dc:date>
      <geo:lat>42.35864</geo:lat>
      <geo:long>-71.05665</geo:long>
    </item>

    …

  </channel>
</rss>
```

There is only one change to the XML, which consists of two new tags—geo:lat and geo:long—to convey the latitude and longitude, respectively. To support the geo namespace, the rss tag provides additional namespace configuration.

■Tip More information on the GeoRSS format can be found at `http://georss.org`. Documentation for the Rome module can be found at `http://georss.geonames.org`.

Configuring the GeoRSS Module

At the moment, the GeoRSS module is not hosted on a Maven repository. This means that before the code can be used, it needs to be installed in your local repository.

To install locally, first download the file from `http://georss.geonames.org/georss-rome-0.9.8.jar`. Once downloaded, use the following Maven command to install the JAR file:

```
mvn install:install-file -DgroupId=rome -DartifactId=georss-rome ➡
    -Dversion=0.9.8 -Dpackaging=jar -Dfile=georss-rome-0.9.8.jar
```

If you are not issuing the command from the directory that the file was downloaded to, simply add a path to the -Dfile property value. Now that the module is installed in your local repository, the Maven configuration can be added to the pom.xml configuration file.

```
<dependency>
    <groupId>rome</groupId>
    <artifactId>georss-rome</artifactId>
    <version>0.9.8</version>
</dependency>
```

Geo-Coding the Address and Creating the Feed Entry

To add the GeoRSS data, you first need to create an instance of the module, then add the required data, and finally add the module to the modules managed for the RSS entry. To abstract the creation of the location information from the core feed entry, a separate method has been created. In the createEntry() method, a call to the new method geoCodeLocation() is made:

```
private SyndEntry createEntry(Event event, TextProvider textProvider) {

    SyndEntry entry = new SyndEntryImpl();
    entry.setTitle(event.getName());
        entry.setLink(
            link.substring(0,link.lastIndexOf("/")+1)+"api/event/"+event.getId());
    entry.setPublishedDate(event.getStartTime());

    SyndContent description = new SyndContentImpl();
    description.setType("text/html");
    description.setValue(createDescription(event,textProvider));
    entry.setDescription(description);
```

```
    entry.getModules().add(geoCodeLocation(event));

    return entry;
}
```

That was the easy part. The geoCodeLocation() method contains the majority of the logic and is broken into two sections. Before you can add the latitude and longitude to the RSS feed, the geo-coded information needs to be obtained. In most cases, this involves making an external call to a service. Because Google Maps is being used in the mashup, Google will also be used to geo-code the address (but this doesn't have to be the case).

■**Caution**   Google can be used in the example because the number of calls to geo-code address information is going to be very small. If you are providing a service or application, there are a number of issues to consider. First is the issue of whether the service restrictions of a free service (such as Google's) are too restricting. When a service is free, typically a maximum number of calls can be made over a set period of time. More important are the legal issues. Are you using the service in a way that is allowed by the terms of service?

Before proceeding, some administrative tasks need to be completed. To use Google's service, you first need to visit http://www.google.com/apis/maps/signup.html to agree to the terms of use and to obtain a developer key. The only information that is needed is the URL of the calling page, and the value to use is http://localhost:8080/app/nodecorate. This particular directory will be discussed in a moment, but for the time being, enter this value and the resulting page should have at the very top an extremely large value for the key that consists of letters, numbers, and some punctuation marks.

With the API key in hand, the Google geo-coding service can be called. The service is invoked with the URL http://maps.google.com/maps/geo. Each parameter for the service is passed as a request attribute:

- q: The address to be geo-coded.

- key: The Google API key (that you just obtained).

- output: The format for the response from the service; the options are XML, CSV, JSON, and KML (KML is a specific XML format for geographic data that is more informative than GeoRSS).

The geoCodeLocation() method needs to create the necessary URL (substituting in the address provided from the Event object), open a connection to the server, request the URL (which is generated on the fly with the event's locations), and parse the results. Here's the first part of the method that performs these functions:

```
private GeoRSSModule geoCodeLocation(Event event) {

    // Geo-code the address
    StringBuilder sb = new StringBuilder()
        .append("http://maps.google.com/maps/geo?q=")
        .append(event.getLocation().getCity().replaceAll(" ","+"))
        .append(",")
        .append(event.getLocation().getState().replaceAll(" ","+"))
        .append("&output=csv")
        .append("&key={googleKey}");

    String[] data = null;
    try {
        HttpURLConnection url =
            new HttpURLConnection(new URL(sb.toString()),"maps.google.com",80);
        url.connect();
        BufferedReader br =
            new BufferedReader(new InputStreamReader(url.getInputStream()));
        String buffer = br.readLine();
        data = buffer.split(",");
    } catch (Exception e) {
        e.printStackTrace();
    }

    ...

}
```

■**Caution** Remember to replace the token {googleKey} with the real Google developer key value you obtained, otherwise, the result will not be as you expect.

A return format of CSV was chosen for simplicity in parsing. The result of the CSV format is one line of text that contains four comma-separated values: the status of the request, the accuracy provided, the latitude of the provided address, and the longitude of the provided address.

■**Note** In the example code, all the exception handling has been removed or simplified for explanation purposes. If you are developing a real application, remember to provide checks for the status, as well as logic to handle when the address cannot be geo-coded.

GEO-CODING STRATEGIES

Geo-coding the physical address to a latitude and longitude, as in the example, is probably not the best way for most applications to interact with the service. In fact, any lookup or external service should be treated the same.

When designing an application that provides an RSS feed or API as well as interacting with external services, the design of the interaction needs to be carefully considered. The implementation options, which are outlined in Table 9-1, need to be taken into account before selecting the final design.

Table 9-1. *Implementation Options for External Service Interaction*

Implementation Option	Description	Considerations
Client Side	The client needs to perform the geo-coding lookup for each address.	This option makes it harder to use the RSS feed or API for the consumer. If consumption is taking place in a browser client via JavaScript, there may be cross-site scripting (XSS) issues (code calling a different host than the one the page was loaded from) as well as other difficulties in parsing the contents to obtain the address information.
Server Side	The server adds the geo-coded address information to the RSS feed or API result.	This option provides the same functionality as the client-side option, only the work is done on the server and returned to the client in the RSS feed or API result. A new call is necessary for each address that needs to be geo-coded. Making an external HTTP call for each address introduces performance delays as well as possible failure points.
No Caching	Each address is geo-coded each time it is used.	The number of calls to the geo-coding service will be high (perhaps requiring a higher subscription level). Performance may also be a problem, especially in the case of results that are lists; each call is a new HTTP request, and a call for each element in the list needs to be performed before the result is returned to the caller.

Implementation Option	Description	Considerations
Runtime Caching	The module performing geo-coding calls manages a runtime cache that is reset when the module is no longer used.	Implementation of this caching style could be client side or server side. There will be a memory requirement to store the cached data, and if you have a clustered application server, there will most likely be a copy of the same information on each server in the cluster. (Clustered cache implementations are possible but nontrivial and complex pieces of code; it's usually just easier to keep duplicates on each server than implement the logic.) The number of calls to the geo-coding server will be reduced.
Database Caching	When the original address information is stored to the database, the geo-coding lookup is performed. To avoid additional external calls, there may be a local database table that is used to check whether the address is already known (most useful when only partial address information is being geo-coded, i.e., city and state).	There are several advantages to this method: a possible failure point (making HTTP calls to the geo-coding service) has been removed; the geo-coding lookup is performed at most once per address but may be performed less if partial addresses are used; there is no additional memory requirement to cache to the geo-coded information; and generating the RSS feed or API result will be faster and better performing because the data is all contained in the database and there are no external HTTP calls (especially problematic in list results). However, this is the most complex option to implement.

The other design question to consider is "how easy will it be to consume the RSS feed or API?" By pushing geo-coding (or other lookup service requests) to the consumer of the RSS feed or API, you are increasing the amount of development necessary to use your service. To drive adoption, the general rule is to make it as easy as possible for those that want to use the service. Hence, providing more information in the RSS feed or API (in the way of geo-coded information for the physical address) is the recommended approach.

Now that the result is parsed, the latitude and longitude values can be used to set a position for the entry. A new GeoRSSModule instance (that, as you have already seen, is added to the RSS entry object) is created and a position set using the latitude and longitude values. This is the second half of the geoCodeLocation() method's logic:

```
private GeoRSSModule geoCodeLocation(Event event) {

    ...

    double latitude = Double.parseDouble(data[2]);
    double longitude = Double.parseDouble(data[3]);

    // Add RSS GeoCoding
    GeoRSSModule geoRSSModule = new W3CGeoModuleImpl();
    Position pos = new Position(latitude,longitude);
    geoRSSModule.setPosition(pos);

    return geoRSSModule;
}
```

In this example, the GeoRSS module used the W3CGeoModuleImpl class implementation. There are two different implementations, each providing a different representation of the latitude and longitude. In the preceding example, the RSS feed output (for the item) is the following:

```
<geo:lat>40.71449</geo:lat>
<geo:long>-74.00713</geo:long>
```

The other option is the SimpleModuleImpl class, and the only change necessary to the preceding code example is the following:

```
GeoRSSModule geoRSSModule = new SimpleModuleImpl();
```

For the new implementation, the corresponding data is represented as the following:

```
<georss:point>40.71449 -74.00713</georss:point>
```

Depending on the intended feed usage, one representation may be preferred over the other. The W3CGeoModuleImpl implementation is used in the example because we expect that the client JavaScript code will need to access the values individually.

Implementing the Mashup Client

Now that the feed has been updated to provide geo-coded information, the last step is to create the JavaScript client that uses the feed information to map the event locations. When you applied for the Google developer key, the page that contained the key value also contained example code for creating a simple map. The client JavaScript code is based on the example with a couple of small additions.

The first step, after creating a GMap2 object for the HTML div tag that will contain the image, is to provide a center point and a zoom level. No specific position was selected but rather a point somewhere toward the center of the United States. This way, when a zoom value is applied (the second parameter in the setCenter() method call), the United States is centered. To allow the user to control navigation, a panning and zooming control is also added. Both of these features are enabled with the following code:

```
map.setCenter(new GLatLng(41.875696,-87.624207), 3);
map.addControl(new GLargeMapControl());
```

Next, the RSS feed needs to be downloaded so the location information can be accessed. Google provides a GDownloadUrl object that accepts a URL for input, and upon loading, calls a user provided function.

```
GDownloadUrl(
  "http://localhost:8080/app/rss.action", function(data, responseCode) {

  var xml = GXml.parse(data);
  var items = xml.documentElement.getElementsByTagName("item");

  ...

});
```

Now that the items to be plotted are known, all that is left is to iterate over them by creating the new marker and adding it to the map via the addOverlay() method. To create a marker for the position (as a GLatLng object) and a pop-up window for the marker (to make it easy just the title is used), use the following code:

```
for (var i = 0; i < items.length; i++) {
    var point = new GLatLng(
        parseFloat(GXml.value(items.item(i).getElementsByTagName("lat")[0])),
        parseFloat(GXml.value(items.item(i).getElementsByTagName("long")[0])));
    var title = GXml.value(items.item(i).getElementsByTagName("title")[0]);
    var marker = createMarker(point,title);
    map.addOverlay(marker);
}
```

Obtaining the value of an XML node gets a little complicated, but the individual steps are straightforward:

1. From the items collection, get the next item.

2. Get the specific tag in this node by its name (either lat, long, or title).

3. The return value is an array with one value, so select the zero index value.

4. Convert the attribute value to a string using the GXml.value() method.

The result of the final code, shown next, can be seen in Figure 9-2.

Caution Don't forget to replace the value token {googleKey} with your Google developer key!

```html
<html >
<head>
  <meta http-equiv="content-type" content="text/html; charset=utf-8"/>
  <title>Google Maps Mashup</title>
  <script src="http://maps.google.com/maps?file=api&amp;v=2&amp;key={googleKey}"
          type="text/javascript"></script>
  <script type="text/javascript">

  //<![CDATA[

  function load() {

    if (GBrowserIsCompatible()) {

      var map = new GMap2(document.getElementById("map"));
      map.setCenter(new GLatLng(41.875696,-87.624207), 11);
      map.setZoom(3);
      map.addControl(new GLargeMapControl());

      GDownloadUrl(
        "http://localhost:8080/app/rss.action", function(data, responseCode) {

        var xml = GXml.parse(data);
        var items = xml.documentElement.getElementsByTagName("item");

        for (var i = 0; i < items.length; i++) {
          var point = new GLatLng(
            parseFloat(GXml.value(items.item(i).getElementsByTagName("lat")[0])),
            parseFloat(GXml.value(items.item(i).getElementsByTagName("long")[0])));
          var title = GXml.value(items.item(i).getElementsByTagName("title")[0]);
          var marker = createMarker(point,title);
          map.addOverlay(marker);
        }
      });
    }
  }

  function createMarker(point,html) {
    var marker = new GMarker(point);
    GEvent.addListener(marker, "click", function() {
      marker.openInfoWindowHtml(html);
    });
    return marker;
  }

  //]]>
</script>
```

```
</head>
  <body onload="load()" onunload="GUnload()">
    <div id="map" style="width: 500px; height: 300px"></div>
  </body>
</html>
```

■Note The `//<![CDATA[` at the start of the JavaScript and the `//]]>` at the conclusion comes from the original example code provided by Google; they are the opening and closing delimiters for a CDATA section. CDATA is an XML directive that tells the XML parser that the contents contain character data, and hence contain no markup characters and can be ignored. When using XHTML (which is XML, and different from HTML which is SGML), enclosing JavaScript code in a CDATA section avoids parsing and potential issues in the browser.

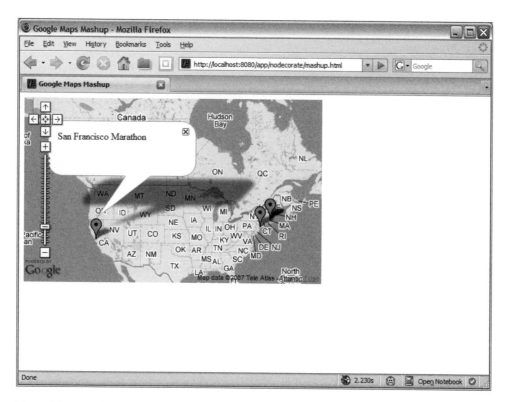

Figure 9-2. *A mashup showing the event locations on a map*

In the example code, this file can be found in the directory /nodecorate/mashup.html. It was placed in the nodecorate directory to avoid being decorated by SiteMesh.

Integrating a Map into the Home Page

With a stand-alone mashup completed, adding the same mashup to the home page is simple. The results can be seen in Figure 9-3.

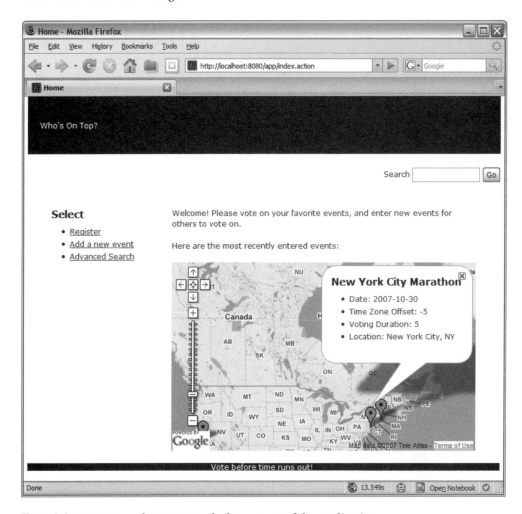

Figure 9-3. *An event mashup map on the home page of the application*

In fact, the only major change that is necessary is in the SiteMesh decorator. Google Maps uses the HTML body tag's attributes onload and onunload to initialize and clean up the JavaScript objects for the map. At the moment, the decorator doesn't use the values provided from the page being decorated. This is easily rectified; for onload, you use the following code to access the decorated page's value:

```
<decorator:getProperty property="body.onload"/>
```

The change to the decorator (from /WEB-INF/decorators/main.jsp) JSP then becomes the following:

```
<body id="page-home"
      onload="<decorator:getProperty property="body.onload"/>"
      onunload="<decorator:getProperty property="body.unonload"/>">

   …


</body>
```

For the index.jsp template, the changes are to replace the Struts2 action tag with an HTML div tag for the map to be rendered in and to add the JavaScript to format the map and render the markers (all of which was covered in the previous section).

To provide a little more information in the pop-up, the title value is bolded and combined with the description of the event:

```
var title = GXml.value(items.item(i).getElementsByTagName("title")[0]);
var contents = GXml.value(items.item(i).getElementsByTagName("description")[0]);
var marker = createMarker(point,"<h3>"+title+"</h3>"+contents);
```

Here is the new index.jsp template:

```
<head>
  <title><s:text name="home.title" /></title>

  <script src="http://maps.google.com/maps?file=api&amp;v=2&amp;key={googleKey}"
          type="text/javascript"></script>
  <script type="text/javascript">

  //<![CDATA[

  function load() {
    if (GBrowserIsCompatible()) {
      var map = new GMap2(document.getElementById("map"));
      map.setCenter(new GLatLng(41.875696,-87.624207), 3);
      map.addControl(new GLargeMapControl());

      GDownloadUrl("http://localhost:8080/app/rss.action",
        function(data, responseCode) {
          var xml = GXml.parse(data);
          var items = xml.documentElement.getElementsByTagName("item");

          for (var i = 0; i < items.length; i++) {
            var point = new GLatLng(
              parseFloat(GXml.value(items.item(i).getElementsByTagName("lat")[0])),
              parseFloat(GXml.value(items.item(i).getElementsByTagName("long")[0]))
            );
```

```
                    var title = GXml.value(items.item(i).getElementsByTagName("title")[0]);
                    var contents =
                      GXml.value(items.item(i).getElementsByTagName("description")[0]);
                    var marker = createMarker(point,"<h3>"+title+"</h3>"+contents);
                    map.addOverlay(marker);
                }
            });
        }
    }

    function createMarker(point,html) {
      var marker = new GMarker(point);
      GEvent.addListener(marker, "click", function() {
        marker.openInfoWindowHtml(html);
      });
      return marker;
    }

    //]]>
    </script>

</head>
<body onload="load()" onunload="GUnload()">

<p><s:text name="home.welcomeText"/></p>

<div>
    <p><s:text name="home.mostRecentTen"/></p>
    <div id="map" style="width: 500px; height: 300px"></div>
</div>

</body>
</html>
```

Implementing Web Services

Along with syndication, web services are the primary means of integrating web applications. Whereas syndication, especially RSS, provides an outgoing read-only information stream, web services allow other programs to interact by submitting data as well as requesting data. There are two types of web services: SOAP (Simple Object Access Protocol) and REST (Representational State Transfer).

SOAP Web Service: This style of web service is a form of RPC (Remote Procedure Call), where both the request and response of the call is XML. Although the calls are primarily transmitted over HTTP, the transport can be JMS, SMTP, or even FTP. SOAP-style web services use WSDL (Web Service Description Language) to define the API, may use UDDI (Universal Description Discovery and Integration) registries to find services, and can use a number of other W3C standards (such as WS-Security, WS-Reliability, WS-Addressing, WS-Transaction, etc.) for application-level cross-cutting concerns. All of this provides a complete and robust infrastructure for web services; however, for the majority of web applications, it is far too complex.

RESTful Web Service: On the other hand, RESTful web services are lightweight, primarily use HTTP, and focus around the concept of using URIs (Uniform Resource Identifiers) to identify integration points. To modify or access the state of the object, the HTTP methods POST, GET, PUT, and DELETE are used. These methods are synonymous with the database operations CREATE, READ, UPDATE, and DELETE (CRUD). It is important to remember that REST is an architectural style rather than a specific implementation.

You can easily think of RESTful web services as objects that actions are performed on. For SOAP web services, think of actions that are performed with parameters (that may or may not be objects).

■**Note** The Wikipedia is a great source for more information on both styles of web services. For more information on SOAP web services, the URL is http://en.wikipedia.org/wiki/SOAP, and for RESTful web services, the URL is http://en.wikipedia.org/wiki/Representational_State_Transfer.

INTEGRATING SOAP WEB SERVICES

Because the SOAP style of web services is RPC based, the integration point is a closer fit to the business services layer than the web layer. For that reason, they will not be covered in this book.

The usual configuration with web applications is a secondary HTTP access point (usually provided via a servlet), which is configured in the web.xml configuration file. Additional web service specific configuration is provided in its own configuration file. If you are using Spring or any of the mainstream application servers, the integration and configuration will be simpler.

Some of the open source projects that can be used are Apache Axis (http://ws.apache.org/axis/), Apache Axis2 (http://ws.apache.org/axis2/), or XFire from Codehaus (http://xfire.codehaus.org), which in the next version is merging with Celtix and becoming Apache CXF (http://incubator.apache.org/cxf).

In this section, a RESTful web service will be implemented.

Mapping URLs to Actions

In Struts2, an action mapper is responsible for determining the configuration for the incoming HTTP request. This is a configurable framework component, with the default implementation being the DefaultActionMapper class. For example, for the URL http://localhost:8080/app/event/list.action, the action mapper maps /event as the namespace (remember /app is the web application context) and list as the action, and uses .action as the action extension. But this doesn't have to be the case.

Several action mapper implementations are already configured in the struts-default.xml (the framework's default) configuration file:

```
<bean type="org.apache.struts2.dispatcher.mapper.ActionMapper" name="struts"
    class="org.apache.struts2.dispatcher.mapper.DefaultActionMapper" />
<bean type="org.apache.struts2.dispatcher.mapper.ActionMapper" name="composite"
    class="org.apache.struts2.dispatcher.mapper.CompositeActionMapper" />
<bean type="org.apache.struts2.dispatcher.mapper.ActionMapper" name="restful2"
    class="org.apache.struts2.dispatcher.mapper.Restful2ActionMapper" />
```

The composite mapper simply allows you to chain together several action mappers, and the restful2 mapper provides URL mapping to simulate RESTful web services. Table 9-2 outlines how the restful2 action mapper maps an action method (the method that is invoked to provide logic) to a URL and HTTP method.

■Note Yes, there is a restful action mapper as well that provides a more simplistic mapping and has been deprecated in favor of the restful2 action mapper.

Table 9-2. *Methods Corresponding to RESTful URIs*

Action Method Name Invoked	HTTP Method	Example URL	Description
index()	GET	/event/	A method is called to perform logic; usually this will return a list of results, in this case, event objects.
view()	GET	/event/3	Returns data on the event with a unique identifier of 3.
create()	POST	/event/	Information submitted to the URI is used to create a new event.
editNew()	GET	/event/new	Similar to create() but using a different HTTP method, this option is provided should you want to differentiate HTTP GET and POST calls.
update()	PUT	/event/3	Information submitted to the URI is used to update the event with a unique identifier of 3.
edit()	GET	/event/3!edit	Similar to update() but using a different HTTP method, this option is provided should you want to differentiate HTTP GET and POST calls.
remove()	DELETE	/event/3	The event with a unique identifier of 3 is removed.

To simulate the HTTP methods of PUT and DELETE (because HTML doesn't support them), there is an additional HTTP parameter __http_method. When used in a form, it will simulate the value provided:

```
<input type="hidden" name="__http_method" value="delete" />
```

■**Caution** In some of the URLs, there is a trailing /. This is important and, if missing, will not cause the expected method to be invoked.

Configuring Action Mappers

To configure a new action mapper, you'll need to change the constant struts.mapper.class in the struts.xml configuration file. Because the classes are already configured (in the struts-default.xml configuration file), only the unique name needs to be specified (rather than a fully qualified class name).

To provide a URL without an extension, the constant struts.action.extension also needs to be set to an empty value. There are two other properties that need to be set, each allowing for nonstandard Struts2 behavior to be overruled for RESTful URLs: struts.enable.SlashesInActionNames (determines whether the action name can include / characters, rather than using the character to differentiate between the namespace and action name) and struts.mapper.alwaysSelectFullNamespace (determines whether the namespace is everything before the last / character).

Following are the changes to the struts.xml configuration file:

```
<struts>

    <constant name="struts.enable.SlashesInActionNames" value="true" />
    <constant name="struts.mapper.alwaysSelectFullNamespace" value="false" />
    <constant name="struts.mapper.class" value="restful2" />
    <constant name="struts.action.extension" value="" />

    ...

</struts>
```

If you were to run the application, it would work correctly but not as required. The goal is to provide a specific package as a RESTful web service and not all the URLs in the application.

To achieve this, the composite action mapper is used. The configuration is basically the same as for the restful2 action mapper; the struts.action.extension property has been removed, the struts.mapper.class changed from restful2 to composite, and a new struts.mapper.composite property (which lists the action mappers in the order that they should be called) added. When using the composite action mapper, only when the first action mapper fails to return a mapping does the next action mapper in order get used (and so forth until the list is exhausted or a mapping returned).

```
<struts>

    <constant name="struts.enable.SlashesInActionNames" value="true" />
    <constant name="struts.mapper.alwaysSelectFullNamespace" value="false" />
    <constant name="struts.mapper.composite" value="struts,restful2" />
    <constant name="struts.mapper.class" value="composite" />


    ...

</struts>
```

■**Caution** If you are including the `struts.properties` file (which has priority over the more common `struts.xml` configuration file) for configuration in your project rather than exclusively using the `struts.xml` file, you must comment out the following line: `struts.mapper.class=org.apache.struts2.dispatcher.mapper.DefaultActionMapper`.

This configuration allows the existing web application to function correctly, but when a RESTful URL is needed, an `.action` extension is also required. The solution to the dilemma is to create a new custom action mapper.

Creating a Custom Action Mapper

When creating a custom action mapper, the `ActionMapper` interface must be implemented. This interface provides two methods: one that converts a URL to an action mapping, and another that converts the other way, from an action mapping to a URL.

```
public interface ActionMapper {

    ActionMapping getMapping(
        HttpServletRequest request, ConfigurationManager configManager);

    String getUriFromActionMapping(ActionMapping mapping);

}
```

The functionality required is that when this new action mapper is being used, the action's extension should be ignored. This way, the `DefaultActionMapper` uses the `.action` extension for the existing functionality (the first mapper checked). When it gets to the new custom action mapper (`FallbackRestful2ActionMapper`), we no longer care about the action extension, and it needs to be ignored to process the RESTful URLs correctly.

By reviewing the Struts2 code for the `DefaultActionMapper`, you'll notice a `dropExtension()` method, which is exactly what is needed:

```
String dropExtension(String name) {
    return name;
}
```

This solution works if only action URLs are passed to the action mapper. As it turns out, all nonaction URLs are passed as well, including HTML, CSS, and JavaScript files. To avoid exceptions being thrown, the dropExtension() method needs to determine if the extension provided is a known extension and, if so, return null (which prevents further Struts2 processing). The final method implementation and the class so far becomes the following:

```
public class FallbackRestful2ActionMapper extends Restful2ActionMapper {

    List<String> knownExtenstions =
        new ArrayList() {{ add("css"); add("html"); add("js"); }};

    String dropExtension(String name) {
        Iterator it = knownExtenstions.iterator();
        while (it.hasNext()) {
            String extension = "." + (String) it.next();
            if (name.endsWith(extension)) {
                return null;
            }
        }
        return name;
    }

}
```

■Note Because we are accessing package-scoped methods of the super classes, the FallbackRestful2ActionMapper class needs to be placed in the same package as the super classes: the org.apache.struts2.dispatcher.mapper package.

The final caveat is that the dropExtension() method is not an abstract method and, hence, the super classes of FallbackRestful2ActionMapper call the dropExtension() method at a local level. This means the getMapping() method also needs to be implemented and is a combination of the getMapping() method from the DefaultActionMapper and the Restful2ActionMapper. Here is the complete class:

```
public class FallbackRestful2ActionMapper extends Restful2ActionMapper {

    List<String> knownExtenstions =
        new ArrayList() {{ add("css"); add("html"); add("js"); }};
```

```java
String dropExtension(String name) {
    Iterator it = knownExtenstions.iterator();
    while (it.hasNext()) {
        String extension = "." + (String) it.next();
        if (name.endsWith(extension)) {
            return null;
        }
    }
    return name;
}

public ActionMapping getMapping(
        HttpServletRequest request, ConfigurationManager configManager) {

    // from DefaultActionMapper
    ActionMapping mapping = new ActionMapping();
    String uri = getUri(request);

    uri = dropExtension(uri);
    if (uri == null) {
        return null;
    }

    parseNameAndNamespace(uri, mapping, configManager);
    handleSpecialParameters(request, mapping);

    if ( mapping == null || mapping.getName() == null) {
        return null;
    }

    // from Restful2ActionMapper
    String actionName = mapping.getName();

    if (actionName != null && actionName.length() > 0) {
        int lastSlashPos = actionName.lastIndexOf('/');

        // try to guess using REST-style patterns
        if (mapping.getMethod() == null) {

            if (lastSlashPos == actionName.length() -1) {

                // Index, e.g., foo/
                if (isGet(request)) {
                    mapping.setMethod("index");
```

```
        // Creating a new entry on POST, e.g., foo/
        } else if (isPost(request)) {
            mapping.setMethod("create");
        }

    } else if (lastSlashPos > -1) {
        String id = actionName.substring(lastSlashPos+1);

        // Viewing the form to create a new item, e.g., foo/new
        if (isGet(request) && "new".equals(id)) {
            mapping.setMethod("editNew");

        // Viewing an item, e.g., foo/1
        } else if (isGet(request)) {
            mapping.setMethod("view");

        // Removing an item, e.g., foo/1
        } else if (isDelete(request)) {
            mapping.setMethod("remove");

        // Updating an item, e.g., foo/1
        }  else if (isPut(request)) {
            mapping.setMethod("update");
        }

        if (getIdParameterName() != null) {
            if (mapping.getParams() == null) {
                mapping.setParams(new HashMap());
            }
            mapping.getParams().put(getIdParameterName(), id);
        }
    }

    if (getIdParameterName() != null && lastSlashPos > -1) {
        actionName = actionName.substring(0, lastSlashPos);
    }
}

// Try to determine parameters from the URL before the action name
int actionSlashPos = actionName.lastIndexOf('/', lastSlashPos - 1);
if (actionSlashPos > 0 && actionSlashPos < lastSlashPos) {
    String params = actionName.substring(0, actionSlashPos);
    HashMap<String,String> parameters = new HashMap<String,String>();
```

```
            try {
                StringTokenizer st = new StringTokenizer(params, "/");
                boolean isNameTok = true;
                String paramName = null;
                String paramValue;

                while (st.hasMoreTokens()) {
                    if (isNameTok) {
                        paramName = URLDecoder.decode(st.nextToken(), "UTF-8");
                        isNameTok = false;
                    } else {
                        paramValue = URLDecoder.decode(st.nextToken(), "UTF-8");

                        if ((paramName != null) && (paramName.length() > 0)) {
                            parameters.put(paramName, paramValue);
                        }

                        isNameTok = true;
                    }
                }
                if (parameters.size() > 0) {
                    if (mapping.getParams() == null) {
                        mapping.setParams(new HashMap());
                    }
                    mapping.getParams().putAll(parameters);
                }
            } catch (Exception e) {
                LOG.warn(e);
            }
            mapping.setName(actionName.substring(actionSlashPos+1));
        }
    }

    return mapping;
}

}
```

Configuring the action mapper is the same as configuring a Struts2-provided action mapper and occurs in the struts.xml configuration file. First is a new bean configuration for the new custom FallbackRestful2ActionMapper action mapper type; then a new struts.mapper.idParameterName property configuring the action property id as the unique identifier for the RESTful calls (i.e., the URL /event/2 will call setId(2) on the action being invoked); and finally, the four property configurations that you saw previously, specifying the fallback action mapper name rather than the restful2 action mapper name. Following is the complete configuration:

```
<bean type="org.apache.struts2.dispatcher.mapper.ActionMapper" name="fallback"
    class="org.apache.struts2.dispatcher.mapper.FallbackRestful2ActionMapper" />

<constant name="struts.mapper.idParameterName" value="id" />

<constant name="struts.enable.SlashesInActionNames" value="true" />
<constant name="struts.mapper.alwaysSelectFullNamespace" value="false" />
<constant name="struts.mapper.composite" value="struts,fallback" />
<constant name="struts.mapper.class" value="composite" />
```

Implementing the RESTful Web Service Logic

All that is left is to implement the action, which provides the logic to perform the RESTful functions that are being requested, and to then configure the action.

To compartmentalize the web service calls, a new api package will be created with a corresponding /api namespace. A RESTful web service is being implemented to access the Event object, so an action configuration is required. The action should look familiar except for the action name, which is event/* rather than event. This mapping allows for the unique identifier value to be specified at the end of the URL; the property of the action (for the unique identifier) has been previously configured using the struts.mapper.idParameterName constant.

```
<package name="api" namespace="/api" extends="base-package">

    <action name="event/*" class="com.fdar.apress.s2.actions.api.EventAction">
        <result name="list">/WEB-INF/jsp/api/eventList.jsp</result>
        <result name="single">/WEB-INF/jsp/api/event.jsp</result>
    </action>

</package>
```

From the configuration, you'll notice that only two methods are being implemented, and from the names, you should be able to guess that one will return a list of events and the other a single event. The URL http://localhost:8080/app/api/event/ returns a list of events and invokes the index() method, and the URL http://localhost:8080/app/api/event/2 invokes the view() method. The resulting action is the following:

```
public class EventAction extends BaseAction
        implements ModelDriven<Event>, Preparable {

    private List<Event> results;
    private EventService service;

    private long id;
    private Event event = new Event();

    public void setEventService(EventService service) {
        this.service = service;
    }
```

```java
    public void setId(long id) {
        this.id = id;
    }

    public long getId() {
        return id;
    }

    public Event getModel() {
        return event;
    }

    public List<Event> getResults() {
        return results;
    }

    public void prepare() throws Exception {
        if(id!=0) {
            event = service.findById(id);
        }
    }

    public String view() {
        return "single";
    }

    public String index() {
        results = service.findAllEvents(10);
        return "list";
    }
}
```

■**Note** When a single event is to be viewed, the work is performed in the `prepare()` method rather than the `view()` method. This is because in the `paramPrepareParamsStack` interceptor stack the `prepare` interceptor is before the `modelDriven` interceptor (which only places the model on the Value Stack if it is not `null`), and by using the `prepare()` method, the `event` object is initialized. Alternatively, all the work could have been done in the `view()` method, but then each property in the JSP template would need to be prefixed with `model.` to reference an initialized object instance.

The final part of implementing a RESTful web service is to implement the JSP templates. The `eventList.jsp` template reuses the `listEvents-partial.jsp` template from searching. Because the `listEvents-partial.jsp` template doesn't provide any of the high-level HTML tags, the `eventList.jsp` template needs to provide them:

```
<html>

<head>
    <title><s:text name="api.eventList.title" /></title>
</head>
<body>

<s:include value="/WEB-INF/jsp/search/listEvents-partial.jsp" />

</body>
</html>
```

The new event.jsp template provides all the information about the event. In this example, it is formatted as HTML. This corresponds to the link that we set in the RSS feed item at the beginning of this chapter so that when the user clicks on the feed link (say /api/event/2), it will render event information in a user-friendly way. Here is the JSP template:

```
<head>
    <title><s:text name="api.event.title" /></title>
</head>
<body>

<table>
    <tr><td colspan="2"><h1><s:text name="event.title" /></h1></td></tr>
    <tr>
        <td><s:text name="event.name" /></td>
        <td><s:property value="name"/></td>
    </tr>
    <tr>
        <td><s:text name="event.startTime" /></td>
        <td><s:date name="startTime" format="MM/dd/yyyy hh:mm"/></td>
    </tr>
    <tr>
        <td><s:text name="event.votingStartTime" /></td>
        <td><s:date name="votingStartTime" format="MM/dd/yyyy hh:mm"/></td>
    </tr>
    <tr>
        <td><s:text name="event.duration" /></td>
        <td><s:property value="duration"/></td>
    </tr>
    <tr>
        <td><s:text name="event.timeZoneOffset" /></td>
        <td><s:property value="timeZoneOffset"/></td>
    </tr>
    <tr>
        <td><s:text name="event.progress" /></td>
        <td><s:property value="status"/></td>
    </tr>
```

```
<tr>
    <td colspan="2"><br/><h3><s:text name="address.title" /></h3></td>
</tr>
<s:if test="location.class.name.endsWith('.Address')">
    <tr>
        <td><s:text name="address.name"/></td>
        <td><s:property value="location.name" /></td>
    </tr>
    <tr>
        <td><s:text name="address.address"/></td>
        <td><s:property value="location.address" /></td>
    </tr>
    <tr>
        <td><s:text name="address.city"/></td>
        <td><s:property value="location.city" /></td>
    </tr>
    <tr>
        <td><s:text name="address.state"/></td>
        <td><s:property value="location.state" /></td>
    </tr>
    <tr>
        <td><s:text name="address.zipcode"/></td>
        <td><s:property value="location.zipcode" /></td>
    </tr>
</s:if>
<s:else>
    <tr>
        <td><s:text name="broadcast.name"/></td>
        <td><s:property value="location.name" /></td>
    </tr>
    <tr>
        <td><s:text name="broadcast.city"/></td>
        <td><s:property value="location.city" /></td>
    </tr>
    <tr>
        <td><s:text name="broadcast.state"/></td>
        <td><s:property value="location.state" /></td>
    </tr>
    <tr>
        <td><s:text name="broadcast.network"/></td>
        <td><s:property value="location.network" /></td>
    </tr>
    <tr>
        <td><s:text name="broadcast.stationIdentifier"/></td>
        <td><s:property value="location.stationIdentifier" /></td>
    </tr>
</s:else>
```

```
<tr>
    <td colspan="2"><br/><h3><s:text name="contestant.title" /></h3></td>
</tr>
<s:iterator value="options" >
    <tr>
        <td colspan="2"><s:property value="name" /> -
            <s:property value="description" /> </td>
    </tr>
</s:iterator>

</table>

</body>
</html>
```

Although HTML is user friendly, it isn't the best format for the data when interacting programmatically. The best format in this case is XML (although JSON, JSONP, and other formats are gaining popularity also). You have several options for creating XML in a Struts2 application: use the xslt result type (especially if you are familiar with XSLT); create the XML directly in the action (using a library such as XStream from Codehaus); or use the resulting JSP/Freemarker/Velocity template to generate XML. Because we've used JSPs until now, the final option of using JSP templates is the approach we'll take.

Generating XML in the JSP template is very easy. In the action configuration, the result value is changed from event.jsp to event-xml.jsp, and then the JSP template is created. The JSP can use any of the Struts2 tags to obtain data, manipulate data, or format data; the only difference is that the JSP is surrounded by XML tags rather than HTML tags. Following is the JSP for creating XML:

```
<%@ page contentType="text/html; charset=UTF-8" %>
<%@ taglib uri="/struts-tags" prefix="s" %>

<?xml version="1.0" encoding="UTF-8"?>

<event id="<s:property value="id"/>">

    <name><s:property value="name"/></name>
    <startTime><s:date name="startTime" format="MM/dd/yyyy hh:mm"/></startTime>
    <votingStartTime>
        <s:date name="votingStartTime" format="MM/dd/yyyy hh:mm"/></votingStartTime>
    <duration><s:property value="duration"/></duration>
    <timeZoneOffset><s:property value="timeZoneOffset"/></timeZoneOffset>
    <status><s:property value="status"/></status>

    <s:if test="location.class.name.endsWith('.Address')">
    <address type="Adress">
        <name><s:property value="location.name" /></name>
        <address><s:property value="location.address" /></address>
        <city><s:property value="location.city" /></city>
```

```
            <state><s:property value="location.state" /></state>
            <zipcode><s:property value="location.zipcode" /></zipcode>
    </s:if>
    <s:else>
    <address type="Broadcast">
            <name><s:property value="location.name" /></name>
            <city><s:property value="location.city" /></city>
            <state><s:property value="location.state" /></state>
            <network><s:property value="location.network" /></network>
            <stationIdentifier>
                <s:property value="location.stationIdentifier" /></stationIdentifier>
    </s:else>
    </address>

    <contestants>
    <s:iterator value="options" >
        <contestant>
            <name><s:property value="name" /></name>
            <description><s:property value="description" /></description>
        </contestant>
    </s:iterator>
    </contestants>

</event>
```

■**Caution** Remember to change the `decorators.xml` file, adding a `<pattern>/api/*</pattern>` entry to the `excludes` tag, to prevent the XML from being decorated with HTML.

The following is the resulting XML when the URL /api/event/3 is invoked:

```
<?xml version="1.0" encoding="UTF-8"?>

<event id="3">

    <name>Boston Marathon 2008</name>
    <startTime>04/03/2008 09:00</startTime>
    <votingStartTime>04/03/2008 07:00</votingStartTime>
    <duration>5</duration>
    <timeZoneOffset>-5</timeZoneOffset>
    <status>NOT_STARTED</status>

    <address type="Adress">
        <name>Boston</name>
        <address>Main St.</address>
```

```
        <city>Boston</city>
        <state>MA</state>
        <zipcode>02140</zipcode>
    </address>

    <contestants>

        <contestant>
            <name>Runner 1</name>
            <description>Runner 1</description>
        </contestant>

        <contestant>
            <name>Runner 3</name>
            <description>Runner 3</description>
        </contestant>

    </contestants>

</event>
```

Caution With the `FallbackRestful2ActionMapper` installed, the web application's starting URL is no longer `http://localhost:8080/app` (as this is now a valid URL), and instead needs to be `http://localhost:8080/app/index.action`.

Summary

With this chapter, boundaries have been broken, and a self-contained web application has been opened up to interact with both people and processes on the Internet.

You have learned how to produce an RSS feed; how to geo-code physical address information into latitude and longitude; how to include latitude and longitude information using a standard format; and how to consume the RSS feed to provide a mashup that is completely external to the application or that resides within the application. Web service functionality was also discussed, concluding with an implementation of a RESTful-style web service.

Even more important than the technologies themselves is that you have learned new ways to integrate new services into the Struts2 framework. In producing an RSS feed, you learned how to implement a new result type, and in producing a RESTful web service, you learned how to implement a new action mapper, which maps a URL to an action configuration and vice versa. Now that you understand and can use the integration points, such as these, you can take advantage of the real power of open source projects. Armed with this knowledge, you will be able to find new and easier ways to implement the new features that your applications require.

CHAPTER 10

■■■■

AJAX

In many ways, AJAX is synonymous with a Web 2.0 application. The term *AJAX*, originally an acronym standing for Asynchronous JavaScript and XML, was coined by Jesse James Garrett in 2005, although the web browser functionality to enable the interactions had been around for many years earlier.

The technology is based around the `XMLHttpRequest` object, which is an object supplied by the web browser that is accessible via JavaScript. It is used to transfer data asynchronously between the browser and a web server. This allows sections of the currently loaded page to be modified (from server-provided data), without the need for a complete page refresh. The advantage to the end user is that a slow, cumbersome web application is now more interactive and reactive to user input. Along with the `XMLHttpRequest` object, many other technologies are used, including XML or JSON (JavaScript Object Notation) as the data transport protocol/ format; HTML to render the page in a browser; CSS (Cascading Style Sheets) for user interface formatting information; DOM (Document Object Model) for modifying a page that has already been loaded by a web browser; and JavaScript to perform the logic to update the necessary information and make the asynchronous calls.

As you can see, many technologies need to work in unison. For this reason, this chapter focuses only on the transport and server-side technologies, and provides simple examples of how the client interacts with the server when appropriate. This allows us to explore the options available to integrate Struts2 with any AJAX client. To provide a solid foundation, we'll start by developing the functionality for the use cases as standard Struts2 actions. From there, you will learn how to modify the HTML and Struts2 tags to use the `ajax` theme. By making simple updates, the standard Struts2 tag can provide asynchronous features without special client programming.

Next, we'll explore some other options for integrating Struts2 applications with AJAX user interfaces. This will include returning XML and JSON responses that can be consumed by JavaScript in the browser. You will also learn how to create Struts2 actions that allow integration with the Google Web Toolkit.

■**Caution** Before the code in this chapter can be run, several artifacts need to be installed into the local Maven2 repository. The instructions on how to install the required artifacts can be found in the sections "Using the JSON Result Type Plug-in" and "Using the Google Web Toolkit."

The Use Cases

During the course of this chapter, the remaining use cases will be developed. They provide the functionality to allow users to vote on an event and to view the outcome of the voting:

Enroll in an Event: The events in the application are searched until an interesting event is found. Once found, the user (if already logged in) is presented with a link to enroll. To enroll in an event, the user first needs to be logged on.

Vote for a Contestant in an Event: Voting is the next step. Similar to enrolling, users need to log on before they can vote. Users can vote only once for each event, and after they have voted, they cannot change their selection.

Find Event Results: During the voting period and after the voting has concluded, any user can view the most recent results for an event. Each contestant's name is listed with the number of votes the contestant has accrued.

These use cases encompass a very simple set of requirements. For a real application, especially for voting and viewing of results, they would no doubt be more complex.

Developing the Supporting Infrastructure

Before the AJAX application elements can be developed, the supporting infrastructure needs to be created. The good news is that you have seen all of these elements before: actions, JSP templates, and the configuration that binds all the elements together. After the base functionality is in place and tested, the AJAX façade can be applied.

■**Tip** This approach is a good foundation for any integration or complex web application development, in particular AJAX applications. The complexity of an AJAX application is not only in the asynchronous nature (a direct opposite to traditional web applications), but it is also due to the melding of technologies—the client side technologies of CSS, JavaScript, and HTML; the server-side technologies (in this case, Java) of Struts2 and J2EE; and the transport technologies of XML, JSON, and JSONP. And, if the shear number of technologies isn't enough, they are being combined in web browsers that still have HTML, CSS, and DOM standardization issues. Fortunately, JavaScript incompatibilities are almost entirely eliminated.

Updating the Menu Options

To make navigating around the application easier, two additional navigational menu items will be added. The first is a link to log on to the application, and the second is a link to view a list of the most recent events. These can be seen in Figure 10-1.

Both these changes are localized to the SiteMesh decorator main.jsp, which is found in the /decorator directory of the web application. The logon link is only shown when the user is not currently logged in, whereas the link for the list of recent events is always shown. The changes to the decorator are shown here:

```
<div id="local">
    <h3><s:text name="leftnav.title"/></h3>
    <ul>
        <s:if test="#session['user']==null">
            <s:url id="register" action="findUser" namespace="/user" />
            <li><s:a href="%{register}"><s:text name="link.register" /></s:a></li>
            <s:url id="logon" action="authenticate" namespace="/" />
            <li><s:a href="%{logon}"><s:text name="link.logon" /></s:a></li>
        </s:if>

        <s:else>
            <s:url id="update" action="findUser" namespace="/user" >
                <s:param name="emailId" value="#session['user'].email" />
            </s:url>
            <li>
                <s:a href="%{update}"><s:text name="link.updateProfile" /></s:a>
            </li>

            <s:url id="logoff" action="logoff" namespace="/" />
            <li><s:a href="%{logoff}"><s:text name="link.logoff" /></s:a></li>
        </s:else>

        <s:url id="newEvent" action="addEventFlow" namespace="/event" />
        <li><s:a href="%{newEvent}"><s:text name="link.addEvent" /></s:a></li>

        <s:url id="recentEvents" action="showRecentEvents" namespace="/search" />
        <li>
            <s:a href="%{recentEvents}"><s:text name="link.recentEvents" /></s:a>
        </li>

        <s:url id="search" action="searchEvents" namespace="/search" />
        <li><s:a href="%{search}"><s:text name="link.search" /></s:a></li>

    </ul>
</div>
```

At the moment, a user is forwarded to the logon page only when the user accesses a secure URL and isn't yet authenticated. The logic for the decorator changes this, and a new action is needed to forward the user to the logon screen:

```
<s:url id="logon" action="authenticate" namespace="/" />
<li><s:a href="%{logon}"><s:text name="link.logon" /></s:a></li>
```

The action's URL corresponds to a new action mapping in the struts.xml configuration file, which uses the BaseAction as a placeholder to forward to the logon.jsp template.

```
<package name="home-package" extends="struts-default" namespace="/">

        <action name="authenticate" class="com.fdar.apress.s2.actions.BaseAction" >
            <result name="success">/WEB-INF/jsp/logon.jsp</result>
        </action>

    ...

</package>
```

■**Caution** Remember that when using internationalization, you cannot call JSPs directly because they do not have access to internationalization information. Instead, always create an action (that can provide access to the internationalized text) with the result being the JSP to be rendered.

Implementing the logic for the view recent events link requires even less work because the action is already developed and configured. The only change to be made is to set a default for the number of results to return (so that it doesn't always need to be specified). This is achieved in the property definition in the ShowRecentEventsAction class:

```
private int number = 10;
```

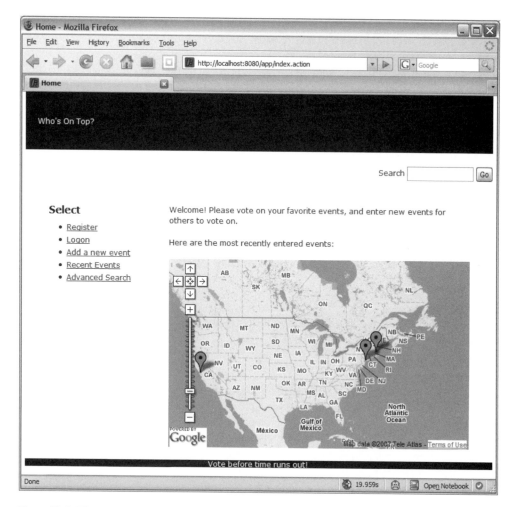

Figure 10-1. *The new navigation options*

Implementing the Voting Use Cases

All three of the use cases for this chapter are accessible from the event list page, which is now easily accessible via the navigation link Recent Events. The rendering of this view is performed by the eventListing.jsp template.

Originally, this template rendered only the core event details of the name, the date of the event, when the event started, and when voting starts. This part of the template will remain the same and, below it, logic will be added to determine what step of the voting process the user is currently at, and what information and links should be available.

The logic also needs to determine if the user has enrolled and whether the user has voted. For this, the JSP template will rely heavily on OGNL expressions. The complete template is shown here:

```
<p>
<h3><s:property value="parameters.event.name" /></h3>
<s:text name="display.event.date"/>
    <s:date name="parameters.event.startTime" format="MMM d, yyyy"/> <br/>
<s:text name="display.event.start"/>
    <s:date name="parameters.event.startTime" format="hh:mm a" /> <br/>
<s:text name="display.event.voting"/>
    <s:date name="parameters.event.votingStartTime" format="hh:mm a"/> <br/>
</p>
<p>
    <s:if test="#session['user']!=null">
        <s:set name="voterSet" value="parameters.event.voters.{➡
            ? #this.user.email == #session['user'].email}" />
        <s:if test="#voterSet.size()>0">
            <s:if test="#voterSet.get(0).voteRecordedTime!=null">
                <s:text name="text.thanksForVoting" />
            </s:if>
        </s:if>
        <s:else>
            <s:url id="enrollUrl" action="enroll" namespace="/voting" >
                <s:param name="eventId" value="parameters.event.id" />
            </s:url>
            <s:a theme="xhtml" href="%{enrollUrl}" >
                <s:text name="link.enroll" /></s:a>
        </s:else>
    </s:if>

  <s:action name="findResults" namespace="/voting" executeResult="true">
    <s:param name="eventId" value="parameters.event.id" />
  </s:action>
</p>
```

■**Caution** When using themes, remember that tags can override the theme in the tags they enclose. You have seen that the form tag does this (where each of the form fields uses the theme specified on the form tag). The eventListing.jsp template is included in other templates by using the component tag, and like the form tag, the component tag overrides the theme for all Struts2 tags in the template. This was the case for the a tag, where the theme needs to be xhtml and not apress. To rectify the behavior, the theme attribute was added to the tag with a value of xhtml, which is the default.

Starting at the second paragraph block, the added code contains various (and sometimes a little confusing) OGNL expressions. Here is the overview of the expressions:

"#session['user']!=null": This expression tests whether the user has logged in to the application. The named object #session refers to the HttpSession object, and it is searching through the attributes for an object with a key of user (the key that the logon action stores the user information under). If there is a value for the key, the user has logged on.

"parameters.event.voters.{? #this.user.email == #session['user'].email}": By far, this is the most complex OGNL expression on the page. The expression parameters.event.voters selects the list of Voter objects from the Event object (which was passed as a parameter via the component tag, and corresponds to the users that have voted for the event). By using parentheses, a subset of the Voter objects in the list can be selected. This is achieved by evaluating an expression (#this.user.email == #session['user'].email) for each element in the set. Only when the expression evaluates as true is the element included in the subset. On the left side of the expression, the user's e-mail address of the current element in the list (denoted by #this) is selected and checked for equality against the e-mail address for the user who is currently logged on. So, in effect, this expression finds the Voter object instances for the currently logged in user. The last piece is the qualifier ?. OGNL allow several qualifiers for the selection expression: ? selects all elements in the list that matches the expression; ^ selects only the first element that matches the logic; and $ selects the last element that match the logic. After calculating the resulting subset, it is placed in a property called voterSet.

"#voterSet.size()>0": To check whether the current user has enrolled to vote, the set of voters that was previously created is checked. Because a Voter object will be created when a user enrolls (but not the contestant voted on or the time the user voted), and the voterSet created only contains Voter objects for the user currently logged on, the size of the list will be greater than 0 if the current user has enrolled to vote.

"#voterSet.get(0).voteRecordedTime!=null": Because the user can only enroll and vote once per event (restricted by the JSP template logic), the size of the voterSet should always be 0 or 1. To check whether the user has enrolled or voted, the voteRecordedTime property is checked (not null signifying that a vote has been cast). This expression is evaluated after the check for an empty list to avoid exceptions.

Depending on the outcome of the OGNL expression logic, either an enrollment link or a "thank you for voting" message is rendered.

> **■Tip** Instead of using OGNL expressions, the logic could have alternatively been implemented as a method on the action class and the method called using the Struts2 `if` tag. This is an option that needs to be weighed during the design and development of your application. Placing the logic in the action provides a central access point for when the same logic is reused often, but the web application may need to be restarted for the changes to take effect. In OGNL, the changes can be tested and applied quickly by refreshing the browser, but developers need to spend more time to understand the expressions, and the expressions are more susceptible to object structure changes (especially with refactoring tools not yet understanding expression language syntax).

To render the results, an `action` tag is invoked in the JSP template. You have seen this tag before, so we'll skip the description. The `eventResult.jsp` template that is rendered is more interesting and can be found in the `/template/apress` directory.

```
<p>
  <h5><s:text name="text.results" /></h5>

  <p>
    <s:set name="canVote" value="results[0].contestant.event.voters.{➥
        ? #this.user.email == #session['user'].email}➥
          .get(0).voteRecordedTime==null" />
    <s:if test="canVote">
      <s:text name="text.canVote" /><br/>
    </s:if>
    <s:iterator value="results">
      ( <s:property value="numberOfVotes" /> )
      <s:property value="contestant.name" />
      <s:if test="canVote" >
        <s:url id="voteUrl" action="vote" namespace="/voting">
          <s:param name="eventId" value="contestant.event.id" />
          <s:param name="contestantId" value="contestant.id" />
        </s:url>
        [<s:a theme="xhtml" href="%{voteUrl}"><s:text name="link.vote" /></s:a>]
      </s:if>
      <br/>
    </s:iterator>
  </p>
</p>
```

For each contestant, the JSP template renders the current number of votes, the contestant's name, and then if the user is logged in and enrolled to vote for the event, a link to vote for each contestant.

In this template, we have another complex OGNL expression: "results[0].contestant.
event.voters.{? #this.user.email == #session['user'].email}.get(0).
voteRecordedTime==null". This expression is very similar to the one previously examined, and
it determines whether the current user has voted by checking the voteRecordedTime property.
There are a couple of differences though. The first is that instead of a parameter, the initial
data is obtained from the action's result property (a list), and instead of an Event object, a list
of Contestant objects is returned. Because each of the contestants returned belongs to the
same event, the zero index contestant of the result list is arbitrarily picked to determine
whether the current user is in the list of voters.

Just like the previous template, this template also places the result of the expression into
a property so that it can be used to determine whether to render the "please vote now" text to
the user, as well as the links to vote for each of the contestants. Figure 10-2 shows three different events, one in each stage of progression and each with different links available.

Actions and business services provide the functionality for the user interface. The new
VotingService sets the stage for the action's logic, and its interface closely resembles the use
cases:

```
public interface VotingService {

    void enroll(User user, Long eventId);

    void vote(User user, Long eventId, Long contestantId);

    Long getResults(Long eventId, Long contestantId);
}
```

You may be surprised to find the getResults() method returning a Long rather than a
List. Returning a List may have consolidated the number of database calls, however, the code
is being developed with a goal of utilizing it in an AJAX application.

A characteristic of AJAX applications is to have the user interface make many small HTTP
requests to update the user interface as needed, rather than making one request that obtains
every piece of data for the entire page. With this is mind, developing the VotingService and
the FindResultsAction will take a slightly different direction.

Three actions provide the endpoints to the links in the JSP templates: EnrollAction,
FindResultsAction, and VoteAction. Each action corresponds to one of the use cases that we
are implementing.

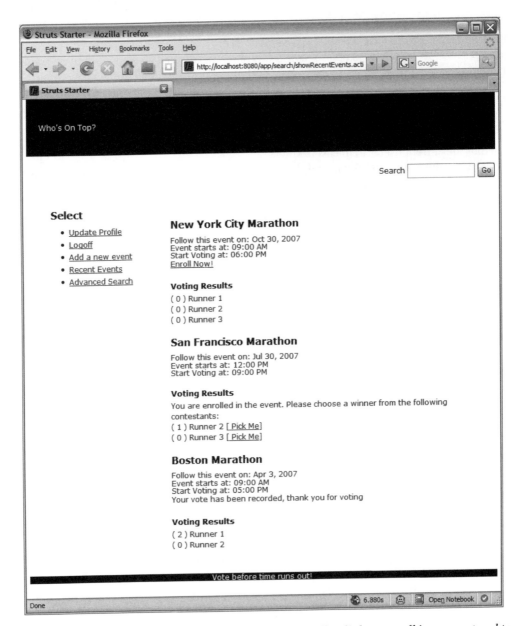

Figure 10-2. *The new event list with the voting results, as well as links to enroll in an event and to vote for contestants*

The EnrollAction obtains the current user from the session and together with the eventId (that was a URL parameter) is used to call the enroll() method on the VotingService:

```
@Result(type= ServletActionRedirectResult.class,
        value="showRecentEvents",params={"namespace","/search"})
public class EnrollAction extends BaseAction implements ServletRequestAware {

    private Long eventId;
    private VotingService votingService;
    private HttpServletRequest request;

    ...

    public void setEventId(Long eventId) {
        this.eventId = eventId;
    }

    public String execute() throws Exception {
        User user =
            (User)request.getSession(true)
                .getAttribute(SecurityInterceptor.USER_OBJECT);
        votingService.enroll( user, eventId );
        return SUCCESS;
    }

}
```

The FindResultsAction is only slightly more complex. Rather than the resulting list type being an existing domain object, a new VotingResult object is used. The VotingResult object is a simple data transfer object containing a Contestant and a Long (for the number of votes accumulated).

To generate the list, the FindResultsAction action uses data from both the EventService and the VotingService:

```
@Result(value="/template/apress/eventResults.jsp")
public class FindResultsAction extends BaseAction {

    private Long eventId;
    private VotingService votingService;
    private EventService service;
    private List<VotingResult> results;

    ...

    public void setEventId(Long eventId) {
        this.eventId = eventId;
    }
```

```
    public List<VotingResult> getResults() {
        return results;
    }

    public String execute() throws Exception {

        results = new ArrayList<VotingResult>();
        for( Contestant next : service.findById(eventId).getOptions() ) {
            results.add( new VotingResult(next,
                votingService.getResults(eventId,next.getId()) ) );
        }
        return SUCCESS;
    }

}
```

The last action is the VoteAction. This action is very similar to the EnrollAction, using the current user, event id, and contestant ids (provided by URL parameters) to invoke the vote() method on the VotingService.

```
@Result(type= ServletActionRedirectResult.class,
        value="showRecentEvents",params={"namespace","/search"})
public class VoteAction extends BaseAction implements ServletRequestAware {

    private Long eventId;
    private Long contestantId;
    private VotingService votingService;
    private HttpServletRequest request;

    ...

    public void setEventId(Long eventId) {
        this.eventId = eventId;
    }

    public void setContestantId(Long contestantId) {
        this.contestantId = contestantId;
    }

    public String execute() throws Exception {
        User user = (User)request.
            getSession(true).getAttribute(SecurityInterceptor.USER_OBJECT);
        votingService.vote( user, eventId, contestantId );
        return SUCCESS;
    }
}
```

Using the `ajax` Theme

With the core infrastructure in place, updating the use cases to be AJAX-enabled should be easy, and in this section, you will learn how to make the changes necessary to utilize the Struts 2.0.9 `ajax` theme.

The `ajax` theme is implemented using the same mechanism as the `xhtml` and `simple` themes. It uses Freemarker templates to provide additional HTML, and in this case, JavaScript code, to decorate the original HTML. To provide AJAX features, the Dojo Toolkit (`http://dojotoolkit.org`) is used. The Dojo Toolkit is one of many different AJAX libraries that could have been used, and work is underway to provide integration with some of the other more popular libraries, including the Yahoo! User Interface Library (`http://developer.yahoo.com/yui`) and the Prototype JavaScript Framework (`http://www.prototypejs.org`).

■**Caution** The Struts 2.0.9 `ajax` theme uses Dojo 0.4.2 (Struts 2.0.10 and higher will use Dojo 0.4.3), which is not the most recent release (currently 0.9). It is very unlikely that the Struts 2.0.x will be upgraded to the most recent release, and it is uncertain as to when the Struts 2.1.x tags will be upgraded. If your project requires utilizing a more up-to-date version of Dojo, the Struts2 `ajax` theme may not be the best option. Your options in this scenario include making changes to the theme's Freemarker templates for the new library version, or using another interaction technique (some of the options are covered in this chapter).

In this section, the Struts 2.0.9 `ajax` theme will be discussed. With the release of Struts 2.1.x, this theme will no longer exist. Instead, all the functionality will be refactored into a plug-in separate from the Struts2 core. The tags, their attributes, and the functionality will be similar, but there will be some changes.

Configuring the Application

As you have already seen, to use a theme other than the default `xhtml` theme, the `theme` attribute is added to any Struts2 tag setting the value to the desired theme name, in this case, `ajax`. For most themes, this is all that is required, but in the `ajax` theme's case, an additional step is needed.

For the `ajax` theme, the Struts2 `head` tag also needs to be added to the result template. The `head` tag, on a per-theme basis, can include additional elements in the page being rendered such as JavaScript, CSS, or HTML files, or adding JavaScript scripts and functions to the page.

To make the `ajax` theme available to all templates in the application, the `head` tag is added to the SiteMesh decorator `main.jsp`. Just like the other tags, the theme attribute is set to the value `ajax`:

```
<html xmlns="http://www.w3.org/1999/xhtml" xml:lang="en" lang="en">
<head>
    <title><decorator:title default="Struts Starter"/></title>
    <link href="<s:url value='/styles/main.css'/>" rel="stylesheet"
        type="text/css" media="all"/>
```

```
    <s:head theme="ajax" />
    <decorator:head/>
</head>
<body>
    …
</body>
</html>
```

Retrieving Action Results

The first change to the web application is that AJAX techniques will be used to display the list of recent events. To reduce the time to render information to the user, the list of events will be rendered in an initial HTTP request, with the results of each event being a subsequent HTTP request.

The existing code in the eventListing.jsp template to render the results is shown here:

```
<s:action name="findResults" namespace="/voting" executeResult="true">
    <s:param name="eventId" value="parameters.event.id" />
</s:action>
```

This makes your job much easier. To refactor this into an AJAX request, the div tag is used:

```
<s:url id="resultsUrl" action="findResults" namespace="/voting">
    <s:param name="eventId" value="parameters.event.id" />
</s:url>
<s:div theme="ajax" href="%{resultsUrl}"
       loadingText="%{getText('text.loadingResults')}" />
```

Note If the code to render the event results is in the same template, rather than in a separate action call, an additional step is required. You need to extract the JSP code, creating a new JSP template, and then create a new action to provide data for the new JSP template.

The div tag is used in exactly the same way as the action tag. It calls a URL, provided by the href attribute, and renders the output as the contents of the tag. The difference being that the request to the URL is performed in the browser using the XMLHttpRequest object and not on the server during the construction of the initial page. Although generated via a url tag, the URL is exactly the same as for the action tag.

Caution Cross Site Scripting (XSS) is a form of security attack where malicious JavaScript code is inserted into a page that accesses a host server other than the one that the page is loaded from. To avoid this type of attack, the div tag will not work correctly unless the URL provided in the href attribute is from the same hostname that the page was loaded from. This is an inherit limitation of the XMLHttpRequest object and AJAX in general (unless coding techniques are used to explicitly work around the limitation, for example, dynamic script tags).

Along with the common Struts2 HTML attributes that you would expect on the div tag, there are a variety of new ajax theme attributes. The first of these is the href attribute, which provides the URL that the XMLHttpRequest object will call. In the preceding code, there is also a loadingText attribute. This attribute provided the text to display to the user while the AJAX request is being made. Many more attributes are available to developers, and the best resource for finding the options available is the Struts2 documentation for the div tag at http://struts.apache.org/2.0.9/docs/div.html.

The final step in the implementation is to prevent SiteMesh from decorating the HTML fragment returned from the server. To do this, the decorators.xml configuration file is modified with a new exclusion pattern matching the URL being invoked:

```
<decorators defaultdir="/WEB-INF/decorators">
    <!-- Any urls that are excluded will never be decorated by Sitemesh -->
    <excludes>

        ...

        <pattern>/voting/findResults*</pattern>
    </excludes>

    ...

</decorators>
```

Figure 10-3 shows the resulting page, with the AJAX calls to retrieve the results in progress. After all the calls are complete, the page is identical to the version without AJAX (refer to Figure 10-2).

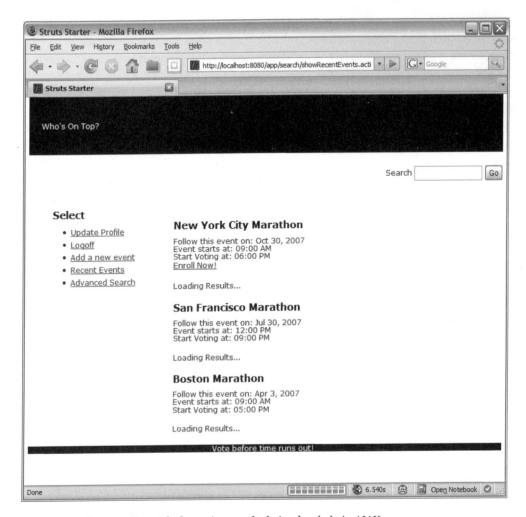

Figure 10-3. *The event list with the voting results being loaded via AJAX*

Invoking Actions as Events

With the event results being returned asynchronously, the next step is to be able to retrigger this process when the user enrolls in an event and after the user has voted for a contestant. Along with retriggering a partial page refresh, Struts2 actions need to be invoked to perform server-side logic for enrolling and voting, and text (not from segments of the page that are being refreshed) needs to be updated with values from the returned page fragment.

The first task is to invoke server-side logic using AJAX calls. In the eventListing.jsp template, the Struts2 a tag was responsible for this call:

```
<s:a theme="xhtml" href="%{enrollUrl}" ><s:text name="link.enroll" /></s:a>
```

Similarly to the div tag, the a tag is updated to use the ajax theme, and similarly a new href attribute is introduced to provide the URL of the action for the server-side logic to invoke. The difference is that for the a tag, a response to calling the URL is not expected.

■Note If a response is returned from the URL invoked when using the a tag, it can be processed by providing the name of a JavaScript function as the handler attribute. For this and other configuration options for the a tag, check out the Struts2 documentation at http://struts.apache.org/2.0.9/docs/a.html.

The resulting code now becomes the following:

```
<s:a theme="ajax"
    notifyTopics="updateResult%{parameters.event.id}"
    href="%{enrollUrl}" ><s:text name="link.enroll" /></s:a>
```

Now that the user is enrolled in the event, the results in the current HTML need to be refreshed to provide the voting options for the contestant. This functionality is already provided via the eventResults.jsp template, and so the div tag that obtains the results needs to be retriggered. The notifyTopics attribute is used for this purpose, sending a message on the topic updateResult%{parameters.event.id}. In response to a message being sent on a topic, any ajax theme tag that has a corresponding listenTopics attribute and a matching value, such as the div tag, will be activated. Here is what the div tag (from the same eventResults.jsp template) looks like now:

```
<s:div theme="ajax" href="%{resultsUrl}"
    executeScripts="true"
    listenTopics="updateResult%{parameters.event.id}"
    loadingText="%{getText('text.loadingResults')}" />
```

Because each event requires a different topic, the value of the notifyTopic/listenTopic attribute value is updateResult%{parameters.event.id}. This combines a static text string updateResult with the ID of the event (provided via the event parameter). The %{parameters.event.id} section is an OGNL expression to be evaluated; for example, if the event had an id of 3, the topic name would be updateResult3. By using an OGNL expression as part of the topic name, a unique topic can be supplied for each event, and a more specific section of HTML can be targeted for update.

Triggering JavaScript Code with Topics

The consumption of topics specified in the `notifyTopics` attribute value can be JavaScript functions as well as other Struts2 `ajax` theme tags. For a JavaScript function to be notified and called when a message is published, the function first needs to subscribe to the topic it is interested in.

Using the Dojo Toolkit makes accessing the topics very easy. The following code is all that is needed to register interest in the `userEnrolled` topic and to have the anonymous function called when a message is published to the `userEnrolled` topic:

```
<script type="text/javascript">
    dojo.event.topic.subscribe("userEnrolled", function(data, type, request) {
        // your logic here
    });
</script>
```

The parameters to the function are the following:

- `data`: The response from the server, which could be HTML, XML, JSON, or anything else.

- `type`: The function can be called at various times during the request life cycle, and this parameter tells the function what the current state is. There are three states: "before" for before the request is made; "load" for when the request succeeds; and "error" for when the request fails.

- `request`: The `XMLHttpRequest` object of the AJAX request.

For the function to be called, it would need to be added to the list of topics being notified. The `notifyTopics` and `listenTopics` attributes are comma-delimited lists of topic names, so the new topic can be added to the existing topics:

```
<s:a theme="ajax"
    notifyTopics="userEnrolled,updateResult%{parameters.event.id}"
    href="%{enrollUrl}" ><s:text name="link.enroll" /></s:a>
```

By providing a topic-based messaging architecture between tags and a mechanism to insert custom JavaScript functions, any type of complex user interface can be constructed.

To complete the `eventListing.jsp` template, three other changes are made: the `div` tag includes a new attribute, `executeScripts`, which executes any JavaScript in the page returned from the AJAX request; the JSP code before the result now only provides the enroll link (and no longer the "thank you for voting" text); and the HTML paragraph tag has an `id` attribute. The form of the HTML paragraph's `id` attribute value is the same as the `notifyTopic`/`listenTopic` attribute value. It combines the static text `eventMessage` with the event ID (this time by using the `property` tag). The complete `eventListing.jsp` template becomes the following:

```
<p>
    <h3><s:property value="parameters.event.name" /></h3>
    <s:text name="display.event.date"/>
        <s:date name="parameters.event.startTime" format="MMM d, yyyy"/> <br/>
    <s:text name="display.event.start"/>
        <s:date name="parameters.event.startTime" format="hh:mm a" /> <br/>
    <s:text name="display.event.voting"/>
        <s:date name="parameters.event.votingStartTime" format="hh:mm a"/> <br/>
</p>
<p id="eventMessage<s:property value="parameters.event.id"/>">
    <s:if test="#session['user']!=null">
        <s:set name="voterSet"
          value="parameters.event.voters.{➥
                ? #this.user.email == #session['user'].email}" />
        <s:if test="#voterSet.size()==0">
            <s:url id="enrollUrl" action="enroll" namespace="/voting" >
                <s:param name="eventId" value="parameters.event.id" />
            </s:url>
            <s:a theme="ajax"
                notifyTopics="updateResult%{parameters.event.id},removeEnroll"
                href="%{enrollUrl}" ><s:text name="link.enroll" /></s:a>
        </s:if>
    </s:if>

    <s:url id="resultsUrl" action="findResults" namespace="/voting">
        <s:param name="eventId" value="parameters.event.id" />
    </s:url>
    <s:div theme="ajax" href="%{resultsUrl}"
            executeScripts="true"
            listenTopics="updateResult%{parameters.event.id}"
            loadingText="%{getText('text.loadingResults')}" />
</p>
```

The eventResults.jsp template is also modified:

```
<p>
    <h5><s:text name="text.results" /></h5>

    <p>
        <s:set name="myVotes" value="results[0].contestant.event.voters.{➥
            ? #this.user.email == #session['user'].email}" />
        <s:set name="canVote" value="#myVotes!=null && ➥
            #myVotes.get(0).voteRecordedTime==null" />
        <s:if test="canVote">
            <s:text name="text.canVote" /><br/>
```

```
            </s:if>
            <s:iterator value="results">
                ( <s:property value="numberOfVotes" /> )
                    <s:property value="contestant.name" />
                <s:if test="canVote" >
                    <s:url id="voteUrl" action="vote" namespace="/voting">
                        <s:param name="eventId" value="contestant.event.id" />
                        <s:param name="contestantId" value="contestant.id" />
                    </s:url>
                    [<s:a theme="ajax" href="%{voteUrl}"
                    notifyTopics="updateResult%{results[0].contestant.event.id}">
                        <s:text name="link.vote" /></s:a>]
                </s:if>
                <br/>
            </s:iterator>
        </p>
</p>
```

Similarly to the eventListing.jsp template, the Struts2 a tag is updated to use the ajax theme, and the notifyTopics attribute is added with a value of updateResult%{results[0]. contestant.event.id}. Because the event id is obtained from a different location in the Value Stack, the expression is different. However, the resulting text is exactly the same as in the eventListing.jsp template.

Along with the updates to the eventResults.jsp template code, the following new code is added:

```
<script type="text/javascript">
    <s:if test="#myVotes!=null && #myVotes.size()>0">
        <s:if test="#myVotes.get(0).voteRecordedTime!=null">
            displayText = '<s:text name="text.thanksForVoting" />';
        </s:if>
        <s:else>
            displayText = '';
        </s:else>
        dojo.byId("eventMessage<s:property ➡
          value="results[0].contestant.event.id"/>").innerHTML = displayText;
    </s:if>
</script>
```

This JavaScript function is executed when the result is received by calling div tag (remember the executeScripts attribute on the div tag is set to true, so this is allowed), and will update the text immediately preceding the results. Depending on whether there is a user logged on and whether they have voted or not, the enrollment link will be removed or change to a "thank you for voting" message.

Using the Dojo Toolkit's helper function dojo.byId() and a naming convention for the id attribute of the paragraph, the specific paragraph matching the current event id is retrieved and the text modified.

■**Note** If you were paying close attention to the OGNL expressions, you may have noticed that they have changed slightly. There are, in fact, two changes: the first is that instead of typing the same expression multiple times, a common expression is broken out into the myVotes parameter; additionally, to avoid exceptions, the myVotes parameter is checked for a null value before calling methods on it. Neither of these changes is important to the logic, but making small refactorings like this keeps the code manageable and makes it easier to read.

Additional ajax Theme Opportunities

The use cases for this chapter provide an introduction to the ajax theme, but they are by no means a complete coverage of the topic. During the development of the example application, there were other opportunities for using AJAX functionality that were not taken. These are the topics for this section.

AJAX Form Submission

A great opportunity for AJAX functionality is when HTML forms are submitted. Instead of loading the entire page, an XMLHttpRequest can be made to the server to invoke the logic and obtain the resulting HTML. The HTML can then be rendered in a particular DOM element.

A good candidate in the example web application is the quick search form on the top right of every page. To enable AJAX functionality, the ajax theme needs to be applied but not on the form tag. Instead, the submit tag is modified. Here is the new quick search div code from the main.jsp decorator:

```
<div align="right" style="position:relative;top:-40px;">
    <s:form namespace="/search" action="searchByTitle"
            method="POST" theme="simple">
        <s:text name="text.search" />
        <s:textfield name="titlePartial" size="15"/>
        <s:submit key="button.search" theme="ajax" targets="main"/>
    </s:form>
</div>
```

Along with the theme attribute, a new targets attribute is added, the value being main, which corresponds to a CSS id attribute available on a current page element. The targets attribute defines the DOM elements whose content will be replaced by the data returned from the AJAX form submission. If you search further down the main.jsp decorator code, you will come across the div tag that matched the main identifier value:

```
<div id="content" class="clearfix">
    <div id="main">
        <decorator:body/>
    </div>
    …
</div>
```

If this was a non-AJAX request, the content being returned would be placed within the same div tag.

Finally, the decorators.xml configuration file needs to be revisited to exclude the URL pattern of the quick search form submission:

```
<decorators defaultdir="/WEB-INF/decorators">
    <!-- Any urls that are excluded will never be decorated by Sitemesh -->
    <excludes>
        ...
        <pattern>/voting/findResults*</pattern>
        <pattern>/search/searchBy*</pattern>
    </excludes>

    ...

</decorators>
```

Tip When you start using a lot of AJAX calls, you will require less configuration if all the URLs being invoked by the AJAX calls are placed under a common package name, for example /ajax. Then, only one pattern (/ajax/*) needs to be added to the decorators.xml configuration file.

AJAX Validation

Validation of fields can also be configured to use AJAX, rather than requiring the user to enter all the information and click the submit button. This feature has been marked as "experimental" and should be used with caution.

When AJAX validation is enabled, a request to the server to validate the current form field is performed as the focus leaves each form element. This allows instant feedback to the user (but only for the form fields that have been in focus) with the cost of more network traffic. The implementation is provided using the DWR (Direct Web Remoting) framework version 1.1.x; however, in Struts 2.1.x, the AJAX validation will use the Dojo Toolkit, which is yet anther reason to consider carefully whether you should use this feature.

DWR allows code in a browser to call server-side Java code as if it were running in the browser. To achieve this, DWR dynamically generates JavaScript that is based on the Java methods, as well as performing the marshalling to transfer data between the JavaScript in the browser and the Java code on the server. More information on DWR can be found at http://getahead.org/dwr.

To enable AJAX validation, configuration needs to be added to two files. First, ensure that the DWR servlet is configured in web.xml:

```
<servlet>
    <servlet-name>dwr</servlet-name>
    <servlet-class>uk.ltd.getahead.dwr.DWRServlet</servlet-class>
</servlet>

<servlet-mapping>
    <servlet-name>dwr</servlet-name>
    <url-pattern>/dwr/*</url-pattern>
</servlet-mapping>
```

Next a `dwr.xml` configuration file needs to be added to the `WEB-INF` directory (this is one of the files that was generated using the Maven2 archetype, or it can be obtained from the Struts2 showcase example application). This file will not be discussed; however, it provides the information necessary to allow DWR to find the Struts2 classes that will perform the validation logic. If you are interested in finding out more about `dwr.xml`, the documentation can be found at `http://getahead.org/dwr/server/dwrxml`.

The final step is to enable AJAX validation in your JSP template by adding the attributes `theme="ajax"` and `validate="true"` to the `form` tag.

```
<head>
    <title><s:text name="user.findUser.title" /></title>
</head>
<body>

<s:form namespace="/user" action="updateUser" method="post"
    enctype="multipart/form-data" theme="ajax" validate="true">

    // form code

</s:form>

</body>
</html>
```

Once again, the Struts2 framework will handle the communication and rendering of the error messages without the need for additional developer interaction.

Validation is an extensive topic, and there is much more than will be covered in this book. The documentation is the best source of information on the more complex configuration, including XML-based configuration, providing a `validate()` method on your actions, and alternate options such as client validation. The URL for the Apache documentation is `http://struts.apache.org/2.x/docs/validation.html`.

Using JavaScript

Using the ajax theme is a good option when AJAX elements need to be incorporated into your web application, and the primary application is rendered by the browser using HTML. When the web application is constructed with only a few HTML pages, which contain mainly JavaScript functions (at this point the application has become a JavaScript application) that obtain data and manipulate the DOM, a different approach is needed.

In the new approach, the Struts2 framework is used only as a data source. Actions are called via URLs, but instead of returning HTML, the result is a more easily parsed format such as XML or JSON. The JavaScript functions process the data, determine what information is to be used for logic and what is to be rendered to the user, and then render the information to the user by manipulating the web browser's DOM directly.

Explaining the nuances of JavaScript to implement the use cases is outside the scope of this book. Instead, this section's focus will be on explaining how Struts2 can be configured to provide data in different forms that can be easily consumed by a JavaScript function.

Using the XML Result Type

The first data format to be explored is XML, and formatting the result into XML is achieved by using the Struts2-provided xslt result type.

This means that if the action has already been developed, you only need to provide a new action configuration in the struts.xml configuration file to return an XML result (an annotation configuration could also be used, but in this case, the action already has an @Result annotation, and an additional configuration is needed). As an example, here is how the ShowRecentEventsAction class would need to be configured to return XML:

```
<package name="xml-services" namespace="/services/xml" extends="base-package" >

    <action name="recentEventsXML"
            class="com.fdar.apress.s2.actions.search.ShowRecentEventsAction" >
        <result type="xslt">
            <param name="exposedValue">dtoResults</param>
        </result>
    </action>

</package>
```

The type attribute of the result tag is set to the value of xslt, as expected. To configure which property is exposed and hence transformed into XML, a param tag is used. The name of the param is exposedValue, and the value is an OGNL expression that returns the objects that will be transformed into XML. For the example, the value dtoResults matches a method on the ShowRecentEventsAction class.

■**Note** For more information on the xslt result type and the configuration options available, check out the Struts2 documentation at http://struts.apache.org/2.x/struts2-core/apidocs/org/apache/struts2/views/xslt/XSLTResult.html.

When using the xslt result type to transform objects, it is important to understand that the value of each and every property will be evaluated. If the property is a complex object, the relationship will be traversed, and then the entire process will start over. In this fashion, the entire object graph will be traversed and transformed into XML.

Initially, this may not seem like a problem for the Event object. However, you must remember that the object to be transformed may have been adorned with additional properties. Because the Event class is also annotated to be persisted using JPA, there is a chance that additional properties are available on the runtime instance. For this reason, the Event object (and the Location object) instance is converted into a simpler DTO (Data Transfer Object) representation. Following is the representation of the Event object, EventDTO:

```
public class EventDTO {

    private long id;
    private String eventName;
    private String startTime;
    private int timeZoneOffset = 0;
    private String votingStartTime;
    private int duration;
    private String lastUpdateTime;
    private LocationDTO location;
    private String status;

    public EventDTO( Event event ) {

        DateFormat df =
            DateFormat.getDateTimeInstance(DateFormat.LONG,DateFormat.LONG);

        this.id = event.getId();
        this.eventName = event.getName();
        this.startTime = df.format(event.getStartTime());
        this.timeZoneOffset = event.getTimeZoneOffset();
        this.votingStartTime = df.format(event.getVotingStartTime());
        this.duration = event.getDuration();
        this.lastUpdateTime = df.format(event.getLastUpdateTime());
        this.location = new LocationDTO(event.getLocation());
        this.status = event.getStatus().name();
    }

    // getters for each of the properties
}
```

DATA TRANSFER OBJECTS

Data Transfer Objects (DTOs), as the name suggests, are objects that transfer data, and were first introduced by Martin Fowler in "Patterns of Enterprise Application Architecture." Another term, *Value Object*, is also used to describe objects that perform the same job. My preference is for DTO, as the name better describes the function of the object in shuttling the data from one layer to another.

In the case of the EventDTO, the object is immutable. This makes sense when transferring data to a user interface, but it isn't always the case. Here are some of the other characteristics that a DTO can exhibit:

- They provide a representation of another object, or they can provide a representation of data elements from multiple objects, which are usually related (i.e., dependent object).

- They can be mutable or immutable.

- They may or may not provide all the properties from the object they represent.

- The properties from the represented object may be simplified (i.e., providing a string representation of a date object).

- There may be multiple DTO representations for a single domain object, with each new representation provided for a specialized task. Multiple objects providing specialized representations is preferred over a sparsely populated DTO because when sparsely populated, the DTO consumer may be uncertain as to whether the property exists and is not available, or whether the value is null.

DTOs are useful, but like any tool, can be overused. When introducing DTOs, make sure there is a specific purpose that they are being used for. Too often, DTOs can complicate an application's architecture by adding unneeded layers of abstraction.

The transformation from Location to LocationDTO occurs in the constructor of the Event-DTO class, and the transformation from Event to EventDTO is performed in the getDtoResults() method on the ShowRecentEventsAction class. This is a new method introduced for the purpose of returning a list of DTO objects. Having it available on the ShowRecentEventsAction class gives the developer the option of obtaining the results as regular objects or as DTOs. The ShowRecentEventsAction now becomes the following:

```
public class ShowRecentEventsAction extends BaseAction {

    ...

    public List<EventDTO> getDtoResults() {
        List<EventDTO> data = new ArrayList<EventDTO>();
        for( Event next: results ) {
            data.add( new EventDTO(next));
        }
        return data;
    }

    public String execute() throws Exception {
        ...
    }
}
```

Because a new package with the namespace /services/xml was configured in the struts.xml, the entire base package can be configured to be excluded from decoration in the SiteMesh decorators.xml configuration file:

```
<decorators defaultdir="/WEB-INF/decorators">
    <!-- Any urls that are excluded will never be decorated by Sitemesh -->
    <excludes>
        ...
        <pattern>/services/*</pattern>
    </excludes>

    ...

</decorators>
```

Using a common package (and hence namespace) for all actions returning XML results will make developing easier. It means that the decorators.xml configuration no longer needs to be updated for each new action configured.

To test that everything is configured correctly, the URL for the action can be called in a web browser. Invoking http://localhost:8080/app/services/xml/recentEventsXML.action will produce a correctly formatted XML response, as shown in Figure 10-4.

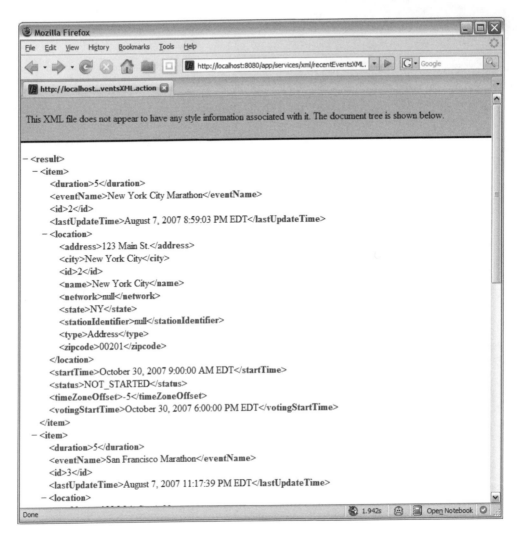

Figure 10-4. *The XML result of calling the* recentEventsXML *action in a browser*

HAND-CRAFTING THE RESPONSE

Another option to using the `xslt` result type is to construct the XML response by hand, either as a JSP, Freemarker, or Velocity template. Using the JSP option, the action is configured to use the default `dispatcher` result type, providing a JSP template to render the response:

```
<action name="recentEventsXML"
        class="com.fdar.apress.s2.actions.search.ShowRecentEventsAction" >
    <result>/WEB-INF/jsp/api/event-xml.jsp</result>
</action>
```

The JSP template would then format the response to any specification that is required. Here is an example of a JSP template that provides a custom XML response:

```
<%@ page contentType="text/html; charset=UTF-8" %>
<%@ taglib uri="/struts-tags" prefix="s" %>

<?xml version="1.0" encoding="UTF-8"?>

<events>
  <s:iterator value="results">
  <event id="<s:property value="id"/>">

    <name><s:property value="name"/></name>
    <startTime>
      <s:date name="startTime" format="MM/dd/yyyy hh:mm"/>
    </startTime>
    <votingStartTime>
      <s:date name="votingStartTime" format="MM/dd/yyyy hh:mm"/>
    </votingStartTime>
    <duration><s:property value="duration"/></duration>
    <timeZoneOffset><s:property value="timeZoneOffset"/></timeZoneOffset>
    <status><s:property value="status"/></status>

    <s:if test="location.class.name.endsWith('.Address')">
    <address type="Adress">
      <name><s:property value="location.name" /></name>
      <address><s:property value="location.address" /></address>
      <city><s:property value="location.city" /></city>
      <state><s:property value="location.state" /></state>
      <zipcode><s:property value="location.zipcode" /></zipcode>
```

```
      </s:if>
      <s:else>
      <address type="Broadcast">
        <name><s:property value="location.name" /></name>
        <city><s:property value="location.city" /></city>
        <state><s:property value="location.state" /></state>
        <network><s:property value="location.network" /></network>
        <stationIdentifier>
          <s:property value="location.stationIdentifier" />
        </stationIdentifier>
      </s:else>
      </address>

      <contestants>
        <s:iterator value="options" >
        <contestant>
          <name><s:property value="name" /></name>
          <description><s:property value="description" /></description>
        </contestant>
        </s:iterator>
      </contestants>

    </event>
    </s:iterator>
  </events>
```

This is a trivial example, and using a style sheet with the xslt result type would be a more efficient option. The key thing to remember is that this technique is not limited to XML and can be used to return JSON, or any other data format that you may require. It is especially usefully when the format being returned cannot be provided in another way easily.

To complete the discussion of returning XML to a JavaScript function, let's take a look at some JavaScript code. As mentioned earlier, this is not a complete implementation of the JavaScript needed to implement the use cases but should be enough to get you headed in the right direction.

Using the Dojo Toolkit, the following javascriptXML.jsp template shows how to invoke a URL and access the data being returned. The result is that the name and the start time of the events returned will be displayed to the user.

```
<html>
<head>
  <title>JavaScript XML</title>

  <script type="text/javascript">
    function loadRemotely() {
```

```
    var kw = {
      url: "/app/services/xml/recentEventsXML.action",
      mimetype: "text/xml",
      method: "GET",
      load: function(type, xml, evt) {

        var entries = xml.getElementsByTagName("item");
        var display = "<h3>Events</h3>";

        for(var e=0;e<entries.length;e++){

          var entry = entries[e];
          var name =
            entry.getElementsByTagName("eventName")[0].firstChild.nodeValue;
          var startTime =
            entry.getElementsByTagName("startTime")[0].firstChild.nodeValue;

          display += "<b>"+name+"</b> - "+startTime+"<br/>";
        }

        dojo.byId("main").innerHTML = display;
      }
    };
    dojo.io.bind(kw);
  }
  </script>
</head>

<body onload="loadRemotely()"></body>
</html>
```

The JSP template consists of two main elements: the HTML part of the page, which consists of an empty body tag that calls the loadRemotely() JavaScript function after the page has been loaded; and the loadRemotely() JavaScript method, which contains the logic to make the HTTP call to obtain the XML data and the logic that processes the results.

At the core of the loadRemotely() method is the Dojo Toolkit's method that makes the HTTP call. First, the configuration is assembled into the variable kw. This consists of the URL to be called, the MIME type, HTTP method, and, most importantly, the function that is called when the response is returned:

```
    var kw = {
      url: "/app/services/xml/recentEventsXML.action",
      mimetype: "text/xml",
      method: "GET",
      load: function(type, xml, evt) {
        …
      }
    };
```

And then the configuration is used in a call to the `bind()` method:

```
dojo.io.bind(kw);
```

If all goes well, the function defined in the configuration will be invoked to process the result obtained from invoking the URL.

■Note For more information on the configuration available for the `bind()` method in the Dojo Toolkit, check out the documentation at `http://manual.dojotoolkit.org/io.html`.

To execute the JSP in Struts2, a simple pass-though action configuration needs to be added to the `struts.xml` configuration file:

```
<action name="javascriptXML" class="com.fdar.apress.s2.actions.BaseAction">
    <result>/javascriptXML.jsp</result>
</action>
```

■Tip This example did not pass any information to the action. If information was needed, it would be added to the URL being invoked as request parameters. On the Struts2 side, the interceptor stack will perform the processing by checking validation and assigning the value to the matching setter on the action.

Using the JSON Result Type Plug-in

Another popular data interchange format is JSON. Like XML, the JSON data interchange format is easy for people to read. Following is what the `EventDTO` and `LocationDTO` representation for a single event looks like:

```
{
    "duration":5,
    "eventName":"New York City Marathon",
    "id":2,
    "lastUpdateTime":"August 7, 2007 8:59:03 PM EDT",
    "location":{
        "address":"123 Main St.",
        "city":"New York City",
        "id":2,
        "name":"New York City",
        "network":null,
        "state":"NY",
        "stationIdentifier":null,
        "type":"Address",
        "zipcode":"00201"
    },
```

```
"startTime":"October 30, 2007 9:00:00 AM EDT",
"status":"NOT_STARTED",
"timeZoneOffset":-5,
"votingStartTime":"October 30, 2007 6:00:00 PM EDT"
}
```

More importantly, the JSON data interchange format can be easily parsed into JavaScript objects.

In the last section, the event name was obtained using the following JavaScript:

```
xml.getElementsByTagName("item")[e]➥
    .getElementsByTagName("eventName")[0].firstChild.nodeValue;
```

After the JSON data format is parsed, the event name can be accessed as a first class property on the object:

```
result[e].eventName;
```

This reduction in complexity makes JSON a desirable data interchange format to use.

■**Note** More information on JSON can be found at `http://json.org/`.

The functionality for the JSON result type is provided via a third-party JSON plug-in. Before it can be used, the plug-in JAR file must be downloaded from its home page at `http://cwiki.apache.org/S2PLUGINS/json-plugin.html` and installed.

For a file name and version of `jsonplugin-0.16-1.5.jar`, the following command will install the plug-in into the Maven2 repository:

```
mvn install:install-file -DgroupId=jsonplugin -DartifactId=0.16 -Dversion=1.5 ➥
    -Dpackaging=jar -Dfile=jsonplugin-0.16-1.5.jar
```

Then, the following code is added to the `pom.xml` configuration file:

```
<!-- JSON Plugin -->
<dependency>
    <groupId>jsonplugin</groupId>
    <artifactId>0.16</artifactId>
    <version>1.5</version>
</dependency>
```

After the plug-in is installed, the actions need to be configured to use the new result type. The best approach is to configure a separate package specifically for JSON results. This package extends the `json-default` package (located in the JSON plug-in JAR) and is configured to use the `json` interceptor as the default interceptor. Using the same example as the XML result type, the following configuration shows an action configuration for the `ShowRecentEventsAction` class that will return a JSON response:

```
<package name="dojo-services" namespace="/services/json" extends="json-default" >

    <default-interceptor-ref name="json" />

    <action name="recentEvents"
            class="com.fdar.apress.s2.actions.search.ShowRecentEventsAction" >
        <result type="json">
            <param name="root">dtoResults</param>
        </result>
    </action>

</package>
```

This configuration looks very similar to the XML result type. The differences are that the name of the result is json, and a param tag with name attribute value of root is needed. The value of the parameter provides the OGNL expression returning an object that will be serialized to a JSON object. In this case, it refers to the getDtoResults() method from the ShowRecentEventsAction class.

■**Note** The SiteMesh decorators.xml configuration file is already configured to exclude the URL pattern /services/*. This includes the URL /services/json, so no further configuration is required.

JSON objects can also be passed to the action, provided valid setters are available. More information on this and other configuration parameters for the JSON result type can be found at http://cwiki.apache.org/S2PLUGINS/json-plugin.html.

The JavaScript that consumes the JSON response is very similar to the XML result type example. As explained previously, the difference is that a valid JavaScript object is passed to the function processing the response, and so navigating to the data that is required is much simpler:

```
<html>
<head>
    <title>JavaScript JSON</title>

    <script type="text/javascript">
        function loadRemotely() {

            var kw = {
                url: "/app/services/json/recentEvents.action",
                mimetype: "text/json",
                method: "GET",
                load: function(type, json, evt) {
```

```
                display = "";
                for( var e=0; e<json.length; e++ ){
                    var name = json[e].eventName;
                    var startTime = json[e].startTime;
                    display += "<b>"+name+"</b> - "+startTime+"<br/>";
                }
                dojo.byId("main").innerHTML = display;
            }
        };
        dojo.io.bind(kw);
    }
    </script>
</head>

<body onload="loadRemotely()">
</body>
</html>
```

■**Note** In the Dojo Toolkit, the JSON text is parsed into a JavaScript object before it is provided as a parameter in the function processing the HTTP response. If you are not using the Dojo Toolkit, you will need to parse the object manually by using `var result = eval('('+json+')');`.

If you are using the Dojo Toolkit as your client JavaScript library, you have another option available. The Dojo Toolkit has defined an RPC (Remote Procedure Call) mechanism that uses an SMD (Simple Method Description) file to describe the services available. By providing a SMD file, the Dojo Toolkit allows the JavaScript code to call methods, rather than using the `bind()` method. More information on the Dojo Toolkit's RPC and SMD can be found at `http://manual.dojotoolkit.org/WikiHome/DojoDotBook/Book9`.

The JSON plug-in can be enabled to return an SMD file by supplying an additional enableSMD parameter (with a value of `true`) to both the `json` interceptor and the `json` result:

```
<package name="dojo-services" namespace="/services/json" extends="json-default" >

    <action name="eventAPI"
            class="com.fdar.apress.s2.actions.search.DojoJSONAction" >
        <interceptor-ref name="json">
            <param name="enableSMD">true</param>
        </interceptor-ref>
        <result type="json">
            <param name="enableSMD">true</param>
        </result>
    </action>

</package>
```

A new `DojoJSONAction` action class is defined, as well. This action class is different from any other action class in the application. In fact, the suffix `Action` is a namesake only. The class, for all intent, is a business service being exposed via a URL.

Each method that you want to expose to the Dojo Toolkit via an RPC must be annotated with the `@SMDMethod` annotation, which unlike a regular Struts2 action, can return any object and may have any number of parameters. Following the same example of returning the recent events, the `DojoJSONAction` class has one method, `findRecentEvents(…)`, which takes an integer value as a parameter and returns a list of `EventDTO` objects. To reuse as much existing logic as possible, this action extends the `ShowRecentEventsAction` class using the `execute()` and `getDtoResults()` methods:

```
public class DojoJSONAction extends ShowRecentEventsAction {

    @SMDMethod
    public List<EventDTO> findRecentEvents(int max) throws Exception {
        execute();
        return getDtoResults();
    }

}
```

■**Caution** This style of writing actions is a significant departure from Struts2. For consistency in the application code base, it may be a better architectural decision to use non-RPC JSON results even when using Dojo as your client-side JavaScript library.

The final step is to update the JavaScript to use RPC calls. Instead of `bind()`, a new `dojo.rpc.JsonService` object is created using the URL configured in the `struts.xml` configuration file. The method on the action, `findRecentEvents()`, can then be called directly, providing the input parameters and attaching a JavaScript function that provides the processing logic for the result. The function processing the logic is the same as when a non-RPC method is invoked.

```
<%@ taglib uri="/struts-tags" prefix="s" %>
<html>
<head>
    <title>JavaScript JSON-RPC</title>

    <script type="text/javascript">
        function loadRemotely() {

            //load dojo RPC
            dojo.require("dojo.rpc.*");
```

```
                    //create service object(proxy) using SMD (generated by the json result)
                    var url = '<s:url namespace="/services/json" action="eventAPI" />';
                    var service = new dojo.rpc.JsonService(url);

                    //function called when remote method returns
                    var callback = function(result) {

                        var display="";

                        for( var e=0; e<result.length; e++ ){
                            var name = result[e].eventName;
                            var startTime = result[e].startTime;
                            display += "<b>"+name+"</b> - "+startTime+"<br/>";
                        }
                        dojo.byId("main").innerHTML = display;
                    }

                    // execute remote method
                    service.findRecentEvents(10).addCallback(callback);
                }
            </script>
</head>

<body onload="loadRemotely()"></body>
</html>
```

■**Note** As well as primitive values, complex objects can be passed to the RPC methods by defining them as a JSON object, for example, `var param = {name: "Boston Marathon"};`.

Similarly to both previous result type examples, an action configuration is also needed to invoke the JSP example:

```
<action name="javascriptJSON-RPC" class="com.fdar.apress.s2.actions.BaseAction">
    <result>/javascriptJSON-RPC.jsp</result>
</action>
```

Using the Google Web Toolkit

The Google Web Toolkit (GWT) is another option for integrating AJAX functionality. Where most AJAX libraries use JavaScript as the client programming language, GWT uses Java. Then, after the development and testing is complete, the Java code is compiled into cross-browser compatible JavaScript for deployment. By encapsulating the quirks of programming JavaScript in the compiler, GWT allows Java developers to use their knowledge of Java to develop browser-based AJAX applications.

■**Note** More information on the Google Web Toolkit can be found at the project's home page at `http://code.google.com/webtoolkit`.

There are some disadvantages to using GWT. The first is that JDK 1.4 is the highest Java language level that is available for you to work with. This doesn't mean that your main project needs to be compiled under JDK 1.4, but rather that the classes being compiled by GWT cannot use the advanced features of generics, enumerations, and so forth. The other restriction is that the classes to be compiled by GWT must all be contained within the `client` package (which is created when the starter code is generated). Although this is not a significant restriction, it may change certain aspects of your project. The main consideration, especially when designing an application that is making remote calls and transferring data, is that any DTOs should be placed in the `client` package and have no external dependencies.

In this section, you will learn how Struts2 and GWT can be combined to produce rich client applications. To integrate Struts2 with GWT, the `struts2gwtplugin` will be used. The documentation and code for this third-party plug-in can be found at `http://cwiki.apache.org/S2PLUGINS/gwt-plugin.html`.

Just as in the previous section, the focus will be on the integration of Struts2 and GWT, and not developing a fully functional GWT application.

Generating the GWT Starter Code

Before proceeding, you need to download the GWT, which can be obtained from `http://code.google.com/webtoolkit/download.html`. Once downloaded, expand the archive into a temporary directory.

To generate the client application code, the `applicationCreator` script is invoked. A single parameter supplies the class name for the entry point into the new GWT application. Following is the command invoked to create the GWT client application:

```
applicationCreator.cmd com.fdar.apress.s2.client.GWTClient
```

When invoked, the command creates several directories and files, as shown in Figure 10-5.

■**Note** There are other ways that the starter application could have been generated. To generate code for the Eclipse IDE, as well as find out about the other options available, consult the documentation at `http://code.google.com/webtoolkit/gettingstarted.html`.

Figure 10-5. *Generating the GWT files for a new application*

The generated code is placed under a single directory. For Maven2, the Java files, configuration files, and web application files need to be moved to the correct root directories, which involves the following steps:

- The Java file GWTClient.java is placed under the /src/main/java root directory, in the same package that it was created in.

- The configuration file GWTClient.gwt.xml is placed under the resources /src/main/resources root directory, in the same package that it was created in.

- The compilation command GWTClient-compile.cmd is placed in the root of the resources /src/main/resources directory (the GWTClient-shell.cmd file will not be used, but can be placed in the same directory as the GWTClient-compile.cmd file).

- The HTML file GWTClient.html is placed in the root of the /src/main/webapp directory.

Because the relative file locations have changed, the GWTClient-compile.cmd file needs to be updated. There are two changes: the classpath is modified to reference the new file location where the command is located, the /src/main/java directory, rather than the /src directory; and the compilation output directory is set to be the /src/main/webapp directory. The updated GWTClient-compile.cmd file (where C:/devapps/gwt-windows-1.4.10 is the directory that the GWT archive has been expanded to) becomes the following:

```
@java -cp "%~dp0;%~dp0/../java;%~dp0\bin;➥
    C:/devapps/gwt-windows-1.4.10/gwt-user.jar;➥
    C:/devapps/gwt-windows-1.4.10/gwt-dev-windows.jar" ➥
    com.google.gwt.dev.GWTCompiler ➥
    -out "%~dp0\..\webapp" %* com.fdar.apress.s2.GWTClient
```

To confirm that the directories are configured correctly, run the command GWTClient-compile.cmd. If everything is configured correctly, a new directory called com.fdar.apress.s2.GWTClient is created in /src/main/webapp.

Note At this time, you might have tried to call the URL http://localhost:8080/app/ GWTClient.html to see the application work and been disappointed. There is only one modification needed to fix the problem, and that is to add the directory com.fdar.apress.s2.GWTClient to the beginning of the JavaScript file locations. The reason why will be explained later in the section.

Configuring the Struts2 Plug-in

Before the plug-in can be used, it must be installed in the Maven2 repository. First, download the plug-in from http://code.google.com/p/struts2gwtplugin/downloads/list. The plug-in can then be installed with the following command:

```
mvn install:install-file ➥
    -DgroupId=com.googlcode.strut2gwtplugin ➥
    -DartifactId=struts2gwtplugin ➥
    -Dversion=0.2.1 -Dpackaging=jar ➥
    -Dfile=struts2gwtplugin-0.2.1.jar
```

The plug-in also needs to be added as a dependency for the project, and the following code is added to the pom.xml configuration file:

```
<!-- GWT Plugin -->
<dependency>
    <groupId>com.googlcode.strut2gwtplugin</groupId>
    <artifactId>struts2gwtplugin</artifactId>
    <version>0.2.1</version>
</dependency>
```

Caution There is an unusual spelling in the package name; make sure you use the value googlcode and not googlecode.

Along with the plug-in code, two GWT JAR files also need to be installed. They provide necessary compilation and runtime dependencies. The files gwt-servlet.jar and gwt-user.jar can be found in the directory that the GWT was expanded to. The command to install the files is the following:

```
mvn install:install-file -DgroupId=gwt -DartifactId=servlet ➥
    -Dversion=1.4.10 -Dpackaging=jar -Dfile=gwt-servlet.jar
mvn install:install-file -DgroupId=gwt -DartifactId=user ➥
    -Dversion=1.4.10 -Dpackaging=jar -Dfile=gwt-user.jar
```

The dependencies then need to be added to the `pom.xml` configuration file as follows:

```
<!-- GWT -->
<dependency>
    <groupId>gwt</groupId>
    <artifactId>servlet</artifactId>
    <version>1.4.10</version>
</dependency>
<dependency>
    <groupId>gwt</groupId>
    <artifactId>user</artifactId>
    <version>1.4.10</version>
</dependency>
```

Integrating Struts2 and GWT

To integrate Struts2 and GWT, the RPC feature of GWT is used. On the Struts2 side, the magic of the integration all occurs in the `struts2gwtplugin` plug-in (that was previously installed). In fact, if you were not told that Struts2 was involved, you might think that a simple Java class was being used for the server logic.

With this in mind, the remainder of this section focuses on the GWT-specific implementation and requirements. This includes the definition of remote interfaces, matching of remote interfaces with Struts2 action classes, and the GWT client code to invoke the remote calls.

Note The official documentation for the GWT RPC can be found at `http://code.google.com/webtoolkit/documentation/com.google.gwt.doc.DeveloperGuide.RemoteProcedureCalls.html`. As well as providing an overview to the architecture, advanced features for implementing RPC services are covered.

The first step is to define the remote interface that GWT will use to obtain data. For the example, we will be implementing only one remote call. This will be to obtain the most recent events (the same as in the "Using JavaScript" section earlier) and is defined in a `GWTService` interface as the following:

```
public interface GWTService extends RemoteService {

    GWTEventDTO[] findRecentEvents(int max);
}
```

To keep configuration at a minimum, the findRecentEvents() method is defined returning an array of GWTEventDTO objects (although a List could have also been used with additional
special GWT JavaDoc annotations).

Because the EventDTO class and the LocationDTO class are located in a package outside
the client package and contain dependencies on other external classes, matching DTOs for
the GWT interface are created. It is important to ensure that any class being passed over an
RPC to a GWT client be serializable:

```
public class GWTEventDTO implements Serializable {

    private long id;
    private String eventName;
    private String startTime;
    private int timeZoneOffset = 0;
    private String votingStartTime;
    private int duration;
    private String lastUpdateTime;
    private GWTLocationDTO location;
    private String status;

    // getters and setters

}
```

The GWTLocationDTO is also very simple, implementing the Serializable interface and
providing getters and setters for properties:

```
public class GWTLocationDTO implements Serializable {

    private long id;
    private String name;
    private String city;
    private String state;
    private String type;

    private String address;
    private String zipcode;

    private String stationIdentifier;
    private String network;

    // getters and setters

}
```

As well as a synchronous interface, an asynchronous interface is defined. This new interface is related to the original and allows client processing to continue without blocking. When
a response is received, an assigned callback method is invoked. The asynchronous interface
that matched the original interface is the following:

```
public interface GWTServiceAsync {

    void findRecentEvents(int max, AsyncCallback callback);
}
```

From the preceding code, you can see that this relationship is not codified, but rather a pattern in defining the class and methods. The rules are listed here:

- The asynchronous class has the same name as the original, with Async appended.

- The same methods are defined as in the original interface.

- The methods return void rather than a specific type.

- The parameters are the same, with the addition of a new AsyncCallback typed parameter as the very last one defined.

The AsyncCallback class is the key and provides callback methods that the client implements to perform logic under success and failure conditions:

```
public interface AsyncCallback  {

    void onFailure(java.lang.Throwable throwable);

    void onSuccess(java.lang.Object object);
}
```

For now, all you need to know is that by providing both these interfaces and by calling the correct methods in the client, GWT will generate JavaScript that can take advantage of asynchronous remote calls.

The action that implements the remote call functionality, like the asynchronous interface, is similar but not exactly the same as the original interface. Here is the action class, with the method that needs to be implemented:

```
public class GWTServiceAction {

    ...

    public GWTEventDTO[] findRecentEvents(Integer max) {
        ...
    }
}
```

As you can see, the method closely resembles the GWTService interface. The difference is that the method parameters are required to be objects and not primitives (remember no Java 5 and no auto-boxing).

The other changes are that the findRecentEvents() method needs to convert between a list and an array and that the GWTEventDTO and GWTLocationDTO DTOs are created by methods in the action. This is to prevent the GWTEventDTO class from having a dependency on the Event class (and the GWTLocationDTO class on the Location class). The complete action class is shown here:

```
public class GWTServiceAction {

    protected EventService service;

    public void setEventService(EventService service) {
        this.service = service;
    }

    public GWTEventDTO[] findRecentEvents(Integer max) {
        List<Event> list = service.findAllEvents(max);
        GWTEventDTO[] data = new GWTEventDTO[list.size()];
        for( int i=0; i<list.size(); i++ ) {
            data[i] = createDTO(list.get(i));
        }
        return data;
    }

    private GWTEventDTO createDTO( Event event ) {
        // creates and returns a GWTEventDTO
    }

    private GWTLocationDTO createLocationDTO( Location loc ) {
        // creates and returns a GWTLocationDTO
    }
}
```

■**Note** Unlike regular Struts2 actions, action classes that implement GWT remote functionality do not need to have an `execute()` method. For all intents and purposes, this makes the action class just a regular class that is configured within the `struts.xml` configuration file.

On the server, the final step is to configure the `GWTInterceptor` interceptor and apply it to all actions that are being used as GWT RPC endpoints. Because a common namespace will most likely be used for all GWT endpoints, a new package is created in the `struts.xml` configuration file, and the interceptor is configured as the default for the package. The action configuration is as simple as it gets; only the action name and the action class from the preceding code are required:

```
<package name="voting" namespace="/voting" extends="base-package" >

    <interceptors>
        <interceptor name="gwt"
            class="com.googlcode.strut2gwtplugin.interceptor.GWTInterceptor" />
    </interceptors>
```

```
<default-interceptor-ref name="gwt" />

<action name="GWTService"
        class="com.fdar.apress.s2.remote.gwt.GWTServiceAction" />
```

`</package>`

Next, the GWT client code needs to be implemented. The code is comprised of three classes: the GWTClient class that provides the entry point for GWT (specified when generating the starter code); an EventTableWidget that provides the visual representation of the event data to be displayed; and the EventProvider class that provides the logic to make the RPC and update the model being rendered by the EventTableWidget class.

Caution All code that is used by the GWT client and compiled by the GWT JavaScript compiler needs to be placed under the `client` package.

The EventTableWidget class is the core element in the client code, containing both the user interface element to be rendered (the Grid property) and the data provider that obtains the information (the EventProvider property and inner class) to be rendered. By extending the GWT Composite class, access is provided to several lifecycle callback methods. The one implemented is the onLoad() method, which calls the data provider's method updateRowData(). All other initialization is performed in the constructor, as follows:

```
public class EventTableWidget extends Composite {

    private EventProvider eventProvider;
    private EventTableWidget eventTable;
    private final Grid grid;

    public EventTableWidget() {
        eventProvider = new EventProvider();
        grid = new Grid();
        initWidget(grid);
    }

    protected void onLoad() {
        eventProvider.updateRowData();
    }

    private class EventProvider {
        ...
    }
}
```

■**Note** The user interface code being presented is not even breaking the surface of the functionality that is provided by GWT. For more information on the available widgets, as well as properties, methods, and styles, check out the GWT documentation at `http://code.google.com/webtoolkit/documentation/` `com.google.gwt.doc.DeveloperGuide.UserInterface.html`.

The inner class `EventProvider` is much more interesting. It is responsible for making the RPC call to the Struts2 action and updating the information being rendered to the user. In the constructor, there are several lines of scaffolding code that construct an instance of the `GWTService` service class and then set the endpoint on the service. The endpoint URL assigned to the service matches the one configured for the `GWTServiceAction` action class in the `struts.xml` configuration file.

The `updateRowData()` method does all the work. This method is called from the `onLoad()` method of the `EventTableWidget` class and uses the asynchronous service interface that calls the `findRecentEvents()` method. The last parameter, being an anonymous inner class, provides the callback methods for the success and failure cases:

```
private class EventProvider {

    private final GWTServiceAsync gwtService;

    public EventProvider() {
        gwtService = (GWTServiceAsync) GWT.create(GWTService.class);
        ServiceDefTarget target = (ServiceDefTarget) gwtService;
        target.setServiceEntryPoint("/app/voting/GWTService.action");
    }

    public void updateRowData() {

        gwtService.findRecentEvents(10, new AsyncCallback() {

            public void onFailure(Throwable caught) {
                // do nothing
            }

            public void onSuccess(Object result) {
                pushResults((GWTEventDTO[])result);
            }

        });
    }
```

```
private void pushResults(GWTEventDTO[] events) {
    grid.resize(events.length,3);
    for (int i = 0; i<events.length; i++) {
        GWTEventDTO event = events[i];
        grid.setText(i,0, event.getEventName());
        grid.setText(i,1, event.getStartTime());
        grid.setText(i,2,event.getLocation().getCity()+
            ", "+event.getLocation().getState());
    }
}
}
```

When successful, the returned results are updated in the Grid user interface element, and the new information is reflected in the browser to the user.

The GWTClient class is by far the easiest and is required to implement a single method onModuleLoad(). This method is the first to be invoked and provides the initialization and startup code for the GWT client. A single method is used to access the HTML DOM element with an id attribute of slot1. To this element, a new EventTableWidget is added:

```
public class GWTClient implements EntryPoint {

    public void onModuleLoad() {
        RootPanel.get("slot1").add(new EventTableWidget());
    }

}
```

The HTML entry point to use the GWT module is the GWTClient.html code. This was one of the generated files, which needs one small adjustment. Instead of loading the JavaScript file from the current directory, the relative directory needs to be specified. The following line of code is the only one needing modification:

```
<script language='javascript'
    src='com.fdar.apress.s2.GWTClient/com.fdar.apress.s2.GWTClient.nocache.js'>
</script>
```

Tip GWT modules can be deployed in any HTML page or HTML-generated page (for example, JSP). All that is needed is to include the correct JavaScript files and make the id attributes referenced in the GWT client code available.

To complete and run the example, you need to do the following:

- Change to the /src/main/resources directory, and run the GWTClient-compile.cmd command.

- Run the mvn jetty:run command from the same directory that the pom.xml configuration file is located.

At this point, you can point your browser to http://localhost:8080/app/GWTClient.html, and the GWT client code will make an asynchronous RPC to the matching Struts2 action on the server (see Figure 10-6).

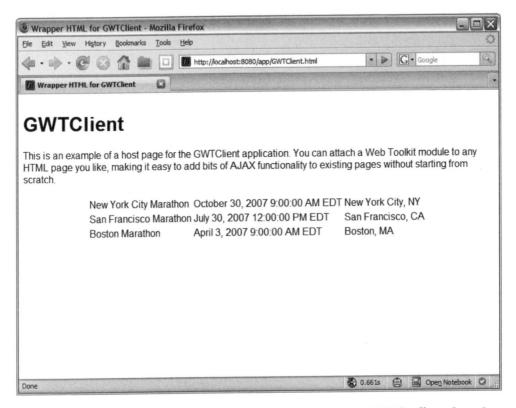

Figure 10-6. *The resulting screen of the example code performing a GWT RPC call to a Struts2 action*

Summary

This chapter focused on how Struts2 can be a data provider for many different types of AJAX interactions.

You learned how to use the Struts2 ajax theme, which allows URLs to be called asynchronously and the user interface to be updated with the information returned, and how existing JSP templates can be updated to provide AJAX functionality with only a few changes.

Several methods for providing data were also discussed, including returning an XML result and JSON result. If you are using the Dojo Toolkit, you learned how the Simple Method Description feature can be used to provide an RPC interface rather than an action URL-based interface, making the client development a little easier. Finally, the Google Web Toolkit (GWT) was explored, and we discussed how Struts2 actions can be used as data providers.

To learn more about AJAX, especially the client-side development that was not the focus of this chapter, check out these Apress books: Foundation of AJAX, Practical AJAX Project with Java Technology, and Practical JavaScript, DOM Scripting, and AJAX Projects.

Index

You Need the Companion eBook

Your purchase of this book entitles you to buy the companion PDF-version eBook for only $10. Take the weightless companion with you anywhere.

We believe this Apress title will prove so indispensable that you'll want to carry it with you everywhere, which is why we are offering the companion eBook (in PDF format) for $10 to customers who purchase this book now. Convenient and fully searchable, the PDF version of any content-rich, page-heavy Apress book makes a valuable addition to your programming library. You can easily find and copy code—or perform examples by quickly toggling between instructions and the application. Even simultaneously tackling a donut, diet soda, and complex code becomes simplified with hands-free eBooks!

Once you purchase your book, getting the $10 companion eBook is simple:

❶ Visit **www.apress.com/promo/tendollars/**.

❷ Complete a basic registration form to receive a randomly generated question about this title.

❸ Answer the question correctly in 60 seconds, and you will receive a promotional code to redeem for the $10.00 eBook.

THE EXPERT'S VOICE™

2855 TELEGRAPH AVENUE | SUITE 600 | BERKELEY, CA 94705

Offer valid through 5/08.